POSTSCRIPT TO VICTORY

British Policy and the German-Polish Borderlands, 1919-1925

Patricia A. Gajda

UNIVERSITY
PRESS OF
AMERICA

Copyright © 1982 by
University Press of America, Inc.
P.O. Box 19101, Washington, D.C. 20036

All rights reserved

Printed in the United States of America

ISBN (Perfect): 0-8191-2204-1
ISBN   (Cloth): 0-8191-2203-3

Library of Congress Catalog Card Number: 81-40634

To My Mother

ACKNOWLEDGMENTS

I wish to extend my thanks to all those who have offered assistance and encouragement during the completion of this work, only a few of whom can be mentioned here. Marion C. Siney taught me what history is and became my friend in the process. The staff of the Public Record Office, London, unfailingly and cheerfully helped put their treasures at my disposal. The British Museum and its newspaper depository at Colindale provided material that would otherwise be unobtainable. The University of London Institute of Historical Research and the School of East European and Slavonic Studies assembled valuable resources and made their use not only possible but convenient. The managers of the Polish Institute and Sikorski Museum in London and the Bibliothèque Polonaise in Paris graciously gave me access to their private library collections. The Beaverbrook Library, London, which houses *inter alia* the massive collection of the Lloyd George Papers, welcomed me. Its fine facilities and the assistance of the staff, especially of the director, Mr. A. J. P. Taylor, made my visit there both historically valuable and personally memorable.

My thanks also go to those who provided maps for this work. The maps on pages 28 and 151 appear by permission of Oxford University Press. The maps on pages 89, 135, and 137 from Crown-copyright records in the Public Record Office appear by permission of the Controller of Her Majesty's Stationery Office.

Finally, my heartfelt thanks are extended to Digby Stuart College, Roehampton Institute of Higher Education, London, without whose interest and hospitality this study quite literally could not have been done--and certainly could not have been done so enjoyably.

Patricia A. Gajda

TABLE OF CONTENTS

PREFACE ix

NOTE ON DOCUMENTARY CITATIONS xi

LIST OF MAPS xiii

Chapter   Page

   I. GREAT BRITAIN AND THE NEW DIPLOMACY AT PARIS
      (January 1919 to June 1919) 1

      Historical Background and the British Position
      Development of British Policy
      The Polish Question and the Peace Terms

  II. BEFORE THE NEW REGIME
      (June 1919 to January 1920) 29

      Keeping Order in Danzig
      Danzig before the Allied Administration
      Upper Silesia before the Allied Occupation
      Anglo-Polish Ties

 III. A YEAR OF OBLIGATIONS
      (January 1920 to March 1921) 53

      The Interim Regime in Danzig
      The New Regime in Upper Silesia

  IV. INTERREGNUM: LOST PRESTIGE AND DUTY UNFULFILLED
      (March 1921 to June 1921) 79

      Aftermath of Allied Administration in Danzig
      Upper Silesia after the Plebiscite
      Insurrection and the Breakdown of Allied Authority
      The Attempt to Restore Order

   V. BRITISH INITIATIVE: INVESTMENT AND RESTORED PRESTIGE
      (June 1921 to October 1921) 111

      A Renewed British Interest in Danzig
      Restoration of Allied Prestige in Upper Silesia
      Crisis for the Entente
      Towards a Final Upper Silesian Settlement

Chapter	Page

    VI. TOWARDS THE RETURN TO A FAMILIAR ROLE
        (October 1921 to July 1922) 141

        Danzig: The International Company
        Danzig, the Allies, and the League of Nations
        Expediting the Settlement in Upper Silesia
        The End of the Interlude
        Investment in Upper Silesia

    VII. BRITISH PRESENCE IN A TRADITIONAL ROLE
        (July 1922 to December 1923) 165

        Britain and the Crisis in Polish-Danzig Relations
        Danzig before the League
        The Financial and Economic Crisis of 1923
        Upper Silesia after Allied Withdrawal
        An Improved State of Anglo-Polish Relations

    VIII. BRITAIN AND THE CHANGES IN THE STATUS QUO
        (1924 to 1925) 189

        Danzig and Anglo-Polish Relations
        Danzig and the League of Nations
        Economic Deterioration in Upper Silesia
        Origins of British Revisionism

    IX. CONCLUSIONS 211

BIBLIOGRAPHY 217

PREFACE

It has become customary, when viewing the inter-war period through the developments of British diplomatic history, to focus upon the Anglo-French relationship and to subordinate or adjust to it the various other relations maintained by both of these western democracies with other European states. Another convention perpetuated by either convenience or disinterest is the neglect of the study of Great Britain's relationship with the new Republic of Poland until on the eve of the Second World War, when seemingly out of a vacuum, arises the British promise of guarantee to that nation. This study is an attempt to remedy the shortcomings of these procedures although it, too, necessarily in part sees the British motivation behind the Anglo-Polish relationship as subsidiary to and tempered by the Anglo-French alliance and Anglo-German understanding. It is not a comprehensive investigation of the relations between Britain and Poland in inter-bellum Europe. Such a broader study will be left to others to explore. It proposes, however, to trace the relations between the two states in the first half-decade following the Great War emphasizing the interest Great Britain expressed, especially regarding two of the most difficult Polish questions arising out of the Treaty of Versailles--the status of Danzig and the fate of Upper Silesia. It is hoped that once having ascertained British policy toward two of Poland's major problems in the years 1919-1925, this study will act as a beginning of a much-needed investigation into Britain's interest or lack thereof in Polish problems during the early inter-war years.

> Patricia A. Gajda
> Tyler, Texas
> 1981

NOTE ON DOCUMENTARY CITATIONS

Major documentary collections used in this study are part of the archives of the British Foreign Office. Citations for those documents which appear in a Confidential Print Series (e.g., FO 417) indicate the collections, the volume number of the series, and the document rather than the page number. In all citations used here for the massive General Correspondence collections (FO 371), the number following the stroke indicates the volume. The key to the final series of numbers which is used to identify the document (e.g., N 1700/335/55) is as follows: (1) the initial specifies the department of the Foreign Office (Northern, Central, Western) which dealt with the paper; (2) the first set of digits is the registry number of the specific paper; (3) the center set of digits indicates the file number assigned on an annual basis to the topic with which the paper deals; and (4) the last set of digits is a permanent code to specify which country the paper refers to (e.g., 55 indicates Poland, 18 indicates Germany). In some Foreign Office collections, the number immediately following the designation of the collection is a piece rather than a volume number, e.g., FO 688 (The British Legation at Warsaw Archives) is collected into boxes; FO 890 (British Section, Upper Silesia Plebiscite Commission Archives) may be in the form of boxes, bundles, or large envelopes. Other variations, when they are peculiar to a collection, are specified in the footnotes.

Another important source, catalogued by the Beaverbrook Library in London which houses it, is the collection of private papers of David Lloyd George, composed of some 1,041 boxes of documents. It has been divided into Series A through I. The only series cited in this study are F (Lloyd George as Prime Minister, 1916-1922; 254 boxes) and G (Lloyd George Papers, 1922-1945; 264 boxes). The style of citation used here is that of the cataloguer (e.g., F/3/2/16); the initial indicates the series; the digits specify box number/folder number/ and document number.

LIST OF MAPS

Map	Page
1. Danzig and Environs	28
2. Upper Silesia: The Plebiscite Commission Report .	89
3. Upper Silesia: The August 4, 1921 Proposals . .	135
4. Upper Silesia: Final French and British Proposals of August 11, 1921	137
5. Upper Silesia: The Final Award	151

CHAPTER I

GREAT BRITAIN AND THE NEW DIPLOMACY AT PARIS

The day was nothing special. Trading at the Paris Bourse was rather moderate and the eyes of French society were again turning to traditional concerns like fine fashions, although the new décolleté styles raised a few traditionalist eyebrows. The English were slipping back to as uncomplicated a pre-war existence as possible. Once-popular war plays were closing today at the Princes and presently at the Haymarket, and Moss Brothers in Bedford Street, who had recently sold military dress to officers, now advertised that they were retooling "from khaki to mufti," the latter notably rendered from nearly all pre-war materials. The Americans basked in their newly-acquired prohibitionist sanctity, their virtuous status having been announced in Congress only two days earlier when Nebraska had supplied the 36th vote necessary for ratification of the constitutional amendment. The Italians were still wrestling with a new cabinet, an exercise whose repetition they would apparently not tire of for at least another two generations.

Like on most Paris winter days, the gray, cloudy sky held promise of nothing either better or worse to come. Taxis and occasional private cars pulled up, their occupants singly, in pairs, in groups, hurrying inside to the ornate gilt and crimson Clock Room, more in a spirit of business than excitement. Invariably they carried sheaves of paper, some protruding from large black bags and others neatly bound within orderly foolscap folders. Stately black limousines carrying the greater dignitaries drove directly into the courtyard of the Quai d'Orsay, but even many of these faces went unrecognized by the spare two or three hundred onlookers who had disregarded the cold and gathered for the event. President Poincaré would be there to inaugurate the meeting. Lloyd George, the British Prime Minister, and the other Allied heads of government were expected momentarily. It was Saturday afternoon, January 18, 1919 and the peace conference which, it was hoped, would bring some order from the tumult of the Great War was about to convene.

Just over a century earlier another assemblage of this sort had converged on Vienna, and in the wake of continental chaos had also tried to redraw the frontiers of Europe. Among the many other problems to which they addressed their attention, those men had come to give shape to a Poland. And this they did. It was perhaps not the historic Poland that had once lorded over a good deal of Europe, boasting a "republic" long before it became the fashion. Neither was it by any means an undoing of the eighteenth century partitions which had been carried out while these very allies had looked the other way or had been otherwise engaged.

The "Congress Kingdom" of Poland was carved from the territories of the Napoleonic Grand Duchy of Warsaw and was incorporated in a personal union with the Russian tsar. Within fifteen years, however, this new Poland would disappear from the map as her predecessors had.

Among the questions that demanded the attention of the Paris peacemakers in 1919 was the delineation of the new Polish state whose existence in one form or another had been called for in the war aims of both the Allied and the Central Powers. What shape should the new Poland take? What frontiers should she be awarded at the expense of her neighbors?

Certainly the eastern frontiers of the new Poland were still undeterminable at this conference, for Russia, the power that would share them, consumed in her own revolution, had disengaged herself from the Allied cause and was not now represented at Paris. Thus, the delineation of Polish frontiers in the North and West, where they touched upon the recently defeated Germany, became the primary task at Paris in determining the fate of Poland.

It is difficult, however, to speak of a British policy toward the new country as expressed in the arguments over two of the most hotly contested areas--Danzig and Upper Silesia. Great Britain tended to view the settlements of these particular frontiers less as aspects of Anglo-Polish relations and more as facets of Anglo-German dealings. It is no wonder, then, that Britain's active role in determining both was ever more to be regarded by the Poles as an affront to their sovereignty and national character.

A new mood was abroad that, it was said, should provide loftier motivations for the peacemakers as they tried to relight the lamps of Europe. As these issues and so many others would be taken up, there was talk that the "new diplomacy" would be wielded in place of the old. No more secret agreements. No new imperialism, no matter how benign. Instead, there would be open diplomacy, impartial justice, and self-determination of peoples. Palmerston had once claimed that Britain's friendships were dictated only by her interests. It remained to be seen whether his historic observation would be borne out in the ensuing deliberations or whether the new idealistic spirit would entice the British peacemakers.

Britain fancied herself the practitioner of this new style. As such she called for fair treatment of the enemy, seeking, in this way, to fashion a peace that would prevent future wars. And it was an expression of this policy which prompted Lloyd George to assume the "leadership of compromise." His influence was felt in preserving for Danzig an independent status, neither German nor Polish, and in providing for Upper Silesia a plebiscite rather than complete and immediate Polish sovereignty.

It is evident that at Paris and in the years immediately following, when called upon to deal with either of these territories, Britain appeared to frequently favor the German position over the Polish, always in the name of fairness, justice, and the spirit as well as the letter of the Treaty of Versailles. In the early years following the Great War, Britain could afford to measure justice strictly and observe the niceties of impartiality when dealing with these areas because the world was still large enough for the distant Upper Silesia and Danzig to be irrelevant to her. To use the Poles' assessment of the situation, Britain had lately learned that her defense began at the Rhine but, they said, she had yet to learn that it began at the Vistula as well.

Historical Background and the British Position

Long before the peace conference at Paris, Poland comprised one of the perennial unsettled questions of Europe, but up to about 1917 Britain maintained a "prudent reserve" toward it not so much because of hostility, of which she had so often been accused by the Poles, but rather out of consideration for her Russian ally and perhaps, as sometimes suggested, out of various degrees of "indifference, prejudice and the traditional dictates of British policy." Once Russia withdrew from the war in 1917, Britain's deferring silence, although no longer required, was maintained. No document found in the British archives can provide evidence that official prejudice guided her on this course. The British tradition of non-involvement in eastern Europe did in part contribute to this silence. But the real key to understanding Britain's policy is found in the last of these factors--indifference. But this indifference which characterized the general attitude in Britain was not left unseasoned by doses of irritation and impatience aimed at presumptuous Polish territorial demands, undignified wrangling in the family of nations, or a Polish *fait accompli*. J. D. Gregory, who had, during his years in the Foreign Office, been involved with Polish questions, recalled in his reminiscences an observation of President Masaryk of Czechoslovakia that the Czechs were the head of Slavism, the Poles its heart, and the Russians its body.

> Certainly the palpitations of the great Slav heart of Poland could be heard from one end of the universe to the other from 1918 on. It palpitated in London and Paris and Washington and Rome without ceasing for about five years till everyone got thoroughly sick of it. The hullaballoo indeed got on almost everyone's nerves--and particularly the hypersensitive nerves of Mr. Lloyd George. It was unfortunate, but not surprising.[1]

---

[1] John D. Gregory, On the Edge of Diplomacy: Rambles and Reflections, 1902-1928 (London: Hutchinson and Co. Ltd., 1929), pp. 169-70.

But as a responsible member of the Alliance dedicated to the making of the peace as well as to the winning of the war, Great Britain sought non-involvement only after her duties in this role had been discharged.

When the peace conference convened in January 1919, the cause of Poland was represented by a delegation led by Roman Dmowski, President of the Polish National Committee, and Ignace J. Paderewski, President of the Council of Ministers and Minister of Foreign Affairs, the musician turned diplomat. These two men represented the attempt to heal the rift among Poles which had been evidenced by the *de facto* existence of two Polish governments—one in Warsaw and the other in Paris. The pro-Allied Polish National Committee in Paris with Roman Dmowski at its head had won the recognition of the peace conference as the government of Poland, but an effective government had simultaneously taken over in Warsaw with Josef Pilsudski at the helm. Because of his former cooperation with Austria, collaboration with Germany, and "dangerous" socialist connections, Pilsudski was looked upon with suspicion in the west. Paderewski on January 14 informed the Committee in Paris that he had agreed with Pilsudski about forming a new national government in which the Polish National Committee would participate. With this, Paderewski joined Dmowski in the Polish delegation in Paris.

The Germans had no voice at the conference and it would not be until the Allied peace terms were handed to them on May 7 that their delegation could comment upon the proposed settlement, or *diktat*, as later German observers would have it.

Whether at the conference, in the press, or in public speeches, both countries claimed Upper Silesia and Danzig for themselves on the basis of historic, economic, geographic or ethnographic factors or under the principle of self-determination of nations. The latter sprang from Wilson's Fourteen Points and as one of the guiding ideas of 1919, the Germans expected it to be one of the principles upon which the peace treaty would be based. But the Germans were to be disillusioned in May when harsher terms than they had anticipated were handed to them.

Poles and Germans made simultaneous claims to the coveted territories of Danzig and Upper Silesia using conflicting historical, ethnographical, and economic arguments in their defense. Often sentiment colored their historical perceptions, mathematical acrobatics affected their demographic data and ethnographic evaluations, and bare national coffers dictated their economic philosophies.

Historically, medieval Danzig, like most Polish towns at the time with no sizeable national middle class, was peopled heavily with German and Jewish traders. Although as time passed and other

Polish cities lost their German character and any special privileges, Danzig did not, owing probably to her proximity to Germany and her Hanseatic connections. But her loyalty to Poland was unquestioned and it was under violent protest that she finally passed under Prussian rule during the eighteenth century partitions, retaining until as late as 1815, an expressed preference for affiliation with Poland. The Poles, in claiming this territory at the conference, emphasized this strong allegiance.[2] Poles and Germans also made simultaneous claims to Upper Silesia, each claimant attempting to trace the background of the territory to some historical moment when it had acted as one of the cradles of either Polish or German culture.

It was on the basis of ethnographical data that the Germans made claim to Danzig. Neither the Poles nor any other delegation at the peace conference challenged their claim that Danzigers were essentially a German people in language and culture. Their attempt to juggle the statistical evidence by claiming non-Polish, Slavic-speaking minorities for themselves was a futile exercise which did little to affect the eventual disposition of Danzig. Widespread belief that Upper Silesia was primarily Polish in population and destined to be transferred to the new Polish Republic was complicated as time went on by German-produced ethnographical analyses and reports of German sympathies among many Upper Silesians.

The geological and, particularly, the economic claims had somewhat more substance. Both Poland and Germany claimed that Danzig was necessary for their economic welfare, although experience showed that under German tutelage, the city had been neglected and had fallen into being a second-rate port on the Baltic. For Poland, at least when viewed in 1919, Danzig was its only possible port and link with the sea, a city which under Polish rule would be destined, according to their claims, to become the chief crossroads between east and west in the Baltic.

---

[2]The best account of the historical argument with respect to Danzig is in Charles Homer Haskins and Robert Howard Lord, <u>Some Problems of the Peace Conference</u> (Cambridge: Harvard University Press, 1920), pp. 181 ff., the authors of which were attached to the American delegation at Paris and expressed decidedly pro-Polish leanings there. See also <u>Gdansk and East Prussia</u> by W. Lutoslawski who used the papers prepared for the Polish Delegation in writing this booklet for the Polish Commission of Work Preparatory to the Conference of Peace (Paris: Imprimerie Levi, 1919) and <u>Poland and Danzig</u> prepared by the Polish Research Centre. Figures of the 1910 census indicate that of the 324,000 people in the Danzig area, only approximately 16,000 had Polish as their mother tongue. Haskins and Lord, p. 181.

As for Upper Silesia, it was true that its coal basin geologically formed a unit with the Polish Dabrowa-Jaworzyno and Morawa-Karwina fields in which all of the coal belonged to one formation, although the depth and quality of the deposits varied. The logic of this claim was in part demonstrated in 1939 when the entire system came to be administered as an economic entity, Gau Oberschlesien. Germany played on Allied concerns when she cleverly linked her "need" for Upper Silesia with her ability to pay the reparations that were being demanded of her, a claim not ignored by the British Prime Minister who repeatedly struck the same note in Supreme Council meetings where he tried to temper French demands upon Germany by showing his ally that she would have to buy the reparations settlement with some such compromise.[3]

Development of British Policy

When the peace conference opened in January 1919 the Foreign Office had already produced several statements which articulated its rudimentary position on Danzig and Upper Silesia. The British observation regarding the destiny of Upper Silesia took the form of a single paragraph in an unofficial pre-conference paper on Poland stating:

> The question has been raised whether the coal-mining districts of Silesia should be included in the new State of Poland. As the inhabitants are without doubt mainly Polish, there would seem no good reason for refusing their union with Poland, and there is an important economic reason in favour of doing so, namely, that the coal of these districts cokes, whereas that of Poland proper does not. Their acquisition would therefore be of vital importance for the development of Polish iron industries.[4]

J. W. Headlam-Morley, the Assistant Director of the Political Intelligence Department of the Foreign Office, later in 1921 showed

---

[3] S. Kudlicki, Upper Silesia, 2nd ed. (Perth, Scotland: Munro Press Ltd., 1944), p. 25. See the extensive, particularly statistical presentation of The Economic Value of Upper Silesia for Poland and Germany Respectively: Materials Collected from Official Statistics (London: St. Catherine Press, 1921). For Lloyd George's linking of the Upper Silesian and reparations questions see Meeting of British and French Representatives, November 27, 1920 in Documents on British Foreign Policy, 1919-1939 (London: Her Majesty's Stationery Office), (hereafter DBFP), 1st ser., VIII, no. 96.

[4] Quoted in Memorandum respecting Upper Silesia at the Peace Conference by J. W. Headlam-Morley, April 6, 1921 in DBFP, 1st ser., XVI, no. 13 annex.

this statement to be unclear and erroneous on several counts. He found it vague in delimiting the geographic area in question and nebulous in defining the relationship between that province and the Republic of Poland. Moreover, it was inaccurate in its description of Upper Silesian coal which in reality was similar to Polish coal. Finally, the entire statement, he said, was based upon the premise that a population which was overwhelmingly ethnographically Polish would automatically desire to be part of the Polish state.[5] But this statement remained unchallenged in the early portion of the peace conference.

The original Foreign Office scheme dealing with Danzig was the "Neufahrwasser solution" which Professor Charles Oman had proposed on November 14, 1918. What he suggested was that a major part of West Prussia go to Poland for ethnographic and economic reasons. Since Poland needed access to the sea she should get it, but not at Danzig. This city should remain German while the port of Neufahrwasser at the mouth of the Vistula, about four miles north of Danzig, should go to Poland as a free port on a river open to seagoing vessels capable of ascending the river to the larger city. Both Sir Esme Howard, head of the section of the British peace delegation that dealt with northeastern European questions, and Lord Robert Cecil, Assistant Secretary of State for Foreign Affairs, preferred a German corridor through Polish-inhabited territory or the creation of a small Polish enclave northwest of Danzig where Neufahrwasser, the Polish port, would be established with full guarantees for Polish trade whether by the Vistula or by railway. But these various schemes suffered from inaccuracies that arose out of a lack of information regarding the location of Danzig docks, or technical questions on the navigability of the Vistula.[6] Neither of these schemes comprised official policy as formulated at the Foreign Office and, in fact, members of the British delegation found themselves free agents at the beginning of the peace conference respecting these questions.

Danzigers, whose prospect for the future appeared ominous, saw that they would be called upon in some fashion to provide Poland's

---

[5] Ibid.

[6] Memorandum "Danzig and the Polish Corridor" by J. W. Headlam-Morley, April 4, 1925 in London, Public Record Office, Foreign Office General Correspondence, FO 371/10730, C 5410/459/18; also reproduced in FO 417/18, no. 27 and in FO 371/10097, N 2267/43/55. This memorandum was a chapter of what was projected to be a history of Headlam-Morley's work at the peace conference and has since been published as A Memoir of the Paris Peace Conference by Barnes and Noble in October 1972. Correspondence between him and the Prime Minister concerning these accounts is preserved in Private Papers of Lloyd George, London, Beaverbrook Library, G/257.

outlet to the sea. Prompted by both their fear and their indignation because a majority of them were ethnically German, they demonstrated their nationalist sentiments in violence from October 1918 until the Treaty of Versailles was signed in June 1919.[7]

Although no authoritative Danzig policy existed among the British delegates when the peace conference convened, they tended to disapprove of the transfer of the city to Poland, a point of view which after communications with the Americans, they would to some extent temporarily alter. Influential in the early Anglo-American talks in this regard was the memorandum of January 21, 1919 prepared by a group of geographers from the American delegation. Briefly, their position recommended that Poland should have "secure and unhampered access to the Baltic" at the expense of Germany as the lesser of two evils. With the granting of a corridor and Danzig to Poland, 600,000 Poles of West Prussia would come under Polish rule and 20 million Poles would receive their commercial outlet at the expense and inconvenience of 1,600,000 Germans in East Prussia who would be cut off from the body of Germany. This territorial severing would in no way prevent rail transit across the Polish corridor and, in addition, East Prussia would not have its excellent water communication route via Königsberg and the Baltic affected in the least. This American attitude was to become the dominant one during the first part of the conference.

In a memorandum of February 6, Headlam-Morley recapitulated the original Foreign Office scheme on Danzig and considered the territorial demands being made upon Germany.[8] In order to produce a treaty which the Germans would be willing to sign, he further insisted that the demands "should not go beyond that point at which a strong justification can be put forward which will appeal to German Liberal and Socialist opinion." It was already clear that areas of great industrial importance would be snatched away from Germany with the cessions in Alsace-Lorraine, the Saar, part of the mining district of Silesia, and territories in Posen and on the southern frontier. Headlam-Morley, the source of a thoughtful proliferation of memoranda on Polish questions at the conference, was already evidencing his consistently pro-German attitude for which those who had their own Polish ax to grind would later brand

---

[7]Christoph M. Kimmich, The Free City: Danzig and German Foreign Policy, 1919-1934 (New Haven: Yale University Press, 1968), pp. 12-14.

[8]For the Headlam-Morley memorandum of February 6, 1919 see Confidential Print 11338, "Papers and Correspondence Dealing with the Establishment of Danzig as a Free City," in FO 608/65, file 130/6/1, no. 20216.

him as the pliable tool of Lloyd George.[9]

Sir Eyre Crowe and Lord Hardinge both agreed, the former noting that it was important for Howard's Special Mission to Warsaw to "avoid staying or doing anything to give rise to the expectation in Poland that Great Britain is favorable to her annexing or acquiring Danzig," and the latter commenting that a free port at Danzig and the free transport on the Vistula "should meet all the economic needs" of Poland to "render her in no worse a condition than Czechoslovakia, Yugo-Slavia or Hungary."[10]

Speculations on the land settlements in the Polish area abounded at Paris and less than a week after Headlam-Morley's observations on Danzig, the Council of Ten on February 12, established the Polish Commission, on the initiative of Lord Balfour, to handle the reports and requests for instructions from the inter-allied mission which had recently been dispatched to Poland.[11]

While the Commission proceeded to work on its report on the German-Polish boundary question, a new, more convincing statement was produced within the British delegation which helped to confirm the preferred policy of non-cession of Danzig to Poland. This confirmation came in the form of a memorandum of February 20, by Dr.

---

[9] Lord Derby reported to the Foreign Office that Pertinax in the *Echo de Paris* saw Lloyd George's replacement of other representatives at Paris with a "more tractable person," Headlam-Morley, as part of a grand design which included the British Prime Minister's intention to appoint as the League of Nations High Commissioner for Danzig a British functionary holding his own views. Derby to FO, no. 876, July 13, 1919 in FO 608/65, file 130/6/1, no. 15284.

[10] A message was telegraphed from Lord Balfour to Howard in Warsaw to this effect on February 26, in which Howard was specifically instructed not to commit himself in any direction regarding the future disposal of Danzig. Balfour to Howard, no. 21-22, February 26, 1919 in FO 608/65, file 130/6/1, no. 20216.

[11] Sir Esme Howard and General A. Carton de Wiart were the British representatives in this special mission to Warsaw. Howard, who was admittedly "out to help Poland as far as I could to re-establish herself as a strong and independent State," while he respected his one-eyed oft-wounded colleague as the "bravest man in the British Army," was nevertheless disappointed that the indomitable Carton de Wiart was selected to replace South Africa's Prime Minister Louis Botha, the original appointee who held more sway with Lloyd George. See Sir Esme Howard, Lord Howard of Penrith, *Theatre of Life*, Vol. II: *Life Seen from the Stalls* (London: Hodder & Stroughton, 1935), pp. 307-14.

G. W. Prothero, the historian then working in the Foreign Office, which heavily emphasized the historic aspect of the issue. Since the fourteenth century Danzig had been primarily German, he maintained, and for 350 years while nominally under Polish sovereignty, it had been practically a free city like the other towns of the Hanseatic League. All of the things that comprised its civilization, whether related to educational institutions or commercial prosperity, were German. Furthermore, two-thirds of the population was Protestant, unlike the population of Catholic Poland. Perceiving that Polish annexation of West Prussia and Danzig would create "a sense of gross injustice in the mind of Germany which might be fatal to the peace of the world," Prothero called for a fulfillment of Allied commitments by either of two courses: (1) by bringing the Vistula or part of it under regulations applicable to international rivers and similarly arranging the railway communications or (2) by neutralizing Danzig including the district between it and the sea and placing it under League of Nations protection.[12] The British delegation was much impressed by this proposal--which appears to have been the first one for providing a special regime for the city--for they saw how they could simultaneously satisfy Poland's need for access to the sea without turning over to her the unquestionably German city.

An unofficial meeting of the British and American delegations took place on February 21 at the Hotel Crillon at which the Howard-Lord agreement was reached,[13] and which in effect reversed the original Foreign Office scheme. Sir Esme Howard and Robert H. Lord, the American representative, agreed that it would be an "economic absurdity" to leave Danzig, Elbing and Königsberg as East Prussian ports while the entire Polish state and population were deprived of a proper seaport and direct control over its access to the sea. National sentiments and the economic interests of Danzig notwithstanding, it seemed necessary to include the city in the entire strip of Polish-speaking country along the Vistula's left bank which would be awarded to the new Poland. In an attempt to prevent German interference with rail communications, they proposed to allow Germany to retain the administration and control of

---

[12] Quoted in memorandum by Headlam-Morley of April 4, 1925 cited above.

[13] This agreement appears in British files as part of Headlam-Morley's memorandum of April 4, 1925 cited above. Nelson records that the Howard-Lord agreement does not as such appear in the papers of the American delegation, but he notes the existence of an undated memorandum entitled, "The German-Polish Frontier" which is signed in typescript "R. H. Lord." Harold I. Nelson, Land and Power: British and Allied Policy on Germany's Frontiers, 1916-1919 (Toronto: University of Toronto Press, 1963), p. 148

the main Berlin-Königsberg railway from Könitz to the Vistula near Dirschau. Such an agreement appeared a substantial success for the American Harvard professor who was able to win over to his point of view the British career diplomat whose government's Foreign Secretary, Foreign Office, and General Staff had consistently opposed both the creation of a Polish Corridor and the Polish acquisition of Danzig. But in reality Howard had from the beginning been more generous in his attitudes toward the new Polish state than most of his colleagues had been.

From the evidence available, it appears that the Howard-Lord agreement was unauthorized and no sooner had it been reached then both Sir Eyre Crowe, plenipotentiary to the peace conference, and Lord Hardinge of Penshurst, Permanent Undersecretary of State, commented unfavorably upon it. Both agreed that Poland must secure adequate guarantees for free transit of her trade through the port of Danzig but both rejected outright the territorial separation of East and West Prussia by means of a Polish Corridor. The amiability exhibited between the American and British delegations notwithstanding, the fact remained that the peace conference had been in session now for some five weeks and still the British delegation had no formal policy respecting Danzig or Upper Silesia. The German-Polish frontier question, having been consigned to the Commission on Polish Affairs, His Majesty's Government was not moved to favor any particular settlement in anticipation of the Commission's recommendations--surely a proof of British disinterest and impartiality. From such circumstances could spring the diplomacy of compromise in the latter part of the peace conference which was dominated by Lloyd George.

Finally on February 25, Headlam-Morley, who later became the author of the clauses regarding Danzig which almost without challenge or change found their way into the final draft of the treaty, put forward a memorandum which seriously contemplated only two alternatives for the settlement of the Danzig question:

> (a) The City of Danzig should be incorporated in Poland. But the Government of Poland should, by a special charter to be deposited with a guarantee with the League of Nations, grant to Danzig and the adjoining districts autonomy with regard to matters to be determined, and in particular, religion, the use of language, the local government and administration of the civil and criminal laws, and education.
>
> (b) Danzig and the adjoining district [should] . . . remain under German sovereignty but it [should] . . . receive the position of an autonomous State in the German Federation, and shall be made, for purposes of

commerce, a free port under the guarantee of the League of Nations.[14]

A prompt retort came on the following day from H. J. Paton, an Oxford professor and wartime civilian appointee to the Admiralty, who was perhaps the most knowledgeable person on Polish affairs at the conference. He recognized that Germany had legitimate claims to both West Prussia and Danzig and that her loss of these territories could potentially "arouse a spirit of bitterness in Germany" and become a "certain source of future wars." But on the other hand, he deplored the remnant of *realpolitik* which advised the Powers to direct injustice, when its execution was inevitable, toward the smaller nations because they could more easily be made to acquiesce in unfavorable states of affairs. Certainly the settlement of this question should not be left to be decided after the treaty, he pleaded, because sentiment being involved in it, a definite, clear decision was sure to cause less difficulty and danger than a "policy of postponements and compromise." If injury was to be unavoidable, it should be made unquestionably and promptly clear. "To raise hopes on both sides and to keep both sides for long in a state of suspense is merely to inflame passion and to make an ultimate settlement more difficult."[15] The truth of his statement was borne out in the results of the interminable postponement of the Upper Silesian settlement. Without the uncertainty alternating with hope and frustration, there probably would not have been an insurrection in May 1921 nor even those in the summers of 1919 and 1920. This is the kind of situation Paton foresaw for Danzig if the issue were left dangling after the peacemakers went home.

At the same time that Headlam-Morley's proposal was put forward, C. W. C. Oman resurrected the old Neufahrwasser scheme and coupled it with the concept of a Polish Corridor for access to the sea.[16] He proposed to leave Danzig under German sovereignty on the principle of self-determination, but to assign the port town of

---

[14] Memorandum by Headlam-Morley of April 4, 1925 cited above.

[15] Memorandum by Paton, Confidential Print 11338, "Papers and Correspondence Dealing with the Establishment of Danzig as a Free City," no. 7. When writing his 1925 memorandum on Danzig and the Corridor (which often reads like a personal panegyric), Headlam-Morley, after discussing his February 26, 1919 proposals only parenthetically mentions this Paton response before continuing at length with his own March 3 response to Paton. But the Paton memorandum appears in full in the confidential print cited here.

[16] Memorandum by C. W. C. Oman, February 26, 1919 in FO 608/54, file 130/6/1, no. 3333.

Neufahrwasser to Poland along with the Polish-speaking regions of West Prussia, thereby creating a corridor and German enclaves of Danzig and East Prussia. This, Oman justified on the basis that "it is the interests of Poland rather than those of Germany which the Allies must consider first." Other such proposals were developed and discussed as the work of the Commission continued on its report to the peace conference concerning the German-Polish boundary.

Interestingly, the disposition for ownership of Upper Silesia at first was not an issue of controversy within the British delegation or among the Allied delegations in Paris. There was no argument over the province's Polish ethnic composition and the general assumption at the peace conference was that the contested territory should go to Poland.[17] There is no more than parenthetical reference to the province in the available documents of the peace conference and in the major national newspapers of Great Britain in early June. Upper Silesia did not become an issue until the Germans protested against its proposed assignment in the draft treaty to Poland and linked their loss of it with claims of their inability to make reparation payments to the Allies.

But ethnographic considerations were proving to be an inadequate basis for arriving at a Danzig settlement, and whatever remnant of support among the British delegation which remained for the old Neufahrwasser scheme was finally dissipated on March 1 with the presentation of the Admiralty memorandum which left no consistent policy to direct the delegation.

The document in question was a lengthy memorandum which put forward the arguments for and against the inclusion of Danzig in the new Polish state. It came from the Admiralty, largely the

---

[17] Representative of general views on the province was the reference to Upper Silesia as "purely Polish in its population" and as such the subject of no major debate. See The Times [London], March 8, 1919, p. 9. Before the conference Balfour and the Foreign Office had advocated a partition of the province based primarily on ethnographic considerations. See Nelson, p. 169. It was precisely because the Upper Silesian boundaries were not disputed among the Allies before the completion of the draft treaty until Lloyd George made a crusade of "saving" the province for Germany, that Gregory Macdonald criticized the Prime Minister. To him it appeared that Lloyd George had irresponsibly and singlehandedly rejected the boundaries which had been "unanimously agreed upon by responsible diplomats and scholars." See Gregory Macdonald, "Polish Upper Silesia" (Prepared for New Fabian Research Bureau, Unpublished manuscript deposited at Polish Institute and Sikorski Museum Library, London, 1935), p. 93.

product of Paton and other civilians, and it appeared to carry much weight with the British peacemakers.[18] It examined the economic, strategic, and historical bases of the claims made by Poland and Germany in the Danzig and Corridor region and suggested modifications of the ethnographic frontier. Using evidence emanating from the Prussian Statistical Office, the memorandum indicated that West Prussia was inhabited by a Polish-speaking population and the subject of justifiable cession to Poland.

Next, the "Admiralty" memorandum considered the question of Poland's claim to a port, especially Danzig, and to practicable means of communication between it and Poland proper. Poland maintained that a purely ethnographic solution would provide her with no serviceable port, no possible railway connection to the sea, no site for possible erection of a port, and would give a geographically and historically Polish river to Germany whose only value would be to serve as an obstacle to Polish economic independence. After considering the alternatives of creating an artificial port for Poland at Putzig with rail or canal connections and ceding Neufahrwasser to Poland as an outlet to the sea, the document rejected both in favor of the unconditional transfer of the sovereignty of Danzig to Poland. It shattered the old Neufahrwasser scheme by observing the situation which occurred in the years between the first and second partitions of Poland when Danzig was under Polish control and Neufahrwasser under Prussian sovereignty. Frederick II had diverted trade from Polish Danzig to Prussian Neufahrwasser until the population of Danzig had been cut by more than half.

Headlam-Morley, however, remained opposed to Polish annexation of the city and wrote on March 3 that he preferred an autonomous or semi-independent state for Danzig. It was with the historian's broad view that he saw the dealings of 1919.

> We want to shake ourselves free of the obsessions of the unified and centralised national State, which is the growth of the period since the French Revolution. It is the exaggeration of this which is the cause not only of the war, but of the difficulties with the peace. We are still under the obsession of the political ideas which created pan-Germanism and threaten to bring about an equally aggressive and uncompromising spirit among the new nationalities.[19]

---

[18]"Memorandum Outlining Arguments for and against the Inclusion of Danzig in the New Polish State," undated and unsigned, in FO 608/54, file 130/6/1, no. 3339. However, it appears as a secret print in FO 374/20 as no. 42 and is identified in the catalogue as originating in the Naval Intelligence Staff on March 1, 1919.

[19]Memorandum by Headlam-Morley of April 4, 1925 cited above.

To render Danzig autonomous would be to assure the city control of its own affairs and to rescue it from the fear of being subjected to Polish propaganda and dominance. From such autonomy would grow improved relations between Danzig and Poland who would discover the commercial advantages of cooperation as neighbors. What he aimed to prevent was the categorical annexation of a people to an alien state without securing for them some degree of autonomy under international guarantee. Already evident in the design is the concept of the settlement eventually arrived at in the draft clauses and then in the final articles of the Treaty of Versailles which settlement was primarily a British brainchild. It proved to be in outline the compromise solution between the two extremes of German and Polish annexation, but unlike the lukewarmness and pure expediency usually at the heart of compromise, this solution was based upon a positive and firm belief that it was the most suitable course for all involved, not merely the best bargain that could be struck under the particularly difficult circumstances.

No matter what the speculation was, the question of Poland's boundaries had, after all, been given to the inter-allied Commission on Polish Affairs to examine and report upon. By March 12, their first report was completed and delivered to the Supreme Council, and on March 19 it was discussed at the Council of Ten meeting where it was greeted with denunciation by Lloyd George.[20]

The Commission sought to grant to the Poles everything that they had asked for, and more. First, it recommended that the city and port of Danzig be assigned to Poland in response to that country's "legitimate aspirations" for an outlet to the sea. As a corollary to this, the corridor to the sea should also go to the new state in view of the fact that it was more possible to secure the right of transit for 1,600,000 East Prussians across the Polish strip than for some 25,000,000 Poles across a German area. The creation of the corridor was deemed necessary in order to prevent the 600,000 Poles in West Prussia from remaining under German sovereignty. In order to achieve a rail connection, the Commission favored Polish control of the Danzig-Dirschau-Mlava-Warsaw railway, even though it necessitated the annexation to Poland of those Germans in northern West Prussia who lived east of the Vistula River. Other considerations dealt with territory to be included or excluded from various plebiscite areas. With respect to Upper Silesia about which quick agreement had been reached, as already seen, the report sought to cede the territory on purely ethnographic grounds and failed to consider the serious economic and industrial problems that would ensue from such treatment. The upshot of the entire report was that Poland should walk away as the victor.

---

[20] A print of the full text of the First Report of the Commission on Polish Affairs, March 12, 1919 appears in FO 608/69, file 135/1/3, no. 4118.

Basing his objections on the principle of self-determination and upon the belief that too large a German minority within the new state would be detrimental to Poland, the Prime Minister launched his objection, which was destined to take on the proportions of a full-scale campaign. Such a solution, in his estimation, would be unsuitable not only because it was a potential threat to Polish unity, but also because no German government would sign a treaty making such demands upon it. Moreover, a railway could be removed but not a large settled population. Where centuries-old German aggrandizement was merely reversed, he thought, the decision might be palatable to the Germans, but the areas to which Poland had no clear ethnographic or historic claim, Lloyd George believed, would become a *Germania irredenta* and contain the "seed for future war." He queried whether the Allies would ever be willing to go to war to prevent the secession of these areas in the future. At this time his objections, it will be noted, centered on the corridor district alone, implying the Prime Minister's acceptance, in theory at least, of a Polish Danzig.[21]

Following the lengthy discussion, the report was returned to the Commission for further consideration; on the following day it was unanimously determined on the recommendation of Colonel Frederick M. Kisch, who had replaced Sir William Tyrrell as the British representative, to maintain the report in its entirety.[22] It is important at this point to note that it was upon British initiative that the Commission's report was affirmed because Lloyd George later suggested that "British representatives had given their assent with reluctance." Evidence does not uphold the truth of this statement, and rather, it seems that following lengthy discussion, the British representatives decided that all things being considered, it would be better to assign Danzig to

---

[21] This does not mean that British opinion was unanimous on the question of Danzig's going to Poland. H. A. L. Fisher, one of the few Liberal ministers in Lloyd George's coalition cabinet, in his letter of March 17, 1919 to the Prime Minister urged Lloyd George to prevent such an eventuality which, it seemed, would give rise to a German irredentist movement. See London, Private Papers of Lloyd George, F/16/7/37. An interesting opinion on the disposition of Danzig was that expressed by General Henry Wilson, the Chief of the Imperial General Staff, who in his diary entry for March 17 noted that Danzig ought to be forfeited to Poland on condition that Poland withdraw from the Eastern Galician town of Lemberg. Lee Major General Sir Charles E. Callwell, Field-Marshal Sir Henry Wilson, His Life and Diaries (London: Cassell, 1927), II, p. 174.

[22] Minutes of Meeting of Council of Ten, March 22, 1919 in Foreign Relations of the United States, Paris Peace Conference, IV, 448-58. (hereafter FRUS, PPC)

Poland. As Headlam-Morley wrote in 1925, "They had perhaps done so reluctantly in the sense that they recognized the grave objections to this procedure, but their vote was an honest and considered decision which they were not prepared to recant, and to which they adhered."[23]

News of Lloyd George's criticism of the report and subsequent statements allegedly made by him to the effect that use of the Vistula and the Danzig-Thorn railway would constitute the access to the sea which Poland desired and would suffice to insure that nation's economic independence were received with some alarm in Warsaw by Sir Esme Howard. He telegraphed Balfour that such utterances had produced a "painful impression" in Warsaw and, doubting that the Prime Minister had actually made the statements in question, sought confirmation of their authenticity. Howard consistently maintained a sympathetic attitude toward the Poles and believed that in any such halfway solution as was proposed by the Prime Minister, Germany would always be in a position to interrupt traffic on the Vistula and on the railway, and that no international arrangements would successfully secure Polish free transit should the Germans employ their brand of "trickery." So strongly did Howard and General Adrian Carton de Wiart feel on this point that the former offered to come to Paris to put forward the Polish case in this regard.

A leak to the press exposed in France and Poland a full account of the Council of Ten sessions and Lloyd George angrily threatened to leave the conference.[24] Critics attacked his unwillingness to accept a unanimous report of the inter-allied Commission on Polish Affairs. Headlam-Morley, in considering this moment in retrospect, sought to white-wash the Prime Minister. He agreed, that had the Commission's work been purely technical, the criticism

---

[23] Memorandum by Headlam-Morley of April 4, 1925 cited above.

[24] Lord Northcliffe's Paris Daily Mail followed suit and attacked the Prime Minister on grounds that he had no right to override the Commission and it revealed passages from his statements made in the ostensibly secret sessions of the Council of Ten. See Winston S. Churchill, The Aftermath (New York: Charles Scribner's Sons, 1929), p. 196. Lord Northcliffe, owner of The Times and the Daily Mail, wanted to head a delegation to Paris. Lloyd George's rebuff led to a war between them which took the form of mutual vilification. Part of The Times's attack upon the Prime Minister was demonstrated in that organ's criticism of Lloyd George's Polish policy and in the promulgation of its own pro-Polish viewpoint. See for example, The Times, April 17, 1919, p. 13. On the Northcliffe-Lloyd George altercation see Churchill, p. 213 and Malcolm Thompson, David Lloyd George: The Official Biography (London: Hutchinson, 1948), p. 303.

would have been just, but since it dealt with matters of "the highest political importance" it was proper for Lloyd George to seek to prevent the creation of a situation to which the Germans would find it impossible to submit. Whether prompted by pragmatic politics or principles of the new diplomacy, the fact remains that Lloyd George attempted to dominate rather than lead and to throttle those peacemakers who did not comply with his design.

But the entire press leak escapade led to a remodeling of the conference structure. Up to then, there had been poor liaison between plenipotentiaries and commission members, particularly in the British and American delegations. No clear instructions as to major political principles to guide their work had sifted down to the commissions. Control was therefore tightened when the Council of Four--Lloyd George of Great Britain, Wilson of the United States, Clemenceau of France, and Orlando of Italy--began its sessions on March 20. These meetings were to be completely private unlike those of the old Council of Ten sessions where great numbers of secretaries and subordinates were present--a situation that was so conducive to press leakages. To meet the problem of poor liaison, a system was agreed upon whereby solutions for main political problems were first decided upon by the Council and then small committees were appointed to carry out the decisions in detail. These groups worked informally and in such immediate touch with the plenipotentiaries that any problems which arose were speedily referred to and settled by the Council. Under the new system, Danzig was the first important matter to be considered.

What Lloyd George was saying publicly merely reiterated the stand he had taken all along on the Polish question. In his famous memorandum of March 25, the Prime Minister recognized Poland's right to a corridor but he said that that area should be drawn "irrespective of strategic or transportation considerations so as to embrace the smallest number of Germans."

> The proposal of the Polish Commission that we should place 2,100,000 Germans under the control of a people which is of a different religion and which has never proved its capacity for a stable self-government throughout its history must, in my judgment, lead sooner or later to a new war in the East of Europe.[25]

Little wonder that the Prime Minister did not endear himself in Poland with slighting remarks about that country's political past and administrative capabilities.

---

[25] Great Britain. Parliamentary Papers. *Some* *Considerations* *for* *the* *Conference* *before* *They* *Finally* *Draft* *Their* *Terms* [sometimes known as the "Fountainbleau Memorandum of March 25, 1919"], Cmd. 1614. (London: His Majesty's Stationery Office, 1922).

He led his delegation in expressions of impatience not only toward Poland but toward all the small powers--to him they were costly troublemakers, and until they decided to settle down, there could be no revival of normal trade and commerce which was after all Britain's major interest in securing a prompt peace settlement.[26] Or perhaps it was the taint of "Romanism" about this small state that managed to raise the non-Conformist's ire so often?[27] And, after all, what weight did Polish public opinion carry in Britain? There was no "Polish vote" there to be considered as there was in Wilson's America. So Lloyd George was heard to vent his frustration and unleash his colorful language by declaiming that one might as well "give a clock to a monkey as Upper Silesia to the Poles." Yet, his judgments, when spelled out, were fair. And if he seemed inclined to grant the Germans a sympathetic hearing, he was more farsighted than his French counterpart, Clemenceau, whose concern to extract the pound of flesh from the vanquished only served to feed the coals of hate and invite revenge.

Despite Lloyd George's objections, the report of the Polish Commission held the field at the conference. He summoned his advisers, Kisch and Paton, and his Foreign Secretary, Lord Balfour, who pointed out to him the inevitability of large numbers of Germans going to Poland. Despite the undesirability of such a situation, it was decided at that time not to attempt revision of the German-Polish frontier. As things worked out, this frontier problem was to be dealt with later. Owing to the fact that the Commission's report assigned the Danzig-Mlava-Warsaw railway line, which ran through ethnographically and historically German territory, to Poland, Lloyd George refused to agree. He had come to accept the creation of a Polish corridor which would sever East Prussia from Germany, demonstrating again that the ethnographic factor was of overriding concern to him.

As for the question of Danzig itself, the report had failed to deal with the practicalities of handing over the German city to Polish sovereignty. A political solution to these problems presented to the Prime Minister by his advisers provided that the port city should not be given to Poland but to the Allies who

---

[26]Ray Stannard Baker, Woodrow Wilson and World Settlement, 3 vols. (London: William Heinemann Ltd., 1923), I, 398.

[27]This charge of religious discrimination was frequently leveled but not adequately substantiated in Polish sources, the best example of which is a study in international relations in which Britain emerges as an insensitive, inept, and opportunistic power from the viewpoint of Poland. See Jan Szuldrzynski, Anglia i Polska w Polityce Europejskiej [England and Poland in European Politics] (Jerusalem: Biblioteka Orla Bialego, 1945), p. 267.

"should not transfer Danzig to Poland until they had such arrangements as they might think fit for securing local autonomy to the population." They could thereby delay the settlement pending communication with the Danzigers, without, however, postponing the signature of the Treaty. Lloyd George brought this solution to the meeting of the Council of Four on April 1 whereupon President Wilson called for British and American representatives to draft the treaty clauses providing for the creation of a "free autonomous port and city of Danzig" to be placed under the administration of a League-appointed High Commissioner and to be linked to Poland in a customs union.

Headlam-Morley recalled later that once the French were excluded from this exercise, they took no further part in discussions regarding the status of Danzig outside the Council. This assignment was not consistent with precedent and no record completely explains this abnormal arrangement. Headlam-Morley suspected that France's strong objection to revising the recommendations in the Commission's report which would enrich Poland at the expense of Germany led her to wash her hands of the whole matter. Although France did not help to draw up the clauses, she ultimately agreed to their acceptance and fulfilled her obligations by participating in the subsequent Allied occupation of Danzig.

Accordingly, the two representatives easily came to an agreement. Initially they agreed on three points: (1) that Germany cede Danzig to the League of Nations, (2) that Danzig become self-governing and guaranteed by the League of Nations, and (3) that matters of detail be excluded from the Treaty of Versailles and be dealt with at length later on the spot.

Under scrutiny during these talks were the nebulous references of the Council to a "free and autonomous" Danzig, a statement which might be variously interpreted as indicating Polish sovereignty over the city, Danzig independence, or even a League of Nations mandate. With the new ready-access between Council and committees, Wilson was approached on the question and he demurred at the idea of creating mandates in Europe, a view in which Headlam-Morley heartily concurred. It was decided simultaneously that the High Commissionership should not be an administrative post, but rather that the commissioner should serve as an on-the-spot League representative to settle the difficulties which would undoubtedly arise between Danzig and Poland and between Danzig and Germany. Headlam-Morley and Dr. S. E. Mezes, the American working with him on the draft clauses related to Danzig, were still in doubt as to whether Danzig's sovereignty would be vested in Poland or whether the Free City would be sovereign under the guarantee of the League of Nations. Foreign Office legal advisers indicated that it would be easier to carry out the second alternative, and when Headlam-Morley spoke personally to the Prime Minister on April 5, he received instructions that the sovereignty of Poland should be absolutely excluded.[28]

Along these lines the draft clauses were completed and submitted on April 7 in a form nearly identical with the articles which appeared in the final Treaty. It should be noted that at the time of drafting, it was decided that Danzig's foreign relations should be placed in Polish hands, not so much to strengthen the position of Poland as to prevent potential intrigues which could arise from the situation in which a free Danzig would exchange ministers with Berlin. No one anticipated at this stage how unsatisfactorily this arrangement would develop and how it would virtually allow Poland to exercise sovereignty over the Free City, in fact if not in law.

The Polish Question and the Peace Terms

When the report and draft clauses proposing the establishment of a Free City of Danzig were submitted to the Council of Four on April 7, not everyone in the British delegation regarded them as the best solution to the problem. Sir Esme Howard, for example, proposed that the title *Hansastadt* be removed on grounds that it was anachronistic and evocative of a false impression of a continued connection between Germany and Danzig. Defending the use of the term, Headlam-Morley countered that it had been employed in the hope of easing the transition to the new state of things by recalling the former days when Danzig was not Prussian but an important, prosperous, free city. Further, Howard suggested the inclusion of an additional clause giving Poland the right "to take over and control completely any docks, basins, wharfs and other instrumentalities" within the Free City which then belonged to the German government and to "have the right to erect and own" within the territory of Danzig, docks, basins, wharfs and the like wherever possible. To this, Headlam-Morley was not directly averse but,

---

[28] Memorandum by Headlam-Morley of April 4, 1925 cited above. C. P. Scott, the editor of the Manchester Guardian and Liberal M.P., wrote to J. L. Hammond, the distinguished historian and journalist who acted as the Guardian's special correspondent at the peace conference, how well Lloyd George was performing at Paris and how he had found himself "in the singular position of defending Wilsonian principles against Wilson" with his demand for self-determination for those populations who were ethnically German. See the extract of C. P. Scott to Hammond, April 6, 1919 printed in Trevor Wilson, (ed.), The Political Diaries of C. P. Scott, 1911-1928 (London: Collins, 1970), p. 373. Thirty-five letters from the Lloyd George-Scott correspondence between 1922-29 are preserved in Private Papers of Lloyd George, G/17/11.

given the defective intelligence concerning present ownership and control, he deemed it desirable that this question be taken up in detail later and settled after discussion with the people of Danzig themselves.[29] Later in the month Paderewski, finding himself unable to secure the port city outright for Poland, appealed for such partial ownership as Howard's plan would allow. The Council of Four on April 26 responded negatively, although it preserved for Poland the right to develop the port.[30]

On April 8 the Inter-Allied Mission to Poland supported the original Polish Commission report regarding Danzig, and on April 12 that Commission voted to uphold its report and to resubmit it to the Supreme Council. It was upon Lloyd George that increasing pressure was being applied, for he had made the sole objection to the report on the ground that by it too many Germans would pass under Polish rule.

In mid-April Parliament heard questions from members who found the Prime Minister's behavior regarding Poland disquieting and statements from those who pleaded for an end to British obstruction of the creation of a strong Poland. But, understandably, it was the address of Lloyd George which carried most weight. Before the House of Commons on April 16, he sought a mandate to return to Paris and continue the line he had taken so far. He soundly defended the peace terms as drawn up to that date, and, admitting that the peace would be difficult to attain, he sought parliamentary backing for his position and easily won it, returning to Paris with the added confidence that this support provided.

In response to an Allied invitation to the peace conference, Germany sent on April 30 a delegation of six members, headed by Count Brockdorff-Rantzau, the plenipotentiary who received the Draft Treaty of peace on May 7. The conditions of peace respecting Danzig were substantially those already seen in the Headlam-Morley draft clauses, and provided for a free city under League of Nations guarantee whose High Commissioner would represent the League in differences arising between Danzig on one hand and either Poland or Germany on the other. The mark of the British delegation was stamped indelibly on these clauses, with Lloyd George's categorical exclusion of Polish sovereignty and Headlam-Morley's detailed plan for the transfer of Danzig from Germany, to the Allies, and then finally, to the local authorities.

---

[29] Minutes by Sir E. Howard and Headlam-Morley, April 7, 1919 in FO 608/65, file 130/6/1, no. 6593.

[30] Minutes of Meeting of the Council of Four, April 26, 1919, FRUS, PPC, VI, 291-99.

When the Germans offered their observations on the terms on May 29, they protested that Danzig was ethnographically and historically German, a fact denied not even by the Poles. They invoked Wilson's Fourteen Points and his other pronouncements, which they regarded as part of the pre-armistice agreements, such as his address to the Senate of the United States on January 22, 1917 in which he had said

> So far as practicable, moreover, every great people now struggling toward a full development of its resources and of its powers should be assumed a direct outlet to the great highways of the sea. Where this cannot be done by the cession of territory, it can no doubt be done by the neutralization of direct rights of way under the general guarantee which will assure peace itself. With a right comity of arrangement no nation need be shut away from free access to the open paths of the world's commerce.[31]

In this sense they offered to oblige the Allies by according Poland free and secure access to the sea by making Memel, Königsberg, and Danzig free ports with far-reaching rights being given in all three to Poland. Moreover, they expressed a willingness to conclude a special railway agreement with Poland to assure her of ready passage to and from these ports. But the German objections added nothing new to the spectrum of solutions which the Allies had studied in drawing up the peace terms, and the conference, having already bowed to British objections and withdrawn its plan for a thoroughly Polish Danzig, contemplated no change in Articles 100-108 to oblige Germany.

Another German loss was recorded in the clauses of the draft treaty regarding Upper Silesia into which the original proposals of the Commission on Polish Affairs were incorporated. Briefly, the western boundary of the ethnographically Polish territory served as the proposed frontier between Germany and Poland except in the ethnographically German Leobschutz "peninsula" which, had it been assigned to Germany, would have produced an impracticable frontier. Of the nearly 2,000,000 people who would be taken from Germany in this partition, two-thirds were Polish and one-third German.

Germany's lengthy response to these draft clauses again called upon the Wilsonian Fourteen Points and maintained that neither historically nor ethnographically did Poland have a right to Upper Silesia. Germany claimed that economically it was mandatory for her to retain the province if she were to face reparations payments particularly in the wake of the loss of Alsace-Lorraine and the

---

[31] H. W. V. Temperley (ed.), A History of the Peace Conference of Paris, 6 vols. (London: Oxford University Press, 1920) II, 291.

Saar Basin. This plea did not fall on deaf ears. Furthermore, Germany made a serious charge that the majority of the population in the province favored German sovereignty. German arguments provided misleading statistical "proof" in support of this claim and charged that the existence of the diluted "Wasser-Polnisch" language spoken by some Upper Silesians could in no way justify a Polish ethnographic claim to the territory. With these German allegations, the ownership of Upper Silesia became for the first time a controversial question at the peace conference. Still believing, as many delegations in Paris did, that the populations of the province preferred to be incorporated into Poland, Lloyd George proposed that the Allies hold a plebiscite there. However, the notion of holding a plebiscite to determine the interests of the Upper Silesian populations was not popular at the conference, but not because the conference thought poorly of the principles of self-determination of nationality. In fact, the actual trend of the conference was to favor these principles over economic or strategic considerations. But the unwillingness to concede to or to take a "soft line" toward Germany, which characterized the French attitude, also strongly influenced the delegations of those states which for the next decade and more were called non-revisionists in Europe.

Upon the receipt of German observations on the terms of peace, the Allies passed a busy month before the final Treaty was actually signed. June saw a great deal of activity particularly on the part of the British Empire Delegation and the newly-formed Committee on the Eastern Frontiers of Germany. Deliberations began on the nature and degree of concession necessary to produce a treaty which Germany would be willing to sign. On June 1 a special meeting of the British Empire Delegation was arranged to discuss the situation.[32] Delegates were in agreement that all terms must be fair, so that in the event of German refusal to sign, it would be justifiable to renew the war against that country. The members almost unanimously favored an alteration in the draft clauses relating to Upper Silesia. Lloyd George won his delegation's acceptance of his proposal to hold a plebiscite in that territory. Armed with this new backing, he returned to the Council of Four with his demands on June 3. He was not questioning Upper Silesia's Polish character in his demand, he said, but he wished to prevent German talk of revenge and to strengthen the Allies' hand in the face of public opinion should they be forced to march on Berlin if Germany refused to sign. In addition, he believed that the Allies should not impair German capacity for making reparations payments by automatically severing from her the rich province of Upper Silesia.[33]

---

[32] Minutes of a Meeting of the British Empire Delegation, June 1, 1919 in Cabinet Papers, Cab 29, box 28.

[33] Lord Riddell recounts in his diary a conversation with Lloyd George on May 30, 1919 during which the Prime Minister handed the

Five sessions of the Council were devoted to the question of holding an Upper Silesian plebiscite, but the heads of the major delegations adamantly polarized, with Lloyd George favoring and Clemenceau and Wilson opposing it. The Prime Minister acknowledged the need for an Allied military presence in Upper Silesia to insure a fair vote and he asked for a guarantee that Germany should be able to purchase coal on the same terms as Poland in those regions which might be transferred from her control. With the implementation of these safeguards, both Wilson and Clemenceau relented and on June 4 the Supreme Council resolved to hold a plebiscite in Upper Silesia to determine the wishes of the inhabitants. The fact that in the end Lloyd George's course in this matter seemed to please neither Germany nor Poland was in itself a possible indication of its impartiality.

A new Commission on the Eastern Frontiers of Germany, consisting of the chairman, General Lerond, Headlam-Morley, Pietro della Torretta, and R. H. Lord, was appointed at the same meeting. It was charged with drafting new clauses for the Treaty of Peace dealing with a plebiscite in Upper Silesia, a guarantee to Germany that she could purchase coal from the area on the same terms as Poland, and the modification of economic clauses dealing with German property in the event the territory was transferred to Polish sovereignty.

There was disagreement among the members of the Commission over the timing of the plebiscite. Headlam-Morley attempted to scale down Lerond's proposal for a three-year waiting period by claiming that six months would suffice. Besides, once she dispatched them, Britain was not anxious to keep her troops in central Europe for an extended period of time. Neither Britain nor any other of the Allied powers had yet dispatched troops to the area. The armistice agreements had made no provision for the immediate occupation of central or eastern Europe; hence, the Allies had no real control there to implement the decisions which they had reached in Paris. Lerond favored the longer interval because he viewed it as providing a necessary period within which Upper

---

note with German comment on the peace terms to him and asked for his comment. The Prime Minister was concerned because the disposal of Upper Silesia was linked with reparations and the Allies might be "cutting off their noses to spite their faces if they hand[ed]the mines to the Poles without regard to the question of the indemnity." See Lord George A. Riddell, Lord Riddell's Intimate Diary of the Peace Conference and After, 1918-1923. (London: Victor Golancz Ltd., 1933), pp. 83-4. On the following day Andrew Bonar Law addressed a note to Lloyd George with his observations on the German reply and urged that the Prime Minister prevent Germany's loss of Upper Silesia which he felt would inevitably hamper her industry and ability to pay. See A. Bonar Law to Lloyd George, May 31, 1919, Private Papers of Lloyd George, F/30/3/71.

Silesia could become "liberated from Prussian administration and the grasp of land owners and big industrialists as well as of the German clergy." But he finally agreed to an eighteen-month minimum and three-year maximum period.

After some debate whether the vote should be recorded by commune or *en bloc*, Headlam-Morley found it necessary to abandon the Prime Minister's position favoring the latter. The Commission, after six meetings, drew up and submitted its report to the Council of Four which considered it on June 11.[34]

At this session of the Council Lloyd George decided not to press for the shorter time before the plebiscite, but he refused to agree with Lerond who favored the exclusion from the plebiscite areas of those places where Polish members had been elected to the German parliament. Because the population had returned ethnically Polish members, the Prime Minister argued, did not necessarily indicate that they favored separation from Germany. Upon withdrawal of the Commission, the Council of Four discussed the report in greater detail and, with minor modifications, accepted it. Upon Lloyd George's recommendation, it was decided that the vote would be held under the auspices of the Allied and Associated Powers and not under the League of Nations. And finally on June 14, they agreed that the Upper Silesian plebiscite should be held from six to eighteen months from the coming into force of the Treaty. With these major decisions having been reached and the interested governments informed, the Allies replied to the German observations on the peace terms with a summary of those terms and a formal detailed answer to the German lengthy observations. And after more than five months of deliberation, revisions, and bargains, the Treaty of Versailles was set before the Germans who signed it in most ceremonious surroundings on June 28.

Throughout the months that had led to this moment, Lloyd George had been attacked by the French and the Poles as anti-Polish and his past critical statements against that country had been revived to haunt him. Polish newspapers took a dim view of his actions and until the day he relinquished power would remember him as the man responsible for snatching away from them the jewels of Danzig and Upper Silesia. Yet the evidence is unmistakable that regarding Danzig, the Prime Minister was no innovator. The charge that he "threw over the advice of Foreign Office experts" in order to keep Danzig out of Polish hands is misleading and inadequate. Neither the polonophile H. J. Paton nor Sir Esme Howard who supported the widest Polish claims was representative of the advisers who collaborated with Lloyd George during the conference. Even

---

[34]Minutes of Meeting of the Council of Four, June 11, 1919 in FRUS, PPC, VI, 311-15.

before the peace conference convened, the Foreign Office had favored withholding Danzig from Polish sovereignty. During the first months of the conference the British delegation generally agreed with this position, although His Majesty's Government seemed slow in formulating an official policy for its representatives in Paris and those on-the-spot in Poland to follow. If at first the British government showed itself to be disinterested in the issues, the Prime Minister took up a position favoring a non-Polish Danzig on clearly identifiable ethnographic grounds, which he consistently emphasized in Paris regardless of which claimant benefitted. He rescued the British representatives from their temporary lapse into heresy spawned by the Americans, and in the latter part of the conference led his delegation decisively.

In the Upper Silesian issue he never questioned the ethnographic basis upon which the mineral-rich province was originally to have been partitioned. It was not until the serious German charges that the population of that territory preferred German rule were made that he considered a plebiscite. As a most practical politician, he wanted to produce a treaty that the Germans would sign. The sooner such an instrument could be produced, the sooner normality would return.

Was Lloyd George an exemplar of the new diplomacy at Paris? He tried to treat Germany justly but probably for the "old diplomacy" reason that ultimately the European economy and stability depended upon the German hub, and enlightened self-interest dictated good treatment of her. He was called upon to honor no secret wartime agreements with respect to Danzig or Upper Silesia and instead could speak for the ideals of the Fourteen Points—self-determination of nations and Poland's access to the sea. He was more daring in defying the bonds of the Entente than old Foreign Office hands liked. Crowe must have winced more than once at the Prime Minister who operated spontaneously and often dictatorially, but Lloyd George could with some degree of satisfaction walk away from the table in the Hall of Mirrors knowing that regarding the German-Polish problems he had done the best that time and circumstances had allowed.

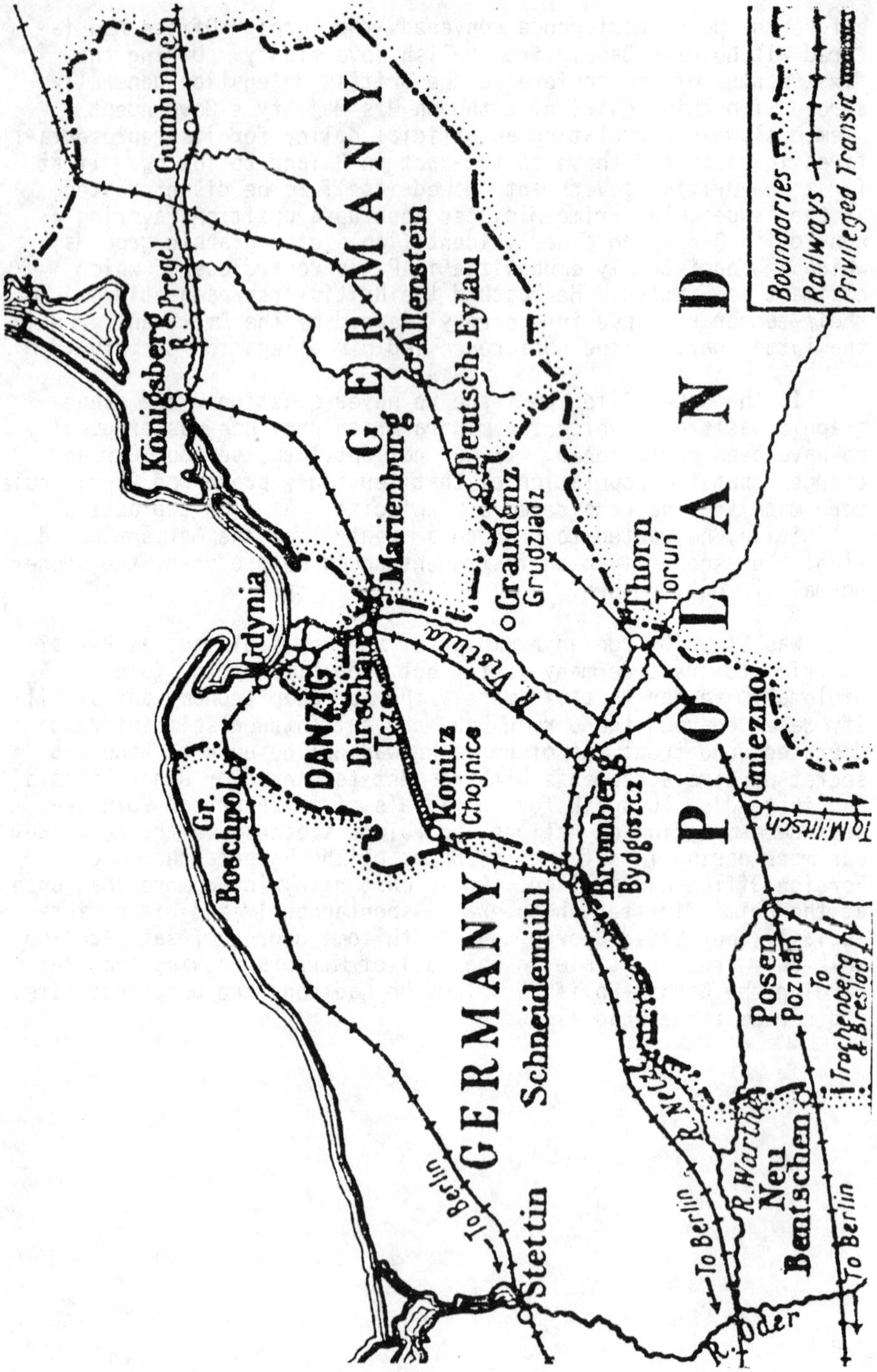
GERMANY
POLAND
Königsberg
R. Pregel
Gumbinnen
Allenstein
Deutsch-Eylau
Marienburg
Graudenz
Grudziadz
Thorn
Torun
Gdynia
DANZIG
Dirschau
Tczew
R. Vistula
Konitz
Chojnica
Gr. Boschpol
GERMANY
Schneidemühl
Bromberg
Bydgoszcz
Gniezno
To Militsch
Posen
Poznan
To Trachenberg & Breslau
Stettin
To Berlin
R. Netze
R. Warthe
Neu Bentschen
To Berlin
To Berlin
R. Oder
Boundaries
Railways
Privileged Transit

CHAPTER II

BEFORE THE NEW REGIME

(June 1919 to January 1920)

For Poland the Paris Peace Conference was over when the Treaty with Germany was signed on June 28, 1919, although the conference did not formally terminate until January 21, 1920. Of course, the question of Poland's eastern frontiers with Lithuania and Russia remained unsettled and the status of the Ruthenian territory which she preferred to call Eastern Galicia was still undecided. But settlements of the questions touching her that could be reached in Paris instead of on a field of battle, by and large, were written into that Treaty. By it she had won recognition by Germany of her resurrection, although she had failed to secure unquestioned sovereignty over the much-coveted Danzig and Upper Silesia. If it was owing mainly to the policy pursued by the British representatives that she was deprived of these, the solution did not altogether work for the convenience of Britain.

Ironically, considering that Poland was a state about which she cared little, Great Britain led the move to reverse the proposed assignments of territory made in the draft treaty and thereby incurred widespread obligations--perhaps not overwhelming in magnitude, but, nevertheless, sources of irritation and inconvenience for a long time to come. Under the articles of the Treaty dealing with Danzig, she was obliged, as a major member of the Allied Powers, to appoint a representative to a commission charged with delimiting the frontiers of the Free City within fifteen days of the Treaty's coming into force. Further, she had to cooperate in the establishment of the Free City and participate in selecting a High Commissioner whose job would include not only assisting in drawing up a constitution but also negotiating on Danzig's problems with Poland or Germany, particularly those problems arising out of the peace settlement. Still more, as one of the Allies, Britain had to undertake to negotiate a Polish-Danzig treaty that was to regularize relations between the two states for the six purposes carefully delineated in Article 104 and, finally, to receive former property of the German government in this territory and oversee its assignment and transfer of ownership to either Danzig or Poland.

The obligations she incurred in Upper Silesia under Article 88 and its annexes were long to be the source of frustration, irritation, and even concern about the strength of the Anglo-French Entente. Britain was required to name a representative to sit on the Inter-Allied Plebiscite Commission who would help provide the administration for the province for a period of some six to eighteen months in length. He and his colleagues would have at their disposal the troops Britain and her allies would be called upon to contribute to pacify the area in order to organize, administer, and report to the Supreme Council upon the plebiscite. To what extent Great Britain was able or inclined to prepare to discharge these duties between the signature of the Treaty of Versailles and the date of its coming into force, January 10, 1920, provides the focus of this chapter.

Before a week had elapsed after the signature of the Treaty in the great Hall of Mirrors, the Prime Minister introduced that document to the House of Commons. There on July 3 he eloquently and at length defended the Conference's handiwork, highly praising his colleagues in the delegation who assisted in the Treaty's preparation, before launching into a discussion of its major principles and provisions. When he took up the question of territorial adjustment as delineated in the Treaty, he defended it on the grounds of self-determination for both the victors and the vanquished. He viewed Danzig as one of the territories rescued from the German grip and restored to a former state of independence. Without specifically naming Upper Silesia he nonetheless referred to it as he continued:

> However unjust it was to take Polish populations and put them under German rule, it would have been equally unjust to take German populations and place them under Polish rule--and it would have been equally foolish. Whether for strategic or economic reasons, it would do nothing but produce mischief in Europe. Europe has the lesson of Alsace-Lorraine, and it would be folly on our part to create any more Alsace-Lorraines to Europe. It would have been a wrong to Europe. Perhaps in fifty years' time Poland would have had to pay the penalty of the blunder committed by the Allies in this year. For that reason the British Delegation--and I have no hesitation in claiming a share in it--resolutely opposed any attempt to put predominantly German populations under Polish rule. I think Poland will have good reason to thank us for the part which we took in that action.[1]

He defended the territorial adjustments as being consistent with the terms of justice "judged by any principle of fairness." It is a matter of record that Parliament with little negative discussion accepted the Treaty with Germany.

---

[1]117 H. C. Deb. 5 S, 1211-1232. Lloyd George discusses the event of its delivery to Parliament in Memoirs of the Peace Conference, 2 vols. (New Haven: Yale University Press, 1939), II, 631.

Keeping Order in Danzig

Danzig, the German city destined to become independent, the site where the Allies and especially Great Britain would soon discharge some of their duties accruing from the Treaty, was not entirely satisfied with the future which the peacemakers had designed for her. *Oberbürgermeister* Heinrich Sahm communicated his fear to the British Mission's General Neill Malcolm that, should the ratification of the Treaty end the supply of German coal destined for the city, upon consumption of the few days' reserve supply, Danzig's industry would be seriously affected. The city would then be unable to produce the wares needed to compensate Germany for further coal supplies.[2] Moreover, the administration of the city, in submitting to the principle of enforced secession, pressed for a revision of the boundaries of the Free City for economic and especially ethnographic reasons. In order to preserve the city's food supply, the Danzig government wished to include many neighboring villages within its frontiers and, in the name of self-determination, they provided statistical evidence that, ethnographically, Poland had no claim to these territories. What the compilation of data came to was the same argument so often presented by the Germans during the course of peace negotiations that the Kassubian population[3] was not Polish and the territories inhabited by these people, therefore, rightly belonged to Germany. Not only was this an exercise in flawed logic, but also an error in ethnography. This argument had been neither vindicated nor perpetuated in the Treaty.

Attempting to avert collisions between ethnic Germans and Poles in the restive Danzig population, Sir Percy Wyndham, the British minister at Warsaw, late in May requested the dispatch of a warship to Danzig without delay. Paton responded with enthusiasm to such a move, hoping that it would prod the Germans into demonstrating their good faith in the Danzig settlement, a development which he regarded as "very improbable" in ethnically Polish districts.[4]

---

[2] Sahm to Malcolm (not dated; about July 1919) in Documents on British Foreign Policy 1919-1939, 1st ser., VI, no. 66, enc. 1.

[3] The Kassubes who inhabited the territory in the environs of Danzig spoke a nearly extinct western Slavic language akin to Polish. Ordinarily, in statistics presented by Poles, the Kassubes were included as part of the Polish-speaking population; in German statistics, they were usually not included as Germans but were listed in a class of their own.

[4] Wyndham to Balfour, no. 111, May 26, 1919 in FO 608/70, file 135/2/1, no. 10969 and the attached minute by Paton of May 27, 1919. There is a question as to the date of dispatch of this telegram, but the date is confirmed in FO 371/3922, file 67716,

Before the new administration took over, British representatives issued warnings to both Germans and Poles ordering them to refrain from provocative action in both military and commercial spheres. General Carton de Wiart reminded the Poles that, under the peace terms, the territory of Danzig was to be ceded to the Principal Allied and Associated Powers rather than to Poland and that only by abstaining from aggressive action could they expect the Allies to safeguard Polish interests there.[5] Britain also proposed to bring pressure on the Germans who were already obstructing the passage of British goods destined for Poland through the port of Danzig.[6]

Although the Treaty of Versailles did not specifically charge the Allies with occupying Danzig, it implied that order should be maintained to provide the atmosphere in which constitution-making and treaty-making could proceed. The Allies could not readily agree that their military presence was essential to ease the transfer of authority there. At their meeting on June 18, the Foreign Ministers discussed the detailed arrangements regarding the cession of Danzig by Germany to the Allied and Associated Powers as laid down in the conditions of peace.[7] These called for

---

no. 79954 where the telegram is recorded without the minutes.

[5] Balfour to Carton de Wiart, no. 149-50, May 30, 1919 in FO 608/65, file 130/6/1, no. 10952.

[6] British firms were about to make large shipments of wool via Danzig to supply the raw material for Polish textile industries and were understandably concerned about their safety in the light of recent occurrences. What caused their apprehension was the German refusal, until they were obligated by the Armistice Commission at Spa, to permit to go forward a consignment of foreign goods for the relief of the Polish population sent by the British Red Cross Society from London. A Foreign Office representative in a telephone conversation with Peters of the Department of Overseas Trade concerning this problem suggested that a telegram be dispatched to the Supreme Economic Council in Paris "pointing out the vital necessity of anticipating any possible obstruction on the part of the Germans" in connection with trade between Great Britain and Poland via Danzig. On the following day, the Foreign Office followed through with a verbal rather than telegraphic communication to this effect with Sir William Goode, a member of the Supreme Economic Council. Foreign Office minute, unsigned, June 3, 1919 in FO 371/3921, file 48888, no. 83673.

[7] The minutes of the I. C. 197 secret meeting of the Conference of Foreign Ministers, June 18, 1919 are recorded in FO 371/3899, file 73, no. 92864 and the British Delegation Military Section secret minute W.C.P. 1005 is annx B to the same document.

the appointment of the Commission which was described in Article 101 to delimit the frontier of the Free City, as well as a High Commissioner who would be the League's representative resident in the city. As a direct outgrowth of these talks, military and naval representatives were appointed, among them Britain's General C. Sackville-West and Admiral Sir George Hope. The new interallied commission deliberated and promptly agreed that German troops should be forced to withdraw from the Danzig area and that Polish troops should be prohibited from entering.

The Allies found it difficult to reach unanimity, however, when they tried to decide whether a military presence at Danzig was mandatory and what the composition of such a force would be should it prove necessary to form one. The French and Italian generals believed that the High Commissioner required an Allied force to assist him in discharging his duties while the British and American generals thought such a force to be unnecessary for various reasons. Besides the general reluctance of the British and the Americans to get very deeply involved in continental affairs, their dissent also stemmed from their presumption that both the Polish and German governments intended to act in good faith with respect to the Free City and that the German government would realize that it was in the interest of the German population of Danzig to maintain order and support the authority of the League's High Commissioner. Furthermore, an inter-allied military force would have irritating effects on the people, and would be potentially productive of internal disorders. Should the High Commissioner evidence an inability to maintain his authority by moral influence and a locally raised police force, then, they conceded, it would no doubt be within the powers of the Allied and Associated states to send the men necessary to enforce the conditions of the Treaty. But the cost also had to be considered, especially in view of the general post-war lack of shipping. Even if the troops were made available, an interval before their arrival would be inevitable and possibly critical.[8]

In response to Lord Balfour's request, General Malcolm in Berlin sent two British officers to Danzig accompanied by a German staff officer to collect on-the-spot information which was needed by the British delegation to determine the "least number of troops required to safeguard the port and maintain lines of communication with Poland along the railway and Vistula."[9] Malcolm himself be-

---

[8] Major General Sackville-West's report S.W.C. 430/1 on the occupation of Danzig and Memel appears in FO 371/3899, file 73, no. 96830 with Appendix A being the memorandum of the American and British representatives and Appendix B the memorandum of the French and Italian representatives; the latter of these appears as Appendix A of document 2 in DBFP, 1st ser., I, no. 24.

[9] Balfour to Malcolm, no. 26, July 3, 1919 in DBFP, 1st ser.,

lieved that small garrisons at Danzig and Graudenz, which could easily form escorts for trains and large convoys, would be the most suitable of the possible arrangements--an assessment also shared by the German, General Hans von Seeckt. The Germans were eager to greet the arrival of the troops and Malcolm recalled that when speaking of the future League representative, they repeatedly made reference to a "British" High Commissioner.[10]

Investigations, reports, and discussions followed. Even before it was agreed that some type of military presence would be necessary, the Allies found that any theoretical military necessities had to be tempered by other practical factors such as logistics and politics. At the August 8 meeting of the heads of delegations in Paris,[11] Balfour brought up the practical problems in provisioning troops stationed in widely scattered areas of Europe. He proposed that while the Allies fulfilled the provisions of the Treaty by contributing troops in equal number to the total occupation forces, that they consider distributing the troops unevenly. He recognized the symbolic value of having well-functioning, truly inter-allied occupation forces; it showed the defeated Germans that the victors were still working together for the same objectives. But he urged that, for practical reasons of administering and provisioning the troops, places like Danzig and Upper Silesia should have an inter-allied force that had a preponderance of personnel from one nation. He brought up the same subject at a later meeting[12] citing additional problems of troop morale involved when forces were not under a single command. Troops did not like being put under the orders of foreign generals; they liked their own food and their own hospitals. This necessitated, Balfour stressed, multiple sources for each supply and service and all the inefficiency such duplication entailed.

VI, no. 7. Wyndham to FO, no. 64, July 7, 1919 in FO 608/65, file 130/6/1,, no. 14598. If the British delegation was hesitant about sending troops, Balfour was not. He favored the investigation of conditions in Danzig in order not only to survey the situation but also to be in a position to lend assistance to the municipal authorities. See London, British Museum, Balfour MSS, 49751, entry for July 3, 1919.

[10] Report by General Malcolm, July 6, 1919 in DBFP, 1st ser., no. 17. A similar report by Lieutenant Breen that Danzig's *Oberbürgermeister* and citizens were anxious for the early arrival of the English or American garrison appears in General Malcolm to FO, Z33, July 6, 1919 in FO 608/65, file 130/6/1, no. 14784.

[11] Heads of Delegations Meeting, August 8, 1919 in Papers Relating to the Foreign Relations of the United States, Paris Peace Conference, VII, 62-45.

[12] Meeting of the Council of Heads of Delegations, August 23, 1919 in FRUS, PPC, VII, 815-16.

Clemenceau accepted his reasoning. He admitted, however, that political implications also had to be considered. The relationship between Poland and France was an intimate one, and therefore, Clemenceau wanted no military occupation of Poland to occur without French participation.

Subsequently, the Allied leaders appointed a special commission to determine the composition of inter-allied forces of occupation and essentially approved its recommendations which embodied Balfour's proposal.[13] In practice, it turned out that the British came to principally compose and command the forces of the nearby East Prussian plebiscite areas which also served the needs of Danzig.[14] The French came to be primarily responsible for the occupation of inland Upper Silesia.

By the autumn of 1919, Great Britain had a greater stake in Danzig than she had, for example, in Upper Silesia. She had been mainly responsible for the drawing up of the articles of the Treaty dealing with the proposed Free City; she, among the Allied powers, maintained a superiority, even a hegemony, in maritime matters; and in September, she won the Polish government's agreement to construct a new harbor at Danzig.[15]

Word was received at the Foreign Office on October 8 that high tension in German-Polish relations accompanied the anticipated accommodation at the riverport of Graudenz of some German troops under General von der Goltz who were being evacuated from the Bal-

---

[13] The discussions regarding this question came up again several times, for example, in January 1920 when Britain was unable to supply the troops she had earlier committed. Reality did not conform to the theory of these decisions reached in council for many reasons—among them the armistice agreement, domestic questions, and the non-availability of troops and shipping. For the January 20, 1920 meeting of the special commission and the Council of Premiers see FRUS, PPC, IX, 918-21 and 938-41.

[14] In mid-October, the Allied leaders had approved the proposal of the Joint Commission on Polish and Baltic Affairs which recommended that a base at Danzig was necessary to support the troops in the nearby East Prussian plebiscite areas. From these areas troops could immediately be dispatched to Danzig only when commanded by the High Commissioner of the League of Nations, thus not interfering in the Free City's maintenance of its own public order at all other times. Notes of the Heads of Major Delegations Meeting, October 15, 1919 in DBFP, 1st ser., I, no. 74 and also in FRUS, PPC, VIII, 638-68.

[15] Wyndham to FO, no. 248, September 12, 1919 in FO 371/3899, file 73, no. 129059.

tic provinces. Serious disturbances were threatened and feared in nearby Danzig, especially if German troops were withdrawn before Allied troops arrived. Some British military officers called for an Allied naval show of force in the Baltic, but they recognized that until the Peace Treaty came into force and placed the town under Polish sovereignty, the Germans retained the right to place their troops at Graudenz. But the Admiralty would buy none of this. Not only did it doubt the effect of such a demonstration on any rising, since no intervention by force of arms was contemplated, but also it was quick to point out that British naval commitments in the Baltic were already too great, and since reinforcement of the squadron for additional assignments was impossible, the show of force was not feasible.[16] Ordinarily the military and naval establishment was reluctant to involve itself in the Danzig question even though Danzig, presumably a major sea link between east and west, was so situated geographically as to appeal to the maritime and commercial interests of Britain. A parallel situation will be seen in Upper Silesia where the military adamantly opposed the return of a British presence to the plebiscite area and acquiesced only under the pressure of a direct Cabinet order. Whatever the interests the Admiralty had in 1919, Central Europe was not among them.

Yet, the Admiralty had chosen to involve itself to a limited degree in Central Europe in the question of Poland's proposed navy. As early as March 1919, even before the status of Danzig had been finally determined by the peace conference, Count Sobanski and the Polish National Committee had petitioned Britain to send a naval mission to the new republic in the near future. The Foreign Office considered the request premature but communicated it and found the Admiralty well-disposed. Lord Derby, British ambassador in Paris, cognizant of the opportunity for growth of British prestige in Central Europe over that of France, was eager to have the mission dispatched. Accordingly on May 16 Sobanski was informed that the British government would assent to his request.

Instructions for the mission were broad. They provided for advising the Polish government on matters dealing with the development of seaboard, rivers, customs, and water police services, and on matters of navigation and development of the merchant marine. The representatives were to advise the Poles on the organization of a small naval force to implement these services but "in no way to countenance any attempt to create a Polish Navy proper; such action being contrary to the policy of H. M. Government." The mission which arrived in September was purely advisory and sub-

---

[16]Curzon to FO, no. 7237 which transmits the letter from the War Office of October 20, 1919 and from the Admiralty of October 18, 1919 in FO 608/66, file 130/6/1, no. 19894.

ordinate to the British minister at Warsaw.[17]

Danzig before the Allied Administration

Article 104 of the Treaty of Versailles charged the Allies with undertaking to negotiate a treaty between Poland and Danzig which should come into force at the same time as the establishment of the Free City and be completed with six objects in view:

> (1) To effect the inclusion of the Free City of Danzig within the Polish Customs frontiers, and to establish a free area in the port;
> (2) To ensure to Poland without any restriction the free use and service of all waterways, docks, basins, wharves and other works within the territory of the Free City necessary for Polish imports and exports;
> (3) To ensure to Poland the control and administration of the Vistula and of the whole railway system within the Free City, except such street and other railways as serve primarily the needs of the Free City, and of postal, telegraphic and telephonic communication between Poland and the port of Danzig;
> (4) To ensure to Poland the right to develop and improve the waterways, docks, basins, wharves, railways and other works and means of communication mentioned in this Article as well as to lease or purchase through appropriate processes such land and other property as may be necessary for these purposes;
> (5) To provide against any discrimination within the Free City of Danzig to the detriment of citizens of Poland and other persons of Polish origin or speech;
> (6) To provide that the Polish Government shall undertake the conduct of the foreign relations of the Free City of Danzig as well as the diplomatic protection of citizens of that city when abroad.

Although such an agreement had not yet been reached as directed, the Polish government late in October 1919, anticipating the ratification of the Versailles Treaty, sounded the British minister at Warsaw, Sir Horace Rumbold,[18] regarding his views on the proposed

---

[17] The entire collection of documents related to the British Naval Mission to Poland appears in FO 371/3912, file 39818.

[18] Sir Horace Rumbold had been appointed in September 1919 to replace Sir Percy Wyndham whose assignment to Warsaw had been temporary. Lord Hardinge had recommended him for the position because he regarded Rumbold as "one of the shrewdest and cleverest persons in the Diplomatic Service." See Lord Hardinge, Old Diplomacy (London: Murray, 1947), pp. 236-37.

presence of a Polish representative at Danzig for the regularization of Danzig-Polish relations. The Poles won his support when they drew Rumbold's attention to the necessity of establishing passenger and goods traffic between Danzig and Warsaw. Their delegation also submitted the question to the Supreme Council by whose order it was directed to the attention of the German-Polish Commission already sitting in Berlin.[19]

It was not until late November that the peace conference dealt in any substantial manner with the negotiations to be carried out between Poland and Germany and between Poland and Danzig. Some conversations had been going on in Berlin between Poland and Germany, and the missions of Principal Powers had been kept constantly up to date on their progress.

Talks between Poland and Danzig had not yet commenced. Disputes arose over where they should be conducted. The French favored their being based in Paris rather than in the remote Danzig; the British representative, Sir Eyre Crowe, favored Danzig because of the special importance of on-the-spot considerations. Finally, the heads of major delegations decided on November 24[20] that both the Polish-German and the Polish-Danzig negotiations should be moved to Paris. Further, they directed that preliminary discussions be held or preparatory technical studies be made by Poles and Danzigers under the chairmanship of the Allied Representative at Danzig and that he send the report and recommendations to Paris where they would serve as a basis for the Paris deliberations.

The course followed by Sir Eyre Crowe throughout these discussions was one that typified Britain's approach to solving problems in Central Europe, that is, he stressed the importance of on-the-spot information and reliance upon representatives who had been on location rather than attempting to formulate policy on abstract principle. Year's end was to come and go before the negotiations would produce a supplementary treaty for signature. These talks and their results will be seen in greater detail in the next chapter.

If the Allies were to fulfill the stipulations of the Treaty of Versailles with respect to Danzig, it was incumbent upon them not only to make provision for these supplementary agreements but also to agree upon the practical details involved in administering

---

[19] Correspondence between Rumbold and the British Delegation appears in FO 608/66, file 130/6/1.

[20] Notes of Heads of Major Delegations Meeting, November 24, 1919, DBFP, 1st ser., II, no. 29 Appendices H and I; FRUS, PPC, IX, 303-27; Rumbold to Peace Delegation, no. 241, urgent, November 8, 1919, FO 688/1.

the city once the Treaty was ratified. By the terms of the Treaty of Versailles the Allies charged the League of Nations with providing a High Commissioner for the Free City of Danzig. It was decided, however, that during the interim between treaty ratification and the establishment of the Free City, a provisional administrator would be essential.

When, therefore, the Committee for the Execution of the Treaty had met on July 12, the British delegate proposed that the nomination should be made by the British government. Since the most direct communication between the Allies and Danzig was by the sea routes commanded by British ships, it was argued that this predominance of British interest should be recognized by the granting of such a privilege. Secretly, the British believed that the transfer of authority at Danzig could be carried out "with little difficulty" if they directed it themselves.[21] The Committee adopted the proposal when the Americans threw their support to it and neither the French nor any other representatives objected.

Sir Eric Drummond, Secretary-General of the League of Nations, who had learned that the provisional administrator had a good chance of being appointed High Commissioner once the Treaty went into force, doubted the expediency of appointing an Englishman. Such action, he believed, would render the French claim to the Chairmanship of the Governing Commission of the Saar more difficult to resist. The latter position, in his estimation, was being regarded by neutrals as a test of the League of Nations--that is, whether it was a clique to keep Germany contained or a genuine attempt at "world equity." He personally favored the appointment of an American to this post and thought that France would more easily relinquish her claim if a neutral were selected for Danzig. To this end he ultimately suggested the appointment of Hjalmar Branting, the highly respected and trusted Swedish statesman.[22]

By late summer Allied authorities were in agreement that the eventual High Commissioner should be British. This was just the

---

[21] Delegation minute, July 12, 1919 in FO 608/65, file 130/6/1, no. 15290. For a similar assessment see Memorandum by Balfour on Danzig question, July 3, 1919, FO 800/217; the diary entry for July 3, 1919 in British Museum, Balfour MSS, 49751.

[22] Drummond to Balfour, July 17, 1919 in Balfour Papers, FO 800/217. Drummond had also seen, in a telegram not meant for him, that the post was to be offered to General Sir Richard Haking. Haking, he said, would be good for the temporary appointment, given his military knowledge and prestige, but he was no statesman with the skills of constitution-writing and administration that would be needed by the High Commissioner.

beginning of British involvement with the port city. From the time when the Danzig draft clauses had been drawn up, the solution of the Danzig issue seemed to become an Anglo-American project. When America later detached herself from European involvement and refused to ratify the Treaty of Versailles, Britain would virtually be left alone to represent the Allies there.

By late summer Allied authorities were also in agreement that the proposed military force should be British. Sir Henry Wilson, the Chief of the Imperial General Staff, urged against the dispatch of British troops there. He reminded the Council that on March 31, 1920, the conscription act was due to lapse and then no troops except the new post-war volunteer army, which was required for normal overseas duty, would be available. Britain could then spare fewer troops for Allied duties. The British military urged the use of French troops in Danzig but the political leaders were not swayed.

Sir Reginald Tower, a senior member of the British foreign service who had been minister at Munich before the war, accepted the position of provisional administrator with the prospect of becoming High Commissioner when the Allied period of administration expired. He was scheduled to leave London for Danzig during the first week of November, accompanied by an officer and, in view of the British commercial interest there, a commercial adviser.[23]

How this civil administration and military occupation of Danzig would be paid for was also a question which bedeviled the Allies. Tower observed that this experience would prove to be a serious drain on the city and that Polish financial assistance would be necessary. He called for a substantial credit to the city, perhaps through some arrangement with Allied firms whereby a lump sum might be advanced against concessions of special economic privileges. The only other alternative he foresaw was credit furnished by one or more Allied governments, an alternative which he expected would be less than enthusiastically greeted in London and Paris.[24] The question was debated among the Allies. Crowe elucidated the British position which regarded the force as troops of occupation as defined in Article 249.[25] But General Ugo

---

[23] Astoria to Curzon, no. 1492, October 25, 1919 in FO 608/66, file 130/6/1, no. 19872. For details about the assumption of the post as temporary administrator at Danzig see Confidential Print 170657, January 12, 1920 in FO 417/18.

[24] Notes on a Journey to Danzig by Tower, November 17-29, 1919 in FO 608/66, file 130/6/1, no. 20984.

[25] The text of Article 249 reads "There shall be paid by the German Government the total cost of all armies of the Allied and

Cavallero, of the Italian delegation, pointed out that once the Treaty was ratified, the territory would cease to be German and saddling Germany with these costs would be contrary to the spirit of the Treaty. Finally, it was decided that the occupation states should advance the funds needed and receive reimbursement from beneficiary states.

The situation respecting the occupation of Danzig remained so confused and the Allies were so short of troops and the means of transporting them, that the Allied heads of government were still deliberating the make-up of the proposed force on January 20, 1920, the day on which the Treaty of Versailles went into effect and Allied troops ought to have been on the spot. The French, who had voluntarily not participated in drawing up the articles relating to Danzig, did not completely disqualify themselves from its occupation, as Foch's statements at the January 20 meeting indicated, but he was not eager to assume major responsibilities there. Later that day the Allies informed the Germans that there would be a delay in transporting occupation forces to both Danzig and Upper Silesia. In nearby Allenstein, it was British and Italian troops who replaced the Germans who evacuated on February 1.[26] British battalions alone entered Danzig on February 13, replacing the Germans there within an hour of their evacuation.[27]

Associated Governments in occupied German territory from the date of the signature of the Armistice of November 11, 1918, including the keep of men and beasts, lodging and billeting, pay and allowances, salaries and wages, bedding, heating, lighting, clothing, equipment, harness and saddlery, armament and rolling stock, air services, treatment of sick and wounded, veterinary and remount service, transport service of all sorts (such as by rail, sea or river, motor lorries), communications and correspondence, and in general the cost of all administrative or technical services the working of which is necessary for the training of troops and for keeping their numbers up to strength and preserving their military efficiency.

"The cost of such liabilities under the above heads so far as they relate to purchases or requisitions by the Allied and Associated Governments in the occupied territories shall be paid by the German Government to the Allied and Associated Governments in marks at the current or agreed rate of exchange. All other of the above costs shall be paid in gold marks."

[26] Sara Wambaugh, Plebiscites Since the World War, 2 vols. (Washington, D.C.:Carnegie Endowment for International Peace, 1933), I, 113.

[27] John Brown Mason, The Danzig Dilemma: A Study in Peacemaking and Compromise (Stanford: Stanford University Press, 1946), p. 63.

How the territory of Danzig would be transferred from German to Allied administration still remained a matter for settlement until the final week before that transfer took place. Early in January, the Supreme Council, noting that the sovereignty of Danzig *ipso facto* would pass to the Principal Allied and Associated Powers with the ratification of the Treaty of Versailles, agreed that the transfer of the territory should be effected "by the highest functionary of the German administration" to the representative of the Powers "at the request of the latter and under the conditions which he will indicate." Furthermore, upon that transfer German financial, administrative, and judicial registers should close and all archives and registers pass into the possession of the new authority.[28] Although the Treaty came into force on January 10 and theoretically Danzig came under the interim regime of the League of Nations at that time, it was not until February 11 that Tower arrived to formalize the event. He found a satisfactorily run city administration and he hoped to retain some of its leading officials during his tenure. In this way he began his Commissionership which would extend to nearly the end of the year and which, because of his willingness to use the German administrative resources available, would be often looked upon by Poland and France as a pro-German administration taking orders from London.

Upper Silesia before the Allied Occupation

Upper Silesia provided the stage upon which more serious intra-allied differences were displayed. It appeared likely that a partition of this territory between Germany and Poland would ensue from the planned plebiscite. Claims by both nations to the mineral-rich province, already heard at the peace conference, were repeated in the following months.

As early as April 1919, four months before the first insurrection, unrest in Upper Silesia was already in evidence and its strength was ascribed to the Bolshevik influence. To such accusations the British delegation rightly offered criticism. H. J. Paton observed the frequency with which this "red scare" tactic

---

[28] For the minutes of the Council meeting of January 6, 1920 which accepted this "Procedure for the Transfer of the Ceded Territories," see DBFP, 1st ser., II, no. 52 and FRUS, PPC, IX, 806-17. A modification of this would prove necessary as, for example, when it was pointed out to Tower that it was relatively impossible to close all accounts in January when they would have ordinarily been closed at the end of the quarter on March 31. Tower raised no objection to this and it was arranged that on that date the proportionate sums due to the city of Danzig would be assessed. See Tower to Curzon, February 20, 1920, in FO 417/8, Confidential Print 181201.

was employed in that area of the world with no basis in fact. Trouble being imminent, nevertheless, he urged the Allies to send unbiased representatives into disputed areas, a move that had proved successful in Danzig. In the same vein, Headlam-Morley advocated the dispatch of a high-ranking Allied officer to Upper Silesia to supervise the transfer of authority and to ease the situation, although he was skeptical as to the adequacy of the measure.[29] Wyndham reported from Warsaw in July, a month before the insurrection, that German authorities in Upper Silesia were preparing for the deportation of Polish political prisoners and that the Polish government was again complaining of *Grenzschutz* excesses. This latter was a German force established in the first instance to police the border territory of Germany, but its alleged brutality and extended involvement in Upper Silesia were later claimed to be a chief contributing factor to the Silesian insurrection in August 1919.

But in the province which was awaiting the finalization of Allied occupation plans, a grave economic problem existed and the Allies as well as the interested governments addressed themselves to alleviating it. The nature of the difficulty at its simplest was that Upper Silesia, looked upon as the source of the Central European coal supply, was in the throes of a coal shortage. Yet this shortage, according to those who had studied the problem, was linked less to an insufficient supply of resources than to the inability to transport them properly and to the inefficient distribution of food among the miners.[30]

On the eve of the serious disorder and strikes in the mines that summer, Sir Percy Wyndham reported from Warsaw that danger was imminent because of the objections raised by Polish workmen when the coal they had mined was made available for distribution among the Germans.[31] Undoubtedly, the question of coal distribu-

---

[29] Gosling to Balfour, no. 70, April 21?, 1919 in FO 608/140, file 476/1/1, no. 8067. Also see the attached minutes by H J. Paton of April 25 and Headlam-Morley of May 8 concerning methods of dealing with unrest in Upper Silesia in the last months before the final signature of the Treaty.

[30] The American Food Mission studied the question of better food distribution. Specific suggestions on how such a program could be administered were proposed later by British diplomats but not supported by all British personnel then in Upper Silesia. For the American role see Wyndham to Balfour, no. 94, July 23, 1919 in FO 608/71, file 137/5/1, no. 16443. For British proposals see Craig to Wigram, August 27, 1920 in FO 371/4815, C 5010/1621/18.

[31] Wyndham to Balfour, no. 94, July 23, 1919 cited above.

tion, which concerned Germany, Poland, and the Allies in their various negotiations, did have a certain psychological effect on the workers, but the validity of Wyndham's judgment at this time appears questionable in view of the fact that these circumstances were not new ones.

A case can be made that poor or inadequate transportation accounted in large part for the coal shortage in 1919. While Upper Silesia was still under German sovereignty prior to the coming into force of the Treaty of Versailles, an investigation into the causes of the diminution of the coal supply was conducted by a specially assembled Berlin Committee whose findings were later recorded in the October Preussische Jahrbücher. Difficulties of railway transport ranked as the chief cause--difficulties arising out of a lack of available locomotives, many of which were standing idle as those, for example, in the Gleiwitz repair workshops where only half of the previous year's total of locomotives was being repaired by a staff more than doubled in size. Resulting, too, from this shortage, was traffic obstruction at great railway junctions like Brochau near Breslau through which most Upper Silesian coal had to pass.[32]

Mixed reports began reaching London and Paris by August 19 from Allied representatives and from the press, that insurrection had broken out on the night of August 15-16. Polish claims asserted that the immediate cause had been the German attack on the Silesian outpost of Piotrowice where many were said to have been killed or wounded. This was followed by a rising of Polish civilian inhabitants in the Pless and Tychow districts where they disarmed the *Grenzschutz*. Rail traffic at this point ceased in some areas and more serious hostilities broke out in the Rybnik, Pless, and Gleiwitz districts. The insurrection spread to other areas in Upper Silesia and there was talk about Polish insurgents having crossed the frontier where they occupied districts and villages in the province. The Polish government resisted the popular demand for intervention by regular troops in these first days, and Wyndham urged that the Allies exert pressure on German authorities to do the same and to so inform the Polish government.[33]

Balfour responded that any Polish troops entering the disputed area without German invitation would be in violation of the Treaty and that he was taking part in measures aimed at sending Allied representatives to the spot to act as a moderating influence. He and his colleagues were also attempting to agree on an earlier date for the Inter-Allied Commission to take effective control of the plebiscite area. It was, he believed, in the interest of Poland

---

[32] E. Saunders to FO, 697/No. PID 697, December 8, 1919 in FO 371/4384.

[33] Wyndham to Paris, no. 207, August 19, 1919, FO 688, box 1.

and all Central Europe that work in the mines should resume, so he urged the Poles to contribute to an atmosphere of patience and calm in these last weeks preceding German evacuation.[34] Wyndham praised the Polish government for its moderation and its desire to maintain strict neutrality despite the pressures exerted by those Polish civilians who were crossing the frontiers to aid their Silesian countrymen. Repeated urgent requests for Allied troops came from Poland, but the numbers required were never sent. In August an Inter-Allied Mission, hoping to quell the disorder, arrived in Upper Silesia and conducted a thorough investigation.

Three generals were appointed as representatives of the Inter-Allied Commission at Berlin and joined Colonel Anson Conger Goodyear, the American representative on the Allied Coal Commission, who was already in Upper Silesia. Goodyear, at his own request and with the approval of the Supreme Council, had been acting as an arbitrator pending the arrival of the Plebiscite Commission. Because Germany, for internal political reasons, could not request Allied troops to assist in putting down the insurrection, it became the responsibility of this delegation to provide clear and reliable information for the instruction of the Council. As a result of action by German troops and the calming presence of the Commission, fighting came to an end. The Allies adopted the recommendations of the Commission aimed at the removal of acute grievances and the resumption of work in the coal mines.[35]

---

[34]Balfour to Wyndham, no. 291, August 20, 1919 in FO 688, box 1. At the meeting in Paris when this reply was proposed by Balfour, Stephen Pichon, the French Foreign Minister, declared sympathy with it but believed that it was a capitulation to the Poles. "It would appear that the Polish workmen had begun the strikes in Upper Silesia with the purpose of rendering Allied intervention necessary." For minutes of this meeting which considered Balfour's reply see DBFP, 1st ser., I, no. 38 and FRUS, PPC, VII, 730-67.

[35]Supreme Council Meeting, August 22, 1919 in DBFP, 1st ser., I, no. 40 and FRUS, PPC, VII, 780-810. Supreme Council Meeting, August 26, 1919 in DBFP, ibid., no. 43 and FRUS, ibid., 927-40. For an "Appreciation of the situation in the German territory to be occupied by the British Independent Division" see the Secret War Office report, January 12, 1920 in FO 371/4384. A chronology of Upper Silesian events since the end of 1916 with emphasis on 1919 appears in Sir Horace Rumbold's annual report for 1919, May 12, 1920 found in Confidential Print 11549 and also in FO 371/3901, file 73, no. 198528. A detailed account of the 1919 insurrection, particularly the correspondence between the Polish Foreign Office and H. M. Legation at Warsaw is unbound but available from Ashridge Depository at Public Record Office, London, FO 688, box 1.

In early October, a Polish-German amnesty was signed which allowed for the return to Upper Silesia of those refugees who had fled to Poland. In the same month, the Prussian assembly passed an act for the establishment of a more autonomous Silesian province--a law which was never allowed to come into force. Throughout the period of the insurrection and its aftermath, Allied representatives and particularly the British representative urged moderation upon the Polish government and in their successful counsels, they averted the grave danger of war between that country and Germany.

Without minimizing the weight of nationalist agitation, it seems that economic problems, which were in no way peculiar to Upper Silesia, accounted in greatest part for the discontent and uprising. The province shared with other industrial areas of Europe a widespread dissatisfaction with working conditions, the tyranny of endemic profiteering, and a degree of intolerance of authority. These economic-emotional factors, in turn, preyed on minds already swayed by nationalist appeals whose passion was constantly escalating as the Conference persisted in its indecisiveness that merely augmented the uncertainty here about the political future. Some months later, Rumbold wrote that there were considerable grounds for believing that the Prussian administration had deliberately provoked the strikes by encouraging Bolshevik agitation among the workers in order to foment insurrection, and so to discredit the Poles in the eyes of the West and put them at a disadvantage with respect to the plebiscite.[36]

Among the attempts to solve the coal problem before sovereignty passed from Germany was the conclusion of the Polish-German agreement, to go into force on October 22, by which Germany undertook to supply a minimum of 75,000 tons of coal per month to Poland with the specific amount being dependent upon the output. Germany was prepared to provide rolling stock for moving the minimum amount of coal while for an additional 50,000 tons Poland would have to provide her own transport. Details of the agreement

---

[36] Rumbold to FO, no. 326, Confidential Print no. 11549, May 12, 1920 in FO 371/3901, file 73, no. 198528. Two documents of dubious authenticity transmitted from Warsaw to Balfour in July 1919 with a *Note Verbale* from the Polish government who had supplied them to H. M. Legation purportedly indicated direct German involvement and deliberate pressure upon Poles, which contributed to Silesian unrest in the pre-insurrection summer. See Wyndham to Balfour, July 9, 1919 in DBFP, 1st ser., I, no. 36. The point of view of Herbert Hoover, the American Food Administrator, that the insurrection was of a political character instigated by the Germans themselves was referred to in the August 18 meeting of the heads of delegations by Balfour. See the minutes of that meetin in ibid., and FRUS, PPC, VII, 694-712.

were intended to be extended to the lands later allocated to
Poland. Rumbold was surprised by its scope and even the Polish
government claimed to be, although its orders to the negotiators
had been to obtain coal "at any price."[37]

At a meeting of the heads of great power delegations in Paris
on November 14, where Sir Eyre Crowe represented Great Britain, the
Council adopted the proposal of the Committee on Organization of
the Reparation Commission according to which Upper Silesian coal
in the amount of 250,000 tons monthly was to be distributed to
Poland. After the Reparation Commission itself was established,
it presented a note to Germany which required almost doubling the
allotment to Poland at the expense of the German consumer. The
German government protested on both legal and economic grounds,
claiming that there would be a consequent reduction of supplies
available for the Allies from the Ruhr upon whose resources Germany would herself be forced to draw more heavily.[38] This was to
be merely the first of a new set of objections by Germany in which
she claimed to be unequal to the task of payment which the Allies
had foisted upon her.[39]

---

[37] Rumbold to Curzon, no. 365, October 29, 1919 in DBFP,
1st ser., VI, no. 236 and Rumbold to Curzon, no. 366, October 29,
1919, ibid., no. 237.

[38] Notes of a Meeting of Heads of Major Delegations, November 14, 1919 in DBFP, 1st ser., II, no. 22 and FRUS, PPC, IX,
158-74. Note handed to Lord Hardinge by German Chargé d'Affaires,
June 28, 1920 in DBFP, 1st ser., X, no. 164.

[39] A report prepared by the Intelligence Section of the Reparation Commission at Berlin at the time of the London Conference in
February-March 1921 was sent to Paris but was found so unfavorable
to French and Belgian interests that it was immediately suppressed
with all copies being recalled. A copy of the offending paper
which "proved" Germany's inability to pay the reparations demands,
is in the FO files in 131 typed pages and in a 61-page confidential
print. According to Lord D'Abernon, who transmitted it to Lord
Curzon in April 1921, the French and Belgian officials involved
in the preparation of the report "have been severely censured for
giving expression to such inconvenient views." In a subsequent
dispatch D'Abernon attempted to correct what he believed were
exaggerated figures in the report. He thought that even with the
loss of Upper Silesia, Germany's ability to pay reparations would
not be significantly affected. See D'Abernon to Curzon, no. 560
April 12, 1921 in FO 371/5965, C 7970/386/18 and D'Abernon to
Curzon, no. 615, April 20, 1921 in the same volume, C 8420/386/18.

In view of their imminent takeover of the province, the Allies were also interested in the municipal elections scheduled for November 9. The Poles, with Dmowski as their spokesman, protested that the elections, if held, would be so ill-timed as to disqualify many pro-Polish voters who had not yet received amnesty for their activities in the recent insurrection. The Germans verified rumors of their intention to hold the election and claimed that the move was meant as a reform measure to democratize the province which had lagged behind the rest of Germany in this regard; the province had not yet conducted its polling under the new constitution.

Crowe reminded the Council that until the Treaty of Versailles came into force, it could not forbid the elections, but it could warn the Germans that the results would not be recognized by the occupation authorities. It was decided to so inform the German government. When several days later it was learned how favorable the results of the polling had been to the Poles, he helped to amend the note to the Germans which, in effect, diluted the Allied statement by saying that the Allies felt entitled to consider the results null and void if they so chose. So amended, the draft letter was approved and the question came to an end.[40]

Finally, the Allies, under the provisions of the Treaty of Versailles, were charged with the task of administering the plebiscite area of Upper Silesia until the vote could be taken. To the Inter-Allied Commission, therefore, fell the task of governing the area, that is, of having the responsibility for every branch of administration for a period that might extend from six to eighteen months. Plans for this administrative authority were drawn up in the months prior to the arrival of the Commission. Colonel Harold Percival, the British representative on the Commission, reported to his government after conversations with General Lerond, the French representative and president of the body. Lerond's plan for Upper Silesia was based on the assumption that the Commission would directly control and supervise every department and service, for example, justice, railways, post office, telegraphs, labor, finance, and the like. In addition, Allied personnel would be needed to supervise the existing administrative structure, which he proposed to retain. Percival thought the plan was admirable but too costly in military officers and civilian officials as well as in pounds sterling. He preferred, bearing in mind Britain's commitments on other commissions, to modify the plan so that fewer

---

[40] For the history of the Allied response to the Upper Silesian municipal communal elections see the following: Meetings of the Supreme Council held on October 25, 1919, October 29, 1919, November 10, 1919, and November 13, 1919 in DBFP, 1st ser., II, nos. 6, 8, 18, and 21. The same minutes are reproduced in FRUS, PPC, VIII, 763-82, 801-28, and IX, 74-93 and 141-57.

officials would be needed. Lerond, for most part, accepted his counter-proposal which resulted in a saving of 69 officers from the original total of 200.

The two men then, incorporating Percival's measures, drew up a new plan for the Inter-Allied Commission in which the administration would be directed by four commissioners, assisted by a general secretariat. Seven departments were to be established in addition to the secretariat, each under the direction of a representative of one of the Allied governments, with assisting staff personnel representing each of the other Allied governments. The United States, Great Britain, and Italy were each to provide a head and the majority of personnel for one department while France provided for the rest. Lerond, expecting the participation of the United States to be delayed, proposed that Britain temporarily take over the Department of Food Control which was assigned to the Americans. When the United States failed to assume its share in the occupation and administration of Upper Silesia, these enlarged interim duties taken over by the British became permanent. Even more important than the departmental directors in the Commission structure were the *Kreis* controllers, military men of the rank of Major or Lieutenant Colonel, each of whom was assigned to an area to direct the functioning of the local administration and to execute the decrees of the Inter-Allied Commission.[41] The *Statut* of the Commission was signed by the Allied Commissioners on November 12.[42]

---

[41] Crowe to Curzon, no. 2030, October 27, 1919 in FO 608/217, file 460/3/14, no. 19891. The structure of the Commission and the method of administering the plebiscite area were not completely the creations of General Lerond. Before it left Paris, the Inter-Allied Plebiscite Commission drew up its plans, using for its guidance, the Lerond-Von Simpson Agreement of January 9, 1920 and the plans for administration already drawn up by the Schleswig Commission. See Wambaugh, II, 110-11 and 221. The Lerond-Simpson Agreement laid the basis for the relationship between the Allies and the native population in Upper Silesia, Allenstein, and Marienwerder and it provided for the transfer of power to the new Allied administration. For text see Wambaugh, I, doc. no. 25.

[42] The text of the statute does not appear in either Journal Officiel de Haute-Silésie or Wambaugh's volume of documents, but the latter does make reference to it in I, 221. Only the French, British, and Italian commissioners signed the statute. The question of American participation in the occupation of Upper Silesia was one of long standing. In June, Lloyd George had suggested that the Americans undertake the occupation of the province alone (Council of Four Meeting, June 11, 1919 in FRUS, PPC, VI, 316-23) but President Wilson pointed out that such a commitment on his part

Late in 1919, forces of the local German military party began to concentrate in Upper Silesia, probably with the secret protection of the German government, in numbers exceeding the military and interior policing requirements. Police formations of various descriptions likewise were growing and the inhabitants feared that violence would result as the number of agitators grew and evacuation of German forces grew imminent. Marshal Foch informed the Council of the situation and during its December 31 meeting, they decided to urge the German government to take certain immediate measures. Among these were the reduction of troop strength to a point "consistent with the maintenance of order," the evacuation of groups like the Marine Brigade whose attitude was deemed by the Allies "contrary to pacification of the country," the taking of necessary measures to urge residents not to resist the occupation troops, and the discouragement of the influx of non-native demobilized men into Upper Silesia. The Allies specified that the measures were to be carried out immediately so that they would be fully operational by the time the Treaty of Versailles came into force.[43]

Finally, the related question of payment for the occupation was taken up at the same meeting. Crowe circulated a note explaining the point of view of his government toward expenses incurred in the course of occupation of plebiscite areas. This was the same as the position taken with respect to Danzig.

---

was difficult in view of the fact that once peace was declared, American troops had to be withdrawn. (Council of Four Meeting, June 17, 1919 in FRUS, PPC, VI, 529-42). The heads of delegations, throughout the summer and autumn, continued to debate the question. At the October 23 meeting, it was announced that four American battalions were en route to Upper Silesia and would be held at Coblenz. They would not be sent to the zone of occupation until the Treaty was ratified. (Meeting of the Heads of Delegations, October 23, 1919 in FRUS, PPC, VIII, 746-62). The failure of the United States Senate to consent to the ratification of the Treaty prevented American participation in the occupation of the province, leaving the bulk of the work to the French and the most powerful departments of the Plebiscite Commission under their control. In any case the French would have directed the prestigious Interior, Military, and Economic Departments, but an American presence would have lent strength to the image of a neutral Allied occupation force.

[43] Foch to Clemenceau, December 30, 1919 and "Note Concerning the Situation in Upper Silesia" appearing as documents 1 and 2 in Appendix J to Minutes of Supreme Council Meeting, December 31, 1919 in DBFP, 1st ser., II, no. 49 and FRUS, PPC, IX, 721-59.

Article 88, dealing with Upper Silesia, moreover, specified that the expenses were to be paid from "local revenues." Under reserve of Italian approval, the Supreme Council approved the British note.[44]

In January 1920 the Treaty of Versailles came into effect; the occupation forces began arriving later in the month and in February, members of the governing Inter-Allied Commission reached the provincial capital at Oppeln.[45]

Anglo-Polish Ties

The new Polish state in 1919 attempted to enter the family of nations with exaggerated notions of its immediate importance. Even before the Treaty came into force she was already planning to designate a Minister Plenipotentiary and Envoy Extraordinary to the Court of St. James, a move that Britain was not prepared to reciprocate. A proliferation of British embassies in the series of new succession states of Europe was not part of her policy and the British representative at Warsaw in early June urged the Polish government to dispatch a mission to London of a non-permanent character to more or less correspond to the British Mission in Poland. This they did.

The British government accepted Poland's appointment of Prince Eustace Sapieha to the London post. He had been born a British subject and had lived in England many years, his father having served in the Dragoon Guards. Upon inheriting estates in Lithuania he had become a Russian subject.

When the Poles came in search of British approbation in the autumn of 1919, they came, paradoxically, claiming a role as one of the powers and simultaneously seeking a Britain to lean on-- even to some degree, a Britain to dictate policy to them. Some in the Polish Foreign Office feared that the German military still looked upon Poland as a "temporary creation which would inevitably collapse in a few years' time" but also--what was worse--that many

---

[44] Minutes of Supreme Council Meeting, December 31, 1919 cited above.

[45] Allied occupation began with the arrival of French troops after January 20. No British troops were sent at this time. Although the other members of the governing commission had been in the province for over a week, Colonel Percival did not arrive until February 21 at which time he had a cordial reception from the local population. See The Times [London], February 21, 1920, p. 11 and Gregory Macdonald, "Polish Upper Silesia" (Prepared for New Fabian Research Bureau, Unpublished manuscript deposited at Polish Institute and Sikorski Museum Library, London, 1935), p.104.

Allied statesmen especially in Britain shared this view. One spokesman suggested that the British government did not realize that it had the opportunity of "acquiring a dominant position in Poland," being in a position, if it so chose, to "do more to help Poland than any other power." Poland, lavishing the unsought-for attentions of an undesired suitor upon His Majesty's Government, requested British guidance in formulating policy regarding her neighboring countries in order to prevent launching herself "on a policy which might be displeasing" in London.[46] These overtures fall strangely on ears accustomed to hearing about the French-Polish harmony from Versailles to Locarno, but it was again the London visit that was stressed by the new Polish Minister of Foreign Affairs, Stanisław Patek, when he visited the western capitals in December. The historic friendship between France and Poland would be confirmed in February 1921 with the completion of the military alliance assuring Poland a place in the French scheme for her own security in Europe. But Poland had no desire to become a satellite of her western ally; she exercised humility poorly. It was also expedient for Poland, possessed of a desire to be joined again to the sea by the city of Danzig, to count as a friend that nation which controlled the sea and dominated in maritime and commercial spheres.

So, by the time the Treaty of Versailles was ratified, Great Britain had made the correct and necessary preparations to discharge her duty under its provisions, assuming, because it was in her area of interest, a disproportionate responsibility in the port city of Danzig and expecting France to bear the major burdens in Upper Silesia. Whether she discharged these duties with any more enthusiasm or prospect of self-interest is the next question to be considered.

---

[46] Rumbold to Curzon, no. 345, October 5, 1919 and Rumbold to Curzon, no. 416, November 1, 1919 both in DBFP, 1st ser., VI, nos. 199 and 243.

CHAPTER III

A YEAR OF OBLIGATIONS

(January 1920 to March 1921)

On January 10, 1920 the Treaty of Versailles came into force and, with it, new Allied regimes took over in Danzig and Upper Silesia in order to implement the conditions set forth in that document. If Danzig's response to the new situation was restrained and directed toward a postponement of the Treaty's implementation, the vociferous Upper Silesian one, tempered by disillusionment and frustration, was directed toward the achievment of a *fait accompli* to make the province part of Poland. Ensuing months would prove this attempt abortive.

The Allied administration began in Danzig on February 11 charged to be effective until the Free City's constitution could be written and the Polish-Danzig convention ordered in Article 104 of the Treaty of Versailles was concluded. Less than a fortnight after receiving his appointment, Sir Reginald Tower came to Danzig to begin nearly a year's tenure that was to see him vilified as an incompetent administrator, a pro-German, and a puppet of the British Foreign Office who favored collaboration with Germans In Upper Silesia, the arrival of the Inter-Allied Plebiscite Commission was the beginning of an unexpectedly long, and from the Polish point of view, most unwelcome stay. Upper Silesia looked coolly upon the coming of the Allies. Later, it came to resent their presence when it became clear that the Commission planned to genuinely control the province.

Not far from the Free City's borders in the newly-won corridor, the Poles enacted a dramatic coming of age by their country and satisfied their desire to be reunited with the sea. On February 10 General Joseph Haller, the leader of the Polish army which had fought under French auspices during the war, reached the shores of the Baltic near Wielka Wies, which was renamed in his honor to Hallerowo. There he cast a gold ring into the sea symbolizing Poland's renewed contact with the life-sustaining waters.[1] Like the Greeks who had sealed their alliances by dropping iron into the sea, the Poles entered into this marriage, which was more than a mere alliance of convenience, with an eye to permanence and stability. Whether these were to be their lot remained to be seen, but it was unmistakable that both Poland and Germany would have to adjust to a new post-Versailles world in the areas of Danzig and Upper Silesia that so intimately touched them both.

---

[1] Casimir Smogorzewski, Poland's Access to the Sea (London: George Allen and Unwin, Ltd., 1934), p. 146.

The Interim Regime in Danzig

The poor state of Polish-Danzig relations was evidenced when the interim regime took over the city. Despite the attempts of Sir Reginald Tower to promote better relations between the two parties, which were in their own interest, the mutual hatred and suspicion persisted and contributed to the difficulty of the task of carrying out the Treaty provisions. Anxious to glean what they could from the curtailed privileges they had been given in Danzig, the Poles tended to be overzealous, impatient, and exaggerating. Tower's complaints to the Polish Commissioner were successful only in part. On the other hand, Danzigers, a majority of whom preferred to remain German, demonstrated a desire to prevent the execution of the articles of the Peace Treaty which concerned their city. The showdown between these hostile groups was later manifested in the crisis of August 1920.

After his attempts to create a more amicable situation in Danzig had failed, Tower contacted the Conference of Ambassadors in mid-March. This body, composed of the ambassadors of the principal Allied powers in Paris, had been set up in January 1920 upon the closing of the Paris sessions of the peace conference as an executive committee of the Allies.[2] If Polish claims were to be recognized, Tower told the Ambassadors, Danzig would in effect become a Polish city. He refused to honor the claims and to turn over to Poland half of the former German property and everything pertaining to customs, waterways, railroads, and posts. After negotiations in Warsaw between Danzig and Polish representatives had proved abortive because of excessive Polish demands, Tower proposed that a "cooling off period" be instituted by postponing the execution of the Treaty and creating a temporary administration with powers extending over the harbor.[3]

Rumbold's response was negative, showing that he understood, even if he did not condone, the Polish point of view in this regard. He believed that putting off the day when Poland could begin enjoying the privileges in Danzig envisioned by the peacemakers would have serious results. It was well-remembered in Poland that her claim to Danzig had been denied chiefly through the activities of Great Britain at the peace conference. If she should be

---

[2] The most thorough study of this organization is Gerhard P. Pink, The Conference of Ambassadors (Geneva: Geneva Research Center, 1942). A briefer explanation of its constitution and workings is given by Sir Maurice Hankey, Diplomacy by Conference: Studies in Public Affairs, 1920-1946 (London: Ernest Benn Ltd., 1946), p. 32.

[3] Tower to Rumbold, no. 29, March 17, 1920 in FO 688, box 7 which transmits a copy of dispatch no. 43 addressed to the President of the Conference of Ambassadors.

deprived of her rights, he anticipated that a "storm of indignation" would sweep over that country.

Such a course would be most bitterly resented: the responsibility would be once more laid to the charge of Great Britain and what is now being whispered by a few in private, no doubt as a result of German propaganda, that Great Britain wishes herself to control the port of Danzig in her own interests, would be regarded as amply confirmed by any decision to install a temporary administration with extended powers such as is suggested by Sir Reginald Tower.[4]

In a ninety-minute meeting in Warsaw several weeks later, on April 16, which was attended by Tower, Rumbold, and Marshal Pilsudski,[5] the Polish chief of state expressed his country's impatience with the interminable delays connected with implementing the Treaty of Versailles and hinted that his intervention might be demanded by the pressures of public opinion. Rumbold magnanimously chose not to construe this as a threat of Polish occupation despite Pilsudski's recent display of aggression in seizing Vilna which the Poles, Lithuanians, and Russians had all claimed as their own.

In view of the fact that he would in less than a year become High Commissioner himself, it is interesting to note General Sir Richard Haking's attitudes on the Danzig situation in the spring of 1920.[6] Haking, who was in command of the Allied garrison there, was both critical of the way Tower was exercising the rights of the High Commissioner and rash in his own recommendations. He would have liked to have Tower "bluff" his way through the Polish non-cooperation by threatening Allied action. Then, because he thought he could expect little support from the Conference of Ambassadors owing to the friendship between Paris and Warsaw and to the dominant position of France in that body, he called upon

---

[4]Rumbold to Curzon, no. 218, March 29, 1920 in FO 688, box 4. Some weeks later a letter dated in Warsaw was published in the Nation Belge in Brussels with a similar accusation of British self-interest in Danzig. It criticized Tower's friendly relations with Bürgermeister Sahm and charged that Britain was working for Germany against Poland. See Sir F. Villers to FO, no. 270, April 29, 1920 in FO 371/3901, file 73, no. 195335.

[5]Rumbold to Curzon, no. 272, April 19, 1920 in FO 688, box 7.

[6]Secretary of War Office to Undersecretary of State for Foreign Affairs, March 27, 1920 which transmits Haking's letter of March 13 as Appendix B, "Present Situation in Danzig" in FO 371/3901, file 73, no. 188529.

Tower to go directly to the British Foreign Office which, after all, was the authority which had appointed him. Already he was dangerously blurring the lines which separated a British representative from a representative of the League of Nations.

The most startling of Haking's observations dealt with the status of Danzig under the treaty whose conclusion was demanded by Article 104.

> If when the Poland-Danzig Treaty is signed, the Polish Government is to have control of the harbour, the railways, waterways, customs and foreign relations of the Free City, Poland will be compelled to safeguard her interests by establishing her own customs officers, her own harbor, railway and waterway officials and the necessary force to back them up. Danzig will then cease to become a Free City except in name, and it would cause less friction between the Danzigers, the Poles, the Germans outside and the Allies, if the fact was recognised and Danzig made part of Poland. It would also obviate the expense of maintaining Allied Officials in the Free City.[7]

This reckless dealing with the careful distinctions designed by the peacemakers characterized a military man's unconcern with diplomatic subtlety and an almost boorish disregard of the self-consciousness of sovereign states. And this statement was not unique. Repeatedly he claimed that Danzig would eventually become absolutely Polish under the provisions of Article 104 and therefore a prompt Allied withdrawal would not only overcome the immediate impasse but it would also bring the inevitable future into reality all the sooner.[8] Neither the Allied Administrator nor the Foreign Office interpreted the Treaty article in that way, but perhaps Haking's abhorrence of euphemism caused him to foresee a condition that by mid-decade would develop essentially along the lines of his predictions in 1920.

A temporary settlement was reached when Poland and Danzig signed a provisional agreement on April 22 dealing with railway, customs, posts, and other problems outstanding between them. It was meant not to prejudice the final settlement and was to remain in force for four months. But this did not mark the end of the problem.

---

[7] Letter from Haking, "Present Situation in Danzig" cited above.

[8] Haking to War Office, Communicated to Foreign Office, April 3, 1920 in FO 371/3901, file 73, no. 188925. See also the minutes by Crookshank of April 10.

The Poles had long entertained the hope of entering the family of nations and of developing a merchant fleet and navy with a port on the Baltic. They had a plan to establish a naval base on the island of Holm in Danzig Bay--a scheme which was not welcomed by the representatives of the British government. Upon his return to Warsaw from a visit to the Free City, Rumbold requested that the British Mission impress upon the Polish government the fact that the Treaty intended Danzig to be a commercial port, not a naval base.[9] This was consistent with the view of Lord Derby, from the Conference of Ambassadors, who felt that no one ought to be permitted to maintain a base at Danzig, believing that the very existence of the Free City would be jeopardized by a too-literal interpretation of Article 104.[10]

On May 7 the Ambassadors announced several important decisions affecting Danzig: (1) that no military or naval base would be tolerated in that city; (2) that the High Commissioner was authorized to begin the division of German state property there; and (3) that Derby's proposal to create a Harbor and Communications Board in which the harbor, wharves, and appurtenances would be vested, be submitted to the Polish government and the Danzig Council for consideration.[11]

The unanimous resolution of the Conference of Ambassadors was received regretfully by those British officers who were engaged in the preparatory work of establishing a Polish navy. Arrangements for the transfer of six German torpedo boats were practically concluded; naval estimates had been included in the Polish budget and approved. British concessions had been obtained for the sale of one light cruiser, four torpedo boats, and some coastal motor boats and for assistance in officer training. Since Poland had read into these dealings Britain's implicit acceptance of the principle of a small Polish sea-going navy, it was suggested that Poland might

---

[9] Rumbold to Curzon, no. 264, April 19, 1920 in FO 688, box 7. When this question of a Polish mandate over Danzig came up again a few months later, H. A. L. Fisher assessed the ostensible Polish aggressiveness from the point of view held by many in Great Britain. In his estimation, Poland had done much to forfeit British sympathies since her seizure of Vilna that year and British public opinion "would certainly not tolerate occupation of Danzig against the will of the population of that city by a Polish garrison in time of peace." Fisher to Lloyd George, November 18, 1920 in London, Beaverbrook Library, Private Papers of Lloyd George, F/16/7/62.

[10] Derby to Curzon, no. 521, April 29, 1920 in Documents on British Foreign Policy 1919-1939 (hereafter DBFP), 1st ser., XI, no. 262.

[11] Derby to Curzon, no. 547, May 7, 1920 and the resolution of the Conference of Ambassadors in no. 86, May 11, 1920, FO 688, box 7.

find new cause for feeling betrayed by Britain if that country concurred in the decision to prohibit a naval base at Danzig.

About the same time, there was talk in Britain of withdrawing the Naval Mission which had been in Poland since the autumn of 1919. Sir Horace Rumbold strongly objected on the ground that British prestige would suffer, for the vacuum would be filled by the French, and politically it would constitute an admission that Great Britain was disinteresting herself in Poland.[12] In a similar vein, the Admiralty was of the opinion that not only would withdrawal entail a loss of British prestige, but also that in the event of trouble in northeastern Europe, the "task of Great Britain as policeman of the seas" would be made more difficult if existing Polish forces were not under the influence of British ideas and naval officers.[13] Operations, however, were curtailed when the scope of the instructions to the Mission was narrowed to purely naval matters and its personnel cut in the summer of 1920.

The second point of the resolution of the Conference of Ambassadors concerned the distribution in Danzig of former German government property. It substantially reflected the French point of view and was adopted only after the withdrawal of Lord Derby's proposal to provide for the temporary lease of contested properties in Danzig in order to help alleviate the economic stagnation. The Conference authorized the High Commissioner to allocate at once the property which was not disputed between Danzig and Poland and to invite the two parties to submit formal claims for the rest when they submitted their draft treaty.

The last portion of the May 7 resolution of the Ambassadors dealt with Lord Derby's scheme for the creation of a Harbor and Communications Board. What he originally proposed was

> With a view to the maintenance and future improvement of the Port and Harbour of Danzig to the mutual advantage of Poland and the Free City of Danzig it is expedient to set up a Harbour Board composed of an equal number of representatives of Poland and the Free City of Danzig with an independent chairman appointed by the League of Nations. All waterways, docks, basins, wharves and contiguous warehouses and other works shall be vested in the said board, who shall apply all monies received by them to the maintenance and improvement of the Harbour, subject to such payment towards municipal expenditure as may be

---

[12] Rumbold to FO, no. 225, March 30, 1920 in FO 371/3912, file 39818, no. 190058.

[13] Admiralty to FO, N/E 5632/1920, April 6, 1920 in FO 371/3912, file 39818, no. 190361.

hereafter determined on by agreement between the Board and the Municipality of the Free City of Danzig.[14]

While this was generally well received some still expressed the fear that a literal interpretation of this regulation might give Poland complete control over the port.

None of the decisions completely satisfied Derby who believed that they merely provided some elbow room for the High Commissioner but did not find a real settlement to the impasse at Danzig. He was not optimistic that a settlement would be reached either in the port city or in Paris where the French were "clearly determined by a rigid application of the letter of Article 104 . . .to produce a situation in which the 'freedom of Danzig' became nothing but a game." In fact, the French wished to revert to the original recommendation of the Polish Commission at the peace conference and to assign Danzig to Poland outright. Derby, faithful to British policy that supported a genuinely Free City of Danzig, opposed the French in this matter.[15]

Towards the end of the month, on May 27 and 29, two meetings of the Polish and Danzig delegations were held to negotiate a final treaty. Agreement proving impossible, the conversations were adjourned in order that each side could prepare its own draft treaty. The two were simultaneously invited to present their cases to the Conference of Ambassadors and it was hoped that a final treaty could be agreed upon by August 22, the expiration date of the provisional agreement.

It was in July and August that the real crisis arose in the relations between Danzig and Poland over the question of the transport of war material to Poland through that port. Since April 1920, Poland had been fighting a war with Russia which was sparked by Poland's unwillingness to accept the ethnographic line between them, sometimes called the Curzon Line, as her eastern frontier. Toward the end of July the Russian offensive was at its height and the Danzig dock workers refused to handle any war materials passing through that port. Whether prompted by Bolshevik sympathies or Polish antipathies,[16] the fact remains that the dockworkers refused

---

[14] Derby to Curzon, no. 547, May 7, 1920 cited above.

[15] Tower to Rumbold, no. 86, May 11, 1920 in FO 688, box 7 and Rumbold to FO, May 13, 1920 in the same file.

[16] John Brown Mason's account (The Danzig Dilemma: A Study in Peacemaking and Compromise, Stanford: Stanford University Press, 1946, pp. 116-17) of the Danzig dockworkers' strike in July 1920 is based on a study by Ian F. D. Morrow. Mason ascribes the motivation for the strike to the "fairly strong undercurrent of sym-

to discharge the cargo of rifles destined for Poland from the Greek vessel "Triton" when it arrived on July 21. Two possible solutions presented themselves: the British garrison could unload the ship or the High Commissioner could import Polish labor under military protection to complete the task. The second of these was almost certain to precipitate a general dock strike, but the Danzig trades union leaders thought that the first would not. Although the Allies deprecated the use of military labor in principle, the special Allied Mission in Warsaw enlisted the support of the British garrison under the command of General Haking, who discharged the material into barges which were then escorted by Danzig police to Polish territory without incident.[17] A threatened Danzig dock strike and the worsening of Polish-Danzig relations were in some quarters laid at the doorstep of Tower for his alleged poor administration.

Haking, in his characteristic bulldozer style, censured Tower's administration and suggested in such stringent terms that he be recalled that Crowe hesitated to deal with his communication through routine channels. He observed that Haking had been successful in impressing Lord D'Abernon, Britain's representative in Berlin, with Tower's weakness and general mismanagement and in winning the ambassador's consent to do the very thing that the Allies in conference at Boulogne the day before had agreed was undesirable, i.e., to employ British troops in unloading munitions. Crowe was not won over by Haking's arguments and he criticized the General's disloyalty to Tower and his attempted usurpation of more authority at Danzig than was his right, remembering with some cynicism that Haking had once been offered the High Commissionership in the port city but refused the appointment in hope of becoming ambassador or chargé d'affaires at Berlin. There was here,

---

pathy for Soviet Russia rather than to any active hostility to Poland" and like Morrow, he points out that the confrontation between Danzig and Poland at this time was an early manifestation of the divergence in their attitudes regarding their relationship. See also Ian F. D. Morrow, The Peace Settlement in the German-Polish Borderlands (London: Royal Institute of International Affairs, 1936), pp. 67-76.

[17] A personal report of Sir Maurice Hankey on a visit to Warsaw in July 1920 appears in British Museum, D'Abernon MSS, 48923. In this report Hankey indicated that he would have gone further in advocating that the British government as a sea power take as its "sphere" the control of the Port of Danzig and obtain consent of the Allied powers and the Council of the League for this. Such an announcement alone might, he believed, serve as a deterrent to further disorder and might end the strike movement. For the correspondence dealing with the transport of munitions through Danzig in 1920 see Warsaw Archives FO 688, box 7, file 136.

in Crowe's opinion, a clash of personalities which had unfortunately involved the unsuspecting Lord D'Abernon.[18]

Concern over the affair was evidenced in Parliament where a question regarding it was asked the Prime Minster. Lloyd George's answer was circumspect--only reiterating that the British troops were in Danzig to support the authority of the temporary Administrator and that their enlistment in the unloading was considered necessary in order to keep the port open.[19]

When serious disorders did occur during the last days of July, Tower found himself in a difficult position. He was forbidden by the War Office from using military labor until further notice. Nor could he impose martial law to restore order because he lacked the estimated sixteen battalions of reinforcements which would be required for such action. Allied leaders were in agreement that under the terms of the Treaty of Versailles, Poland had a right of unhampered use of the port and that their responsibility lay in securing Poland's fair treatment in that regard. Lloyd George and the Italian Prime Minister, Giovanni Giolitti, informed the High Commissioner to work toward this aim, using any available labor under Allied protection if the Danzig dockers struck. Further, they expressed a willingness to reinforce their troops. This was the only part of the agreement from which the French disassociated themselves, regarding their agreement to dispatch a half battalion from Memel as sufficient.[20] When these instructions arrived in Danzig the effect was immediate. Not only did the demurring railwaymen's movement collapse, but the dockers resumed work on August 31 and no further disorders ensued.

But the crisis of the summer of 1920 had shown Poland that her free access to the sea was not as free as she had bargained for. When her war in the east demanded a ready supply of munitions, her use of the port could not be depended upon and Polish speculations returned to the old idea of finding an alternate, unquestionably Polish port. Later in the year, Lord D'Abernon, expressing a mild, pragmatic revisionism, observed the Polish plight with some sympathy and recommended that a means of communication between Poland and the sea other than Danzig should be found. To him the regime established by the Treaty of Versailles was precarious and German

---

[18] Letter from Sir Eyre Crowe to Lord Curzon with minutes on a telegram to Sir Reginald Tower, no. 129, July 28, 1920 in Curzon Papers, FO 800/156.

[19] 132 H.C. Debates. 5 S, 2029.

[20] Lloyd George to D'Abernon, August 23, 1920 in FO 688, box 7, file 136, no. 24. Prime Minister to Balfour, August 23, 1920 in Private Papers of Lloyd George, F/3/5/6.

intransigence inevitable; this led him to speculate on the suitability of Riga or Memel or some other Baltic port as Poland's outlet. Such an alternative would have been regarded as impossible a year earlier at the peace conference, but perhaps the wounds already incurred would make the Poles more bending and the conciliatory policies of Prince Sapieha, who had only assumed control of the Ministry of Foreign Affairs in June, would convince them to establish friendlier relations with their neighbors to the north, thereby ensuring their freer access to the sea.[21]

With the easing of the summer crisis, negotiations were resumed in Paris in late September for the conclusion of the Polish-Danzig treaty. During the crisis period, while local talks had been suspended, the Allied Conference of Spa[22] on July 11 had contributed in part to the treaty's framing by its decisions concerning the Harbor and Communications Board. Lord Curzon addressed the difficulty of reconciling Articles 104 and 107 of the Treaty of Versailles. What the first one gave to Danzig, the second ostensibly took away by demanding the transfer of ownership of the former German government property not to Danzig alone but to Poland as well. The only solution which presented itself to the Conference was the establishment of a joint authority on which both states could be represented under a League-appointed chairman. Lord Derby emphasized the importance of equal representation, and after discussion it was agreed that the Polish-Danzig treaty, in order to secure for both signatories the advantages envisioned for them by the peacemakers, should establish the board in question which would be "entrusted with the administration and control of the services and means of communication" referred to in Article 104.[23]

This board was written into the document which the Conference of Ambassadors drew up after repeated failures on the part of Danzig and Poland to agree upon a text. It was the major point of contention which was responsible for causing a split in the Polish delegation and sending one fiery negotiator home to inform his government that his moderate colleagues were "giving everything

---

[21] D'Abernon to FO, no. 1110, November 2, 1920 in FO 371/5415, N 1962/1962/55.

[22] The Spa Conference was held from July 5-16, 1920 and among other items had on its agenda the questions of reparations, coal, and Danzig.

[23] British Secretary's Notes of the Inter-Allied Conference at Spa, July 11, 1920 in DBFP, 1st ser., VIII, no. 62. For the resolution regarding Danzig which was approved by the Supreme Council on July 11 see Appendix 8 to the same document.

away." Finally, two conciliatory Polish negotiators followed him to heal the rift and it was probably their assistance, coupled with Allied pressure, which convinced the Polish government to instruct Paderewski to sign the treaty. This he did on November 18, subject to the condition that Poland be given a mandate to protect the Free City. This question of the military mandate was then turned over to the Council of the League of Nations.[24] How this issue developed in the following year will be investigated later.

In planning for the end of the interim regime in Danzig, the Foreign Office assumed that with the signature of the new treaty, Tower's function as Allied Administrator would cease. Early in November Tower informed the Foreign Office of his intention to formally relinquish his post at that time.

As the civilian and military administration came to an end, General Haking addressed some important observations and admonitions to the Chief of the Imperial General Staff.[25] Despite his earlier criticisms, he noted that the Allied Administrator who had taken his instructions partly from the Foreign Office, partly from the Conference of Ambassadors, and partly from the League of Nations had managed to uphold his dignity in a difficult situation and that in the military sphere the French and British troops had maintained a cordial, cooperative relationship. Should troops stay on any length of time, he recommended that they should do so under a single command. Finally, he suggested that the British naval force at Danzig had great moral effect in eastern Europe and should not, therefore, be summarily withdrawn. A British naval presence in the eastern Baltic waters convinced the neighboring countries that Britain "meant business" and though her policy might not have been published abroad, the fleet's presence exercised a considerable effect on their policies.

On October 29, with little fanfare, the Allies had signed the act establishing Danzig as a Free City which was to become effective on November 15 whether or not the Poles accepted the treaty with Danzig which was still awaiting signature at the time.[26] The

---

[24] Rumbold to FO, no. 1002, November 4, 1920 in FO 371/5408, N 1932/373/55. For documents dealing with the question of a Polish mandate over Danzig see FO 688, box 4, file 28.

[25] Director of Military Intelligence to FO, November 15, 1920 which transmits the Confidential letter from Haking to Chief of Imperial General Staff of November 7, 1920 in FO 371/5409, N 2679/373/55.

[26] Lord Derby had urged the Conference to sign the declaration and the Treaty despite the Polish objections. When Jules Cambon argued that they would be void without the Polish signature both

Free City of Danzig was born at 4 p.m. on November 15, 1920.

As usual, attempting to effect an early disengagement of its troops, the War Office urged that the withdrawal of the British battalion not be deferred beyond November 23 owing to lack of winter provisions for them. Lord Derby proposed that date to the Conference of Ambassadors who accepted it and decided that the British and French troops should both depart at that time. By November 29, General Haking and the last of the British troops had left the Free City and the French battalion had departed for Silesia.

When the question of finding a permanent High Commissioner for Danzig had first been considered in October, the Foreign Office favored the selection of a Briton for the post. The French agreed and Balfour, now representing Britain in Geneva, wryly observed that their choice was intelligible when one realized that the High Commissioner of Danzig "would always be having rows with the Poles."[27]

Bernardo Attolico, a skillful Italian administrator, was selected by the Council of the League of Nations on December 10 to act as interim commissioner.[28] He served only until January

---

Derby and the French legal adviser disagreed on grounds that by Article 102 the Allies undertook to establish the Free City of Danzig, and that undertaking was in no way contingent upon the treaty provided for in Article 104. Technically the argument is correct although it is not consistent with common sense. The Free City was constituted but its relationship with Poland undefined; the League of Nations was to protect Danzig, but the city's whole future was still under discussion. The compromise of Lord Derby specified that the act constituting the Free City be signed immediately but that it not become effective until November 15. The same Foreign Office minute, in observing the differences between the British and French representatives, proposed to instruct Lord Derby to ascertain French demands and "tell him to go as far as he possibly can in meeting their wishes: even if we have to give way (which is not clear) it will be best to effect a final settlement of this very tiresome question of Danzig." FO Memorandum by Crookshank, October 29, 1920 in FO 371/5408, N 1626/373/55 and Derby to FO, no. 1241, October 25, 1920 in the same volume, N 1328/373/55.

[27]Balfour to FO, no. 34, November 28, 1920 in FO 371/5409, N 3321/373/55.

[28]Minutes of the 11th Session of the Council of the League of Nations, 10th Meeting, December 10, 1920 in FO 371/5482, W 3564/481/98 and F. P. Walters, A History of the League of Nations, 2 vols. (London: Oxford University Press, 1952), I, 78-79.

1921, however, when the League Council named the permanent High Commissioner--General Sir Richard Haking, who had served on the spot in a military capacity throughout the previous year. Whether his indiscretion would successfully combine with his superior grasp of the situation and his administrative ability to produce a capable League official was something only 1921 could tell.

The New Regime in Upper Silesia

February 1920, the month following the coming into force of the treaty of peace, saw the arrival at the provincial capital at Oppeln of the Inter-Allied Commission which was charged with the administration of Upper Silesia during the period of preparation for the plebiscite. Its reception was quiet, the Germans thinking it would merely choose to supervise the existing administration and the Poles expecting that German officials would, in part, be replaced by their own compatriots. But when the Commission began to take its job seriously and proposed the creation of a High Court and a Court of Appeals for the territory,[29] the Germans in the area protested. Their action fed the hostility existing among some German officials and German labor and led to a series of scattered but serious strikes. The Polish Silesian counterstroke took the form of a press attack on the Germans, which accused them of plotting against the Commission and organizing their own partisans into military formations.[30] Rising political tension was being reported in mid-March and by the end of the month the *Sicherheitspolizei* was already overstepping its authority by becoming a potential military body.[31] It was the existence and activities of this force which contributed in great part to Polish grievances in the insurrections of both 1920 and 1921.

In April serious disturbances occurred in Oppeln after a clash between French forces and a German Silesian paramilitary outfit. In the following month, disorders and miners' strikes occurred several times, sparked by Wojciech Korfanfy, who variously wore the hats of director of Polish propaganda, Polish plebiscite commissioner, and chief insurrectionary.[32] With the

---

[29] Commission Interalliée de Gouvernement et de Plébiscite, *Journal Officiel de Haute-Silésie*, No. 4, June 12, 1920.

[30] An account of the events prior to the insurrection and the insurrection of August 1920 itself can be found in Sir Max Müller's Annual Report for 1920, March 18, 1922 which was transmitted with dispatch no. 144 in FO 371/8143, N 2900/2900/55.

[31] Rumbold to Curzon, no. 222, March 30, 1920 in FO 688, box 8.

[32] Later in the year, the British Commissioner, after hearing complaints of German Silesians, demanded the expulsion of Korfanty from the province. Despite the evidence Percival produced against

return of peace in July, preliminary arrangements for the plebiscite were begun. It was commonly believed among the Allies during the summer months that the plebiscite would take place in November 1920 at the earliest.

When the insurrection broke out in August, British representatives in Poland, because of their Polish sympathies, continued to favor holding the plebiscite before the winter months. Rumbold claimed that "the longer it is delayed the more follies the Poles will commit" to the detriment of their own cause. Percival believed that the extreme weather of the winter months would create difficulties of transport and housing for outvoters (eligible voters who were not currently resident in Upper Silesia) which would certainly hurt the Polish cause.[33] But when the insurrection occurred and put the Poles into a commanding position for a time, the Foreign Office came to favor an extension of the time period before the plebiscite should be held. Lord Hardinge, the Permanent Undersecretary of State for Foreign Affairs, told the Polish Chargé d'Affaires in London, Jan Ciechanowski, that under the changed circumstances, Britain could not press for an early plebiscite and would not do so until equality for the two sides was restored in the area.[34]

While both the Polish and German governments entertained hopes of winning the whole of the plebiscite area and propagandized to that effect, a movement for Upper Silesian independence or autonomy seemed to grow in strength. It was, in fact, not a new movement inaugurated in the immediate pre-plebiscite period. Late in 1918

---

him, Lerond and de Marinis overruled him and called instead upon the Polish government to recall the agitator. Korfanty in the meantime continued his activities and was to play a major role in the following May in the third and largest of the Silesian insurrections. For Colonel Percival's statement before the Inter-Allied Commission see FO 890, part 2, file 2K; for FO correspondence in December 1920 see Curzon to Percival, no. 113, December 11, 1920 in FO 371/4822, C 133398/1621/18. Published documents on the Korfanty affair in the correspondence between the FO, Oppeln, and Paris, appear in DBFP, 1st ser., XI, nos. 117, 119, 121, and 128. For a sympathetic view of Korfanty see the article of Lumby of The Times, "Upper Silesia: Korfanty and the Germans: A Modern Cleon," February 1, 1921.

[33] Percival to Rumbold, September 8, 1920 in FO 688, box 5, file 50, no. 52 and Rumbold to Curzon, no. 597, September 16, 1920 in the same box, file 50, no. 56.

[34] Curzon to Rumbold, no. 458, September 24, 1920 in FO 688, box 5.

a movement for a free Upper Silesia had begun, reaching its zenith in early 1920 about the time the Treaty of Versailles came into force and the province passed from full German sovereignty to Allied administration. Because the newly-arrived Inter-Allied Plebiscite Commission discouraged it as contrary to the Treaty and because of an internal rift, it lost many adherents. It remained sporadically vociferous and at first was largely ignored by the Polish and German governments.

Few British diplomats and military personnel were won over by the movement. Cecil Gosling, British envoy to Prague, had heard some of its adherents in early 1919, as had other British representatives,[35] until he received word from the Peace Conference and from the Foreign Office to lend no encouragement to the movement.[36] Probably the staunchest British advocate was F. Thelwald, the Commercial Commissioner at Berlin.[37] His argument favoring independence as an economic necessity was, however, based upon the commonly-held misconception that Poles were incapable of good administration--a premise which was by no means borne out by productivity figures of Polish Silesia in the years following the partition.

In an attempt to quell the independence movement and at the same time to propagandize prior to the plebiscite, each interested government promised some degree of autonomy to a Silesia which would come under its aegis. The Polish Diet in the course of its

---

[35] Gregory Macdonald, "Polish Upper Silesia" (Prepared for New Fabian Research Bureau, Unpublished manuscript deposited at Polish Institute and Sikorski Museum Library, London, 1935), p. 106. Among the most serious native proponents of independence was the German magnate Count Henckel von Donnersmarck. The Donnersmarck properties were located in the highly contested industrial area and stood to suffer from almost any partition of the province. Late in 1921 the Count sold his estates to a British group with headquarters in London, the Henckel von Donnersmarck Beuthen Estates, Ltd., in which he retained the position of first chairman. The Times, December 7, 1921, p. 10 and The Times Imperial and Foreign Trade Supplement, December 17, 1921, p. 266. The fate of these properties during the frontier delimitation of 1921 is investigated in Chapter VII.

[36] Minute by J. W. Headlam-Morley, March 27, 1919 in FO 608/140, file 476/1/1, no. 5310 and the negative minutes of various members of the FO; Balfour to Gosling, no. 35, May 15, 1919 in FO 608/140, file 476/1/1, no. 9593.

[37] Department of Overseas Trade to FO, Confidential, December 16, 1919 in FO 371/3779, file 4232, no. 163262.

July 15, 1920 sitting, unanimously passed a resolution which favored, for purely economic reasons, the granting of a wide autonomy for the regions which would fall to Poland.[38] In Germany, after negotiation and "violent discussion" between the Center and German Nationalist parties, the former garnered sufficient support, some grudging and resigned, in the Reichstag Foreign Affairs Committee, to insure passage of a law granting "full federal autonomy" to German Silesia if the population of that territory favored it.[39] In each case, Great Britain took little notice of the expressions, failed to consider them with much seriousness, and in effect, shrugged her shoulders even when the German government promised far-reaching Silesian autonomy--that same government for which Lloyd George would soon claim to be doing his utmost to save Upper Silesia.

As preparations for the organization of the plebiscite continued, there were renewed disturbances in early August of an intensity that moved General Lerond to propose the transfer of reinforcement troops from Teschen to Upper Silesia, a proposal which the British supported. Within two weeks the province again erupted into insurrection, almost precisely a year after the last such development.

Indirectly, events in Poland were responsible for the second Silesian insurrection, but more directly, according to British diplomats and military personnel serving in the area, the responsibility lay with Korfanty and the pro-Polish French. Germany had declared her neutrality in the Russo-Polish war that was still raging and local German Socialists in the plebiscite area agitated for a similar commitment by the Upper Silesian authorities.[40] The demonstration of the German Socialists in this sense, coupled with a general strike, led to a clash between the crowds and the French garrison. German mobs arose, Poles staged lynchings and formed armed bands, and Korfanty called upon Poles to defend themselves. With the breakdown of confidence in the Inter-Allied Commission, both sides armed themselves and Percival himself attempted to prevail upon influential German leaders to keep their population

---

[38] Rumbold to FO, no. 475, July 14, 1920 in FO 688, box 5, file 50, no. 21.

[39] D'Abernon to FO, no. 1078, October 24, 1920 in FO 371/4819, C 9838/1621/18.

[40] Wigram had minuted on Percival to FO, no. 79, August 24, 1920 in FO 371/4815, C 4814/1621/18: "It is difficult not to feel that the manner in which the situation has been handled by the Commission, is at least partly responsible for the present position. General Lerond would not have lost greatly in prestige if he had declared the neutrality of the plebiscite area in the . . . War."

quiet. He supported General Lerond's efforts to convince Korfanty to do the same and to disarm.

Polish armed bands appeared in the districts of Kattowitz, Pless, and Beuthen and between August 20 and 25 they extended activities into the districts of Königshütte, Tarnowitz, Rybnik, Lublinitz, and Gross Strehlitz. Although the Commission declared its intention to crush the revolt, French troops failed to take vigorous action against the Poles and this dilatoriness reflected on the authority and tone of the Commission. Local authorities were deposed by the Commission when they refused to cooperate and the *Sicherheitswehr* proved unequal to the task of resisting the large numbers of Poles. According to Percival, evidence pointed to a considerable importation of arms from Poland, a fact which in part contributed to his opinion that the unpremeditated examples of German excesses in Kattowitz and elsewhere were merely a pretext used by Korfanty for putting into operation a carefully laid plan.[41] It was at this time that Percival reversed the policy he had recently followed and proposed to Lerond and to the Director of the Interior Department that the *Sicherheitspolizei* be reissued the arms that had been taken from them. In his estimation, the men of this force generally performed their duty loyally and efficiently, although the French maintained that the opposite was true and greatly mistrusted them.

The French military authorities, not considering themselves sufficiently strong to order the immediate surrender of all arms, were confident that they could negotiate a disarmament of the Polish bands. Meanwhile, the inability or unwillingness of the military authorities to crush the insurrection was destructive to the authoritative image of the Commission and by the end of the first week of the disorders about 75% of the mines were partly or completely closed down.

Even before the negotiations were begun, serious charges of French partiality had arisen, not only on the part of the Germans among the Upper Silesian population but also on the part of the British officers connected with the administration whose protests took the form of tendered resignations. In one of his lengthy dispatches to the Foreign Office, Colonel Percival reported that four of his officers had independently notified him of their desire to terminate their appointments on the Commission. For most part these were district controllers and senior officers who had, in their own estimation, been rendered unfit for duty because they had been so incensed by repeated anti-German acts of their French colleagues that they found themselves becoming sympathetic to the

---

[41] For detailed correspondence on the 1920 insurrection in Upper Silesia see the Central Department papers, volumes 4814-4823 in FO 371, file 1621 and also the Warsaw Archives, FO 688, box 8.

German population rather than remaining entirely neutral. They charged that a fair plebiscite was not possible in view of the high-handed methods of Korfanty.[42] Percival informed the Foreign Office that although these resignations were really directed against the French Section which directed the military operations and the Interior Department, they were a blow to the prestige of the British Section of the Plebiscite Commission.

After a fortnight of serious disorders in Upper Silesia, Percival reported at the end of August that an agreement had been reached between Dr. Urbanek, director of the German Plebiscite Commissariat, and the chief German political parties and trades unions on one hand and Korfanty, director of the Polish Plebiscite Commissariat, and the chief Polish political parties and trades unions on the other. Calm had been restored and work in the mines resumed. Under the Korfanty-Urbanek agreement arms were to be laid down on the following conditions:

> (a) Replacement of the *Sicherheitswehr* by a police force composed of Upper Silesians of German and Polish sympathies in equal proportions.
> (b) Expulsion of persons who have moved into the area since August 1, 1919, with the object of influencing the plebiscite in an unlawful way, or by abuse of their official position. These expulsions to be made on the recommendation of a joint committee of local representatives of the two parties to be constituted in each district (*Kreis*).
> (c) Punishment, with at least a year's imprisonment, for persons found in unlawful possession of arms.
> (d) Prohibitions of all intimidation in industrial or private life, or of differential treatment of persons belonging to particular political or industrial organizations.
>
> A joint committee of representatives of the two parties . . . to be constituted for the plebiscite area as a whole, to supervise the execution of the above terms.[43]

Percival was critical of the agreement. He reported that the replacement of the *Sicherheitswehr* had in reality been agreed upon

---

[42] It is ironic that when Percival wrote unofficially to the FO about the situation in July, he criticized the resignations as "a matter of loss of nerve." This was only months before his own breakdown and replacement on the Commission. Percival to Wigram, July 28, 1920 in FO 371/4777, C 2835/226/18.

[43] Percival to FO, no. 192, August 31, 1920 in FO 371/4816, C 5661/1621/18.

by the Inter-Allied Commission, a fact known to the Polish leaders. The only reason that the orders issued in July had not been carried out was that Lerond, who was abroad, had requested their postponement until his return. Disorders broke out on August 17 before fresh orders could be issued. The second clause was in essence the same as a prior Polish demand. Both Percival and his Italian colleague, General Alberto de Marinis, agreed that under the Treaty of Versailles, only the Inter-Allied Commission had power to expel and that this power was not arbitrary. The third clause, he believed, favored the Poles who could obtain arms and ammunition from across the Polish border to the detriment of the Germans in the province whose disarmament would probably be insured. He believed that the fourth clause was fair to both parties and that the final provision could be successful if the committee would be prepared to accept the Inter-Allied Commission's decision as final in case of disagreement.

When this agreement came to the Commission for approval, Lerond hailed it as a great success and the fruit of his own "tactful" handling of the situation in bringing the Germans and Poles to the conference table. To Percival it appeared rather that the Germans had been driven to the table because of a lack of military protection, and that the Poles had agreed because they sensed British and Italian disapproval. The Poles feared the consequences if they failed to evidence some degree of good faith in trying to put an end to the Upper Silesian reign of terror. Fatalistically, he concluded that he would have to approve the agreement in order to forestall civil war, but in so doing and by preserving Britain from such an indictment, he and the Inter-Allied Commission would in fact be publicizing to the world that the Commission submitted to having its policy dictated to it.[44] He predicted that the Poles would refuse to disarm and, instead, they would merely deposit their arms in convenient caches just across the Polish frontier. The Germans would lose faith in the power of the Commission and arm themselves. Seizures in the industrial area later proved him right. It was at this time when the Poles commanded the fearful respect of most Upper Silesians that they were again unsuccessful in enlisting the support of the British government to set an early plebiscite date. Following Percival's presentation of the case against the French Section and particularly against "the worst offender," General Lerond, the Foreign Office queried whether the time had not come for the British to press for a radical reorganization of the Commission or, failing that, to threaten withdrawal from Upper Silesia and non-participation in the plebiscite.[45]

---

[44] Percival to FO, no. 198, September 4, 1920 in FO 371/4816, C 6029/1621/18.

[45] Percival to Wigram, September 1, 1920 and attached minute by Waterlow, September 9, 1920 in FO 371/4816, C 5700/1621/18. Curzon

It was this question, after Lerond's use of heavy-handed dictatorial methods and serious accusations of French bias, that was to dominate Commission affairs in the autumn months of 1920 before that body could finally take up the question of the actual arrangements for the plebiscite which had in the first instance been its *raison d'etre*. Having come to the conclusion that the Inter-Allied Commission had regretably and irretrievably lost prestige in Upper Silesia, the British government considered that the only means of re-establishing its authority was to recall and replace existing personnel and to reorganize various services of the Commission. Should the French be induced to recall General Lerond, Great Britain would agree to replace Colonel Percival. Judging from the recent Foreign Office criticism of Percival's effectiveness and his own desire to resign, Britain's offer was no sacrifice. The Foreign Office informed Lord Derby in Paris that Lerond was not equal to the task of disarming the Polish bands or of maintaining impartiality and that the very real possibility of war in Upper Silesia, which would lead to a breakdown of coal production, had to be faced unless he were replaced.

Finally, Derby was authorized to use his discretion in intimating to the French that the British might "feel obliged to withdraw altogether from participation in the Commission and to publish our reasons" if British demands were refused. It was an unusually uncompromising stand for Great Britain to take in Upper Silesia and one from which she would soon be forced to retreat.

On September 22, General Lerond came before the Conference of Ambassadors where he made a frank and effective apologia. At that hearing, Lord Derby assessed him as more tactless than deliberately biased, surrounded by his own officers, careless about keeping his colleagues properly informed. The ambassador observed that regulations and rules might be provided which would restrict Lerond without precipitating a confrontation with the French. But he hesitated to act on the unequivocal orders given him because he anticipated voting in the Conference of Ambassadors as a minority of one, which would merely strengthen the French hand. Instead, he believed, his half-way measures of restrictions might more practically be adopted and after some reasonable time Lerond might be quietly appointed to a new and "better" position.[46]

---

to Derby, no. 1000, September 13, 1920 in DBFP, 1st ser., XI, no. 42. Lord Derby recounted his conversation with Millerand in which the latter recognized the necessity for a change but sought a way out to save face for Lerond. It was decided to criticize the organization of the Commission as faulty. See Derby to Curzon, September 20, 1920 in the Curzon Papers, FO 800/153.

[46] Observations by Lord Hardinge on the reports from Derby at the Conference of Ambassadors were recorded in a minute of September 23, 1920 in FO 371/4818, C 7492/1621/18.

But Curzon was adamant and he urged Derby to make use of the hidden threat regarding British withdrawal and to put forward the British proposals for the reconstruction of the Upper Silesia Commission.[47] Among other things, this plan sought to remove the police from the Military Department and to reconstitute them as a separate department under British control. It envisioned a reconstruction of the Secretariat so that all papers should pass through the hands of each member of the governing Commission and not through those of the president alone. The British plan also required that inter-allied secretaries attend Commission meetings for the purpose of recording the decisions reached and action taken. Finally, Britain also desired that the supervision over the accounting of all administrative expenses be vested in the Allies, rather than in France alone whose representative directed the Department of Finance.

France was willing to accept the proposals only in part. She defended her disproportionate weight in Upper Silesia by arguing that France was forced to make good the numbers of personnel for the Commission which Britain and the United States had failed to provide. With respect to British demands for an autonomous police force in Upper Silesia, France sidestepped the issue and offered instead irrelevant concessions which would have augmented the number of secret police.[48]

Derby was dissatisfied with the French concessions. He continued the negotiations until a satisfactory compromise was found. In the end, what he secured was, in effect, the same position of equality for the three commissioners which had existed on paper

---

[47] Curzon to Derby, no. 1047, September 29, 1920 in FO 371/4818, C 7610/1621/18. Both the French and British points of view appear in Derby to FO, October 4, 1920 in FO 371/4818, C 8073/1621/18.

[48] One of the British complaints of longest standing was that the French dominated the police force. As a result of British pressure, France finally consented to placing the police and *gendarmerie* under the direction of the Departments of the Interior and Justice, although a French general remained in command. British and Italian officers with broader powers to enforce discipline were included in the police force. The Plebiscite Police (APO) which had replaced the *Sicherheitswehr* were organized into companies and made responsible to assigned Allied officers. For the text of the Commission's decrees disbanding the *Sicherheitspolitzei* and organizing the APO see **Journal Officiel de Haute-Silésie**, No. 6, August 28, 1920 and the decrees of December 2, 1920 regarding the command and employment of the APO in ibid., No. 10, December 3, 1920. These documents are also reproduced in Wambaugh, II, documents 76, 77, and 83. See also the narrative account of the reform in the Inter-Allied Commission in ibid., I, 240-41.

all along but which Lerond's usurpations, Percival's want of skill, and Marinis's lack of commitment had permitted to evolve into a Lerond dictatorship.

The British government viewed the agreement as a diplomatic success and when Lerond returned to Oppeln on October 19, he was forced to accept a more democratized system. The reorganization was not a panacea for Upper Silesia, but a move toward some needed improvement.

Most pressing among plebiscite questions in the autumn of 1920 was the outvoter or emigrant voter issue which was precipitating a crisis, even a threat of civil war, in the province.[49] It was first raised in a note from the Polish government to the British Legation at Warsaw. The Poles found fault with the Allied interpretation of the Treaty of Versailles which bestowed a vote on all persons born in plebiscite areas without consideration of the length of their residence. They feared that this understanding would invite an influx of disinterested outvoters, lead to disorder, and result in a violation of the spirit of the Treaty. The Polish government's attempt to abolish outvoters was based on an apparent inconsistency in the Treaty between the wording of Article 88, paragraph 1 and the annex to Article 88, paragraph 5, the former describing them as "inhabitants" and the latter specifying those "born or domiciled in the plebiscite area." This vexatious question was turned over to the Conference of Ambassadors when Lerond could not get his colleagues to agree to the Polish interpretation. Rumors abounded that if an unsuitable settlement was arrived at, the inhabitants would take the law into their own hands and prevent the emigrants from voting. The Poles failed to win British support to restrict the outvoter suffrage to those who had "some genuine interest" in Upper Silesia, but the Foreign Office suggested that the Plebiscite Commission and the Conference of Ambassadors consider their other request to hold outvoter polling several days after the general plebiscite in the interest of maintaining order.[50] When the Germans heard reports of the latter Polish proposal which had won French support, they categorically rejected it as prejudicial to German interests.[51] Polish and French resistance to the outvoters stemmed from the belief that the bulk of them would vote for the incorporation of Upper Silesia into Germany and also from the fear that serious disorders would re-

___

[49] FO Memorandum on the Silesian Situation prepared for the Prime Minister, November 25, 1920 in DBFP, 1st ser., XI, no. 86.

[50] Curzon to Lindsay, no. 3824, November 24, 1920 in DBFP, 1st ser., XI, no. 82.

[51] German Chargé d'Affaires to FO, November 26, 1920 in FO 371/4821, C 12341/1621/18.

sult from the influx of an estimated 300,000 people, mainly German, into the plebiscite area.

What the Poles proposed to achieve by separating voters from outvoters in time, Lord D'Abernon, the British ambassador at Berlin, proposed to achieve by a separation in space, that is, he suggested that outvoters record their votes in a fixed place outside Upper Silesia under impartial non-German control. This idea was taken up in the Foreign Office where a polling place like Cologne, an accessible and Allied-occupied city, was suggested.[52]

The outvoter question was considered at the Allied meeting held in London on November 27.[53] Lloyd George, who had taken great part in the negotiations at the peace conference concerning Upper Silesia, reminded the Conference that as Allies they had much to lose in German reparations should the province desire to be annexed to Poland. Such a state of affairs would have to be accepted if it transpired, but he thought that they were not called upon "to concert measures which would facilitate the loss, as this would be an act of self-sacrifice which the Allies could hardly be expected to make."

After debate, it was decided that they should propose to the Polish and German governments that all outvoters be concentrated in an Allied-occupied area of the Rhineland, for example, in Cologne, to cast their votes. Should the Poles and Germans accept the proposal, administrative details would be arranged; should they refuse to accept it, it was agreed to adopt the French scheme which provided for an outvoter poll to be held in the plebiscite territory some days later than the general vote in order to preserve public order in Upper Silesia. If this were to be implemented, it would be a concession on Britain's part because the British had always suspected that French and Polish proposals to delay the voting of outvoters were in reality attempts to prevent their voting altogether. Some British observers in the Foreign Office had wondered whether the French and Polish concern with "maintaining public order" was merely a ploy and whether, once the residents cast their votes, the Poles might foment insurrection and in the disorder prevent the outvoters from casting their ballots.

Public outcry against the Cologne scheme was immediate in Poland; it was directed so particularly against Great Britain that Sir Percy Loraine at the British Legation in Warsaw hesitated to approach the Polish government concerning the matter of Polish

---

[52] D'Abernon to Curzon, no. 590, November 24, 1920 and accompanying minute by S. P. Waterlow in DBFP, 1st ser., XI, no. 81.

[53] British Secretary's Notes of a British-French Conference in London, November 27, 1920 in ibid., VIII, no. 96.

acceptance of the Allied proposal without his French and Italian colleagues being present. Any unilateral action by Britain, he believed, would merely fan Polish resentment against that country which was suspected of having "extorted" this scheme from its reluctant Allies. By the time concerted action was agreed upon and an interview with the Minister of Foreign Affairs had been arranged, Poland had already registered her refusal, having regarded the plan as another betrayal by Britain which sought to augment the German vote. A wave of indignation likewise swept through the German press possibly instigated by the Ministry of Foreign Affairs. The press feared the Cologne plan as a French-backed scheme designed to facilitate the voting of Polish Silesian miners who were employed in great numbers in the Ruhr and in the neighborhood of Cologne. A succinct Foreign Office minute, summarized accurately the overreaction of the interested governments: "The German and Polish reasons for refusing our proposal about the out-voters are a monument of human folly."[54]

In the last months of the old year and the first weeks of January 1921, Polish agitation continued under the inspiration of Korfanty. The methods of terror and intimidation were of such a nature as to insure the alienation of the sympathies of undecided voters and those inclined to reason. Max Müller, the new British minister who had come to Warsaw in January, called upon Prince Sapieha, the Polish Foreign Minister, to cooperate with him in soothing the violence of the armed bands.[55]

February saw preparations for the plebiscite in full swing with joint committees engaged in drawing up the communal voting registers. A semblance of calm prevailed as active propaganda ceased and rival organizations were cooperatively involved in the administrative work.[56] The French continued their policy of searching for arms to which the British Commissioner had repeatedly and strongly objected. He maintained that this policy was stringently carried out only among the German population with the effect of

---

[54] For details of the Polish reaction as recorded by the British Legation at Warsaw between November 27 and December 16, 1920 see FO 688, box 5, file 50. For the German response recorded by the British Ambassador at Berlin see D'Abernon to Curzon, no. 1252, December 6, 1920 in DBFP, 1st ser., XI, no. 99 which does not reproduce Waterlow's minute. The latter can be found in FO 371/4822, C 13496/1621/18.

[55] Correspondence between the British Legation at Warsaw and both the FO and Oppeln is found in FO 688, box 5, file 50.

[56] "Regulations for the Plebiscite" in Journal Officiel de Haute-Silésie in three parts: No. 12, January 3, 1921; No. 14, February 25, 1921; and No. 16, March 2, 1921.

disarming half the population and exposing it to the mercies of the other half. By mid-February Lord D'Abernon noted that the German authorities had recognized their mistake in refusing the Allied proposal for an outvoter polling in Cologne. More than 150,000 eligible voters were refusing to come to Upper Silesia--a state of affairs to which Germany had contributed by generating fear through its advertising campaign against the Polish "reign of terror."[57]

Finally, the question of the outvoters came to an end on the eve of the plebiscite with the announcement that the Conference of Ambassadors had abandoned the split-time voting scheme because it was likely to produce serious disorder. On February 21, 1921 the London Conference issued its decision that residents and outvoters should go to the polls on the same day. Germany, who had feared the other scheme as a plot against her, considered that she had scored a diplomatic victory.

In early March 1921 four battalions of British troops began arriving (about 2,500 men) in Upper Silesia, bringing the total number of Allied forces in the province to about 16,000 men.[58] They moved into areas principally in the eastern districts and in the industrial triangle. Despite the reinforcements and the good behavior of the plebiscite police, Colonal Percival anticipated serious disorder, saw a real chance of civil war, and was convinced that no clear-cut decision would result from the plebiscite. Public demonstrations in the area were banned nearly a fortnight prior to the March 20 voting date and March 11 saw the quiet and orderly arrival of the first outvoters.[59]

After fourteen months of delay since the Treaty of Versailles had come into force, the plebiscite was held on Sunday, March 20, 1921. Thanks to the elaborate arrangements made by the Upper Silesia Commission, the much anticipated event passed off in com-

---

[57] British Museum, D'Abernon MSS, 48953A, Diary entry for February 13, 1921.

[58] Macdonald, p. 107.

[59] On the troop and police situation see Kilmarnock to FO, no. 87, March 7, 1921 in FO 371/5890, C 4775/92/18; Percival to FO, no. 39, March 8, 1921 in FO 371/5891, C 4930/92/18; Director of Military Intelligence to FO, Secret, March 10, 1921 in FO 371/5844, C 5189/5189/62. A summary of the Upper Silesian political situation during the first week of March appears in a letter from Bourdillon, the Acting British Commissioner, to Waterlow, March 9, 1921 in FO 371/5891, C 5451/92/18 which earned a strict rebuke for its anti-Polish bias from Max Müller in Warsaw. See Müller to Lindsay, March 17, 1921 in FO 688, box 10, file 50, no. 112.

plete quiet. Almost a holiday atmosphere prevailed with people already queuing up from 8 a.m. The contested industrial area saw an early vote being cast, with probably the majority being recorded by midday.[60] With early returns indicating a Polish victory, the Poles began their celebration at an open air *Te Deum* attended by thousands. But as the tally of the following days brought disillusionment to them, it was the Germans who held flag-waving celebrations. Germany continued to maintain that the entire plebiscite area was indivisible; Poland had to reconsider her stand on indivisibility.

The final figures giving Germany 707,605 votes and Poland 497,359 votes showed a German victory in industrial communes and a Polish one in the rural communes.[61] It was no easy task to follow the provisions of the Treaty of Versailles which stipulated that the vote should be calculated by communes and that the vote, together with the economic considerations, should provide the basis upon which the partition should be made. A frontier based on the communal totals of the March 20 plebiscite would be tortuous--its delineation perhaps impossible--in the ethnically-mixed, highly industrialized triangle. And so instead of a final settlement to the protracted Upper Silesian involvement, the Inter-Allied Commission found itself as embroiled as ever in the claims and counterclaims to a contested territory that seemed destined to belong to no one.

---

[60] The Times, March 21, 1921, p. 12.

[61] D'Abernon to FO, February 2, 1922 in FO 371/7556, C 2067/2067/18. Müller to FO, no. 582, December 23, 1922 in FO 371/9312, N 30/30/55. Official plebiscite statistics in Journal Officiel de Haute-Silésie, No. 21, May 7, 1921.

CHAPTER IV

INTERREGNUM: LOST PRESTIGE AND DUTY UNFULFILLED

(March 1921 to June 1921)

Having completed her service in the Allied Administration of Danzig by the end of 1920, Great Britain withdrew from the Free City exerting little political pressure there; except for tying up loose ends in the aftermath of the Free City's establishment, she contented herself with activities confined to the commercial sphere which, after all, had provided the impetus for her interest in Danzig in the beginning. But in the disputed plebiscite territory of Upper Silesia her plight was otherwise. Britain had up to now attempted to expedite an implementation of Article 88 and its annexes of the Treaty of Versailles in the province and having weathered the storms of counter-claims, insurrection, and organizational reconstruction, she contributed her share to the preparations for and the holding of the plebiscite on March 20, 1921. But no Conference of Ambassadors would pass a resolution in this case to provide for withdrawing her troops; no new administration was coming to whom responsibility could now be passed; and through no fault of her own, no door could be closed on this unwelcome involvement in Central Europe. She, with her Allies, would lose prestige and authority and be hard-pressed to provide a means of restoring them before taking up again the matter of the liquidation of the Upper Silesian question. If disengagement from Danzig had been routine, disengagement from Upper Silesia would be complex and prolonged. What was worse, the plebiscite provided the Allies with the knowledge that they were a "lame-duck" administration without the certainty of knowing who their successors would be.

Aftermath of Allied Administration in Danzig

General Sir Richard Haking became the High Commissioner of the League of Nations in Danzig in January 1921. His involvement in the Danzig situation in the past equipped him for the position if only he could learn to temper his personal bias and acquire a respect for the niceties of the diplomatic world. His past indiscreet and disloyal behavior toward Sir Reginald Tower had made Haking suspect in the Foreign Office. The news which reached them in early January gave them even further cause for alarm. E. H. Carr, who had represented the Foreign Office during the Polish-Danzig negotiations, learned that General Sir Henry Wilson, the Chief of the Imperial General Staff, wanted Haking to continue sending reports on the situation in Danzig and environs to the War Office. Only his lack of an adequate number of intelligence officers prevented him from complying. Carr informed the Foreign Office of the explosive condition that would develop if a League official acted simultaneously as the head of a British intelligence service. Such a situation actually was not unlike the one in Upper Silesia which had contributed in part to the British demand for reorganization of the Inter-Allied Commission when the French solely staffed the intelligence department and operated the secret police as their own private arm. In the end, the question was referred to Lord Balfour on the League Council and to Lord Curzon at the Foreign Office, and inquiries showed the Haking was aware of the distinction which had to be observed between his roles as British subject and as League High Commissioner. It remained to convince the Director of Military Intelligence, ever operating by the War Office's own design, that *sub rosa* operations would not only be frowned upon by the Foreign Office but would also be detrimental to the relations between Great Britain and the League of Nations.[1]

Among the unsettled questions resulting from carrying out the provisions of the Treaty of Versailles and its detailed adjunct, the Polish-Danzig convention, was the matter of the military defense of the Free City. It will be recalled that Paderewski had finally been authorized by his government to sign the convention in November 1920 with the reservation that Poland be assigned this mandate, a reservation that had been laid before the League of Nations by the Conference of Ambassadors which was supervising the negotiations. On that occasion, the Ambassadors suggested that the Polish government appeared particularly well qualified to receive such a mandate from the League, but they specified that such a right to send troops into Danzig should not be automatic and it should be given only after the League's consideration of each proposed case. A report prepared by Kikujiro Ishii, the League representative who dealt with Danzig affairs, substantially endorsed the Ambassadors' opinion and it was adopted by the Council on November 17, 1920. Paderewski thereupon signed the convention on the following day.[2] He had been offered assurances by the French that Britain would not stand in the way in the matter. But as British policy on the mandate question developed, he had some cause to regret his signature.

The Council of the League on December 12, considered the report of its Permanent Consultative Commission which used as its original premise the notion that Danzig's defense was inseparable from that of the Polish Corridor. Accordingly, the Commission's recommendations included the establishment of Polish defensive works and garrisons, the Polish control of the aerodrome on Danzig

---

[1] E. H. Carr to Spicer, January 6, 1921 in FO 371/6829, N 450 and Hankey to Cirzon, Secret, January 12, 1921, same volume, N 699.

[2] Christoph M. Kimmich, The Free City: Danzig and German Foreign Policy, 1919-1934 (New Haven: Yale University Press, 1968), p. 30.

territory even in peacetime, and the right of Poland in the event of an attack upon the Free City to send immediate reinforcements in response to a summons by the High Commissioner who should be granted a blanket authorization by the League to call up the nearest Polish troops at will. Lord Balfour opposed this position on grounds that the "moral force of the League of Nations would be sufficient to protect Danzig."[3] Both this report of the Commission and the Ishii Report were submitted to the High Commissioner, General Haking, for his observations.

At issue here were two considerations: (1) the expediency of allowing Poland to make military preparations connected with Danzig's defense in peacetime and (2) the giving of a "blank check" authorization to the High Commissioner to summon Polish troops. British and French attitudes diverged widely.

The French favored both the Polish peacetime defense preparations and the "blank check" to the High Commissioner.[4] In an attempt to reconcile their views, E. H. Carr was assigned to confer with M. Laroche and to draft a joint resolution which would assist Haking's decision. The resulting agreement evidenced a decided attempt on the part of the French to meet the British view.[5]

---

[3] When he suggested that the mandate was irregular and that instead the two communities should attempt "to live peaceably side by side," he rather astonished his colleagues in the Council who had anticipated no opposition. It was finally decided to submit the report to the High Commissioner. See Cabinet Offices to FO, no. 32, February 21, 1921 in FO 371/6820, N 2530/283/55.

[4] The French representative Laroche's memorandum on Danzig stated that "les deux gouvernements britannique et français lui promirent d'obtenir pour lui ce mandat" and "leur promesse vis-à-vis de la Pologne de faire tout ce que dependrait d'eux pour obtenir ce mandat." The ensuing argument revolved around the definition of the translation of "mandat" into "mandate," Carr maintaining that "mandate" meant "authority" in this context and not "mandate" in the sense of the Covenant. "I defy M. Laroche to produce any evidence of a promise made to the Poles by or on behalf of H. M. Government." See E. H. Carr to Sir Eyre Crowe, January 27, 1921 in FO 371/6820, N 1432/283/55. During the course of negotiations Carr reported that Laroche came to admit that the Ambassadors "never made or authorised any formal promise to the Poles" and that if any promise had been made it would have been liquidated by Paderewski's acceptance and signature. See Carr to Crowe, February 13, 1921 in FO 371/6820, N 1963/283/55.

[5] FO Memorandum by Gregory, March 14, 1921 in FO 371/6821, N 3469/283/55. This communication includes the full text of the Carr-Laroche Resolution.

Reference to the Polish peacetime military preparation was eliminated and the "blank check" authorization was modified so as to make the operation of the mandate in most instances dependent on a "mature deliberation and pronouncement by the League itself."

Before the deliberations were complete, General Haking issued his report on January 25, 1921.[6] By both military and political arguments, he recommended that the League of Nations virtually reject the principle of a Polish mandate to defend Danzig and in true Haking form, he minced no words in indicating his decision.[7] He was willing to accept the Carr-Laroche resolution subject to some amendments. The most important of these provided that the High Commissioner should not rely solely on his own discretion to summon Polish troops in the event of Danzig's being the victim of aggression but that he should be dependent on instructions emanating from the Council of the League to do so.

The questions was scheduled to come up before the League in February but at French request it was removed from the agenda in order to prevent a public wrangle with Britain and to allow time for the two governments to come to a private preliminary agreement before confronting the forum of other nations. But Britain refused to discuss the matter further until her representatives ascertained the attitude of the Council of the League concerning General Haking's report. Accordingly, Carr was instructed to terminate his negotiations for the present.

At the same time that the Carr-Laroche talks had begun, Prince Sapieha discussed with British representatives the matter of a defense mandate in Danzig for Poland. He recalled his country's plight of the previous summer when Poland had met resistance in the port of Danzig and would have been unable to secure the munitions needed in her war with Russia had not British troops on Allied behalf secured them for Poland. He insisted that his country could not afford to entertain the notion of constructing forts

---

[6] League of Nations to FO, February 5, 1921 in FO 371/6820, N 1892/283/55.

[7] E. H. Carr in a letter to Sir Eyre Crowe claimed that Haking's report "caused considerable flutter in the French dovecots" and that it called "a spade a spade and a Pole a Pole" and contained "a good deal of the kind of truth which is better left untold." What Carr was referring to was Haking's objective military assessment in which he systematically eliminated those nations who by virtue of policy or geographic location were unlikely to launch a land attack on Danzig. Haking ended by seeing Poland as the only potential aggressor in the foreseeable future. See E. H. Carr to Crowe, February 13, 1921 in FO 371/6820, N 1963/283/55.

or garrisoning troops in Danzig. What he sought was merely assurance that in the event of a German attack the Poles would be permitted to defend the port city and in the event of war with any other enemy, they would have the means of importing arms and munitions at Danzig.

The reasonableness of a limited concession in this direction was admitted at a session of the British Cabinet.[8] Sir Eyre Crowe believed, however, that no justification existed for the suggestion that the British government favored conferring on Poland a mandate of the type mentioned in the Treaty of Versailles. The concept of mandates in Europe had been considered and rejected at the Paris peace conference. It was made clear to the ministers, as a result of Balfour's statements, "that the Polish government really wanted to send troops into Danzig not for purposes of defense, but in order to prevent strikes and to coerce the inhabitants." Inasmuch as this was so, the Cabinet agreed to support the view which Balfour had already advanced in the League of Nations.

Upon the suggestion of the French that the London Conference, which was to convene late in February 1921, might provide the opportunity to iron out the mandate question, J. D. Gregory joined the French representative R. Massigli on March 11 and took up the issue where the Carr-Laroche talks had left it. The resolution that had been drawn up by Carr and Laroche and modified by Haking was considered. Where the earlier resolution had given the High Commissioner arbitrary rights to call in Polish troops, whether to protect Danzig from aggression or to keep Polish treaty-given rights in the Free City from being violated, the Gregory-Massigli Resolution subordinated these powers of the High Commissioner to the decisions of the Council of the League. Gregory's aim had been to preserve the original intent of the Conference of Ambassadors which had been endorsed by the League. In this regard it sought to guard against any solution which granted Poland permanent authority to send troops into Danzig arbitrarily or to obtain a military footing there in time of peace. Once agreed upon, the text was communicated to both the British and French representatives at Geneva, Lord Balfour and Léon Bourgeois.[9]

---

[8]Conclusions of Conference of Ministers held February 16, 1921, Appendix II in Cab 23/24.

[9]A summary of the Gregory-Massigli negotiations appears in the FO Memorandum by Gregory, March 14, 1921 cited above and in FO to Hankey, April 8, 1921 in FO 371/6821, N 4265/283/55. The full text of the Gregory-Massigli Resolution, April 8, 1921 appears in FO 371/6821, N 4264/283/55. The French willingness to accept the text is recorded in French Ambassador to FO, April 14, 1921 in FO 371/6821, N 4690/283/55.

Before the question of a Polish mandate to defend Danzig with land forces was brought to the Council of the League, Poland discredited herself in the eyes of Great Britain for her inability or unwillingness to impose a stricter discipline on Polish rebels and military formations in the Upper Silesian insurrection in May. In light of these developments in the plebiscite area, last minute Foreign Office attempts were made to clarify the wording in the resolution with the intent of preventing similar Polish intervention.

At its June 18 meeting, the Council of the League recognized a Polish mandate to defend Danzig with land forces, a right whose exercise was not independent but was subject to the approval of the League Council. Defense of the Free City by sea was not included in this right. Instead, the question of the use of Danzig as a naval base or as a *port d'attache* was submitted to the High Commissioner for consideration. It was, in any event, never contemplated by the Council that the Poles would be permitted to garrison the Free City under any but the most extraordinary circumstances.

The mandate issue represented a tidying up of the issues outstanding in the wake of Allied withdrawal from Danzig in which Great Britain consistently pursued the policy of preserving the "free city" status as provided in the Treaty of Versailles. With its settlement, Britain returned with some zest to her familiar concern with commercial matters. The Foreign Office observed with pleasure the interest certain British firms were evidencing in Danzig and noted that the day was fast approaching when the tentatively interested groups would have to take serious and specific measures toward investment in the port city if they proposed to gain a commercial foothold there. One company which had already taken such specific steps was the Anglo-Polish Steamship Line, Limited, which in the spring of 1920 had announced the beginning of a new weekly service for passengers and freight between Hull and Danzig. Some Poles liked to look upon this venture as the resumption of an old friendship and the revival of a historic trade relationship.[10]

Upper Silesia after the Plebiscite

The story of the spring and much of the summer of 1921 is one of a loss of prestige and authority by Britain and her Allies, especially in Upper Silesia where the most serious of the three insurrections there occurred in May. Interestingly, in the province from which she had so often sought to detach herself, Britain emerged from the chaos of the spring as the new force to be dealt with, providing fresh, able leadership for the Inter-Allied Com-

---

[10]Polish Economic Bulletin, Vol. I, nos. 3-4 (March-April 1920), 9-10.

mission and a returned military presence. June witnessed a new
determination on the part of Britain to stay if she must, employing all the vigor she could muster, and get the job done that she
had first promised to do when she signed the Treaty of Versailles
on June 28, 1919.

After more than a year of preparation, it seemed that the
Inter-Allied Commission had been successful in its work since
the plebiscite had been carried out in a charged but orderly atmosphere. Having assisted in quelling two insurrections and having
survived the internal dissension which finally made necessary an
overhaul of the Commission machinery late in 1920, the Plebiscite
Commission had proved itself capable of wielding authority and
governing a territory to an extent that no other post-Versailles
inter-allied body had been called upon to do.

As more conclusive election returns became available, they
demonstrated the failure of the plebiscite to determine a satisfactory frontier through the contested triangle. This area in the
southeast corner of Upper Silesia was ethnically mixed (although
the towns were heavily German-speaking) and rich in minerals; it
was roughly delineated as a triangle whose points were the industrial towns of Gleiwitz, Tarnowitz, and Kattowitz. During the
meeting of the British Cabinet held on March 22, 1921 it was recalled that recent Upper Silesian events had vindicated the British
position taken at the Paris peace conference and the Cabinet agreed
that the existence of majorities of either Poles or Germans in
isolated areas did not justify the breaking up of the province.[11]
Curzon on the same day telegraphed a private statement to Colonel
Percival indicating that the British government preferred to recognize German claims to the whole of Upper Silesia in the light
of the general German majority. The general tenor of the French
press indicated that the French favored the allocation of the
entire industrial area to Poland in addition to the districts of
Pless and Rybnik which had registered an unquestionably Polish
majority. In Rome, Count Sforza, the Italian Minister of Foreign
Affairs, favored a partition of the contested mining district between the German and Polish claimants. Private talks with General
Marinis suggested to Percival that the Italian representative
agreed with the British attitude toward allotting all of Upper Silesia to Germany.

Public German statements continued the argument for the indivisibility of the plebiscite territory, although within a fortnight's time private conversations revealed that officials would
not be surprised if the Pless and Rybnik areas which had overwhelmingly voted in favor of union with Poland were assigned to

---
[11]Cabinet Session, March 22, 1921 in Cab. 24, meeting 14, minute 17.

that country. The Warsaw press campaign declared that the total of votes taken was irrelevant and that the ultimate decision would be based on the number of communes voting without regard to either the relative size of their population or the size of the majority in each.[12] This argument, like the French one, was in fact based on a literal interpretation of Article 88, Annex 4 of the Treaty of Versailles which stated that "the result of the vote will be determined by communes according to the majority of votes in each commune." Official circles were, however, more realistic and were disappointed with the result. Their hope that Polish majorities in outlying country districts would counterbalance the anticipated German majorities in the west and north and in the large industrial towns had not been satisfied.

Aside from the plane of theory where opinions were formed, expounded, and modified, there was the plane of human experience, frustration, and emotion which exploded in the aftermath of the plebiscite. From March 22-25 a wave of increasingly intense lawlessness directed against those with supposed German sympathies swept over the areas of Beuthen, Kattowitz, Rybnik, and Pless, where Poles were in the majority. Violence took the form of beatings, raiding customs offices, interruptions of railway services, and terrorizing the police. British representatives in all districts were quick to bring the situation to the notice of the Commission which responded by declaring a state of siege until the chances of another serious insurrection were obviated.[13]

Faced with an emergency at home created by the miners' strike which had begun on April 1 and the threatened rail and transport workers' walkout, the British government found it necessary to mobilize and recall all possible units and concentrate troops in Britain. If troops were withdrawn from western Germany for this purpose, this would necessitate a withdrawal of British troops from Upper Silesia to replace them on the Rhine. And so, in drawing up its list of priorities, Great Britain, faced with the threat of serious domestic disorder, again found her participation in Upper Silesia to be expendable.

Under the terms of the Annex to Article 88, the Plebiscite Commission was to communicate the results of the voting to the

---

[12] Müller to Curzon, no. 166, March 24, 1921 in Documents on British Foreign Policy, 1919-1939 (hereafter DBFP) 1st ser., XVI, no. 2.

[13] For a summary of events in the wave of lawlessness see the documents dated March 1921 in DBFP, 1st ser., XVI. Müller to Prince Sapieha (private), March 28, 1921 in FO 688, box 10, file 50, no. 127.

Allied and Associated Powers and make a full report in which it recommended a new frontier. When the British and French representatives could not agree on a settlement, it fell to General Marinis, the Italian Commissioner, to play the mediator. Although personally inclined to support Percival's position on indivisibility, he saw that an implacable stand on this could only end abortively. So he and Percival, instead, came to an understanding on a plan that proposed to assign to Germany the entire industrial triangle and to Poland the southern rural areas of Pless and Rybnik.

Neither the Germans nor the Poles who came to London to plead their case received satisfaction. Curzon heard out Friedrich Sthamer, the German ambassador, but refused to receive a deputation to hear its claim for Upper Silesia. Jan Ciechanowski, the Polish Chargé d'affaires, was unable to obtain the verification of information he had heard about an alleged British decision to hand over the whole of Upper Silesia to Germany.[14] Sir Eyre Crowe denied that his government had yet formed a line of policy; he said that it awaited instead the report of the Plebiscite Commission. Technically, this was true, but a week earlier the Foreign Office had given the green light to Percival to support the Italian compromise scheme which would assign most of the plebiscite area to Germany. Such action taken by the Foreign Office approached duplicity and it did not indicate that the British treated Poland with complete candor. Curzon himself admitted to treating the Poles with curtness because of an unwillingness on his part to be bothered with the perennial Upper Silesian problem.[15]

The British decision to support the Italian compromise in partitioning Upper Silesia was embodied in several subsequent policy statements. One of these was a lengthy memorandum authored by Major L. E. Ottley, who had served in Upper Silesia and who, upon his resignation in late 1920, came to the Foreign Office. It was an economic vindication of Britain's course.[16] Another

---

[14] Curzon to D'Abernon, no. 373, April 7, 1921 in DBFP, 1st ser., XVI, no. 14.

[15] For the Polish attempts to be heard by the British government and subsequent British refusal see the following four documents, all found in DBFP, 1st ser., XVI: Record of Sir E. Crowe of conversations with Polish Chargé d'Affaires and the German ambassador, April 11, 1921, doc. no. 16; Müller to Curzon, no. 190, April 13, 1921, doc. no. 18; Curzon to Müller, no. 96, April 18, 1921, doc. no. 19; and Müller to Curzon, no. 201, April 21, 1921, doc. no. 21. See also Curzon to Müller, April 19, 1921 in FO 688, box 10, file 50, no. 159.

[16] Memorandum by Major Ottley respecting . . . Upper Silesian Question, April 11, 1921 in DBFP, 1st ser., XVI, no. 17.

was a memorandum prepared for the American ambassador justifying the British position by citing topographical conditions and results of the March plebiscite from Rybnik and Pless which heavily favored incorporation with Poland.[17]

Eliminating these areas where the majorities were unquestionable, Great Britain wished to treat the disputed industrial triangle as one commune, in view of the fact that its economic life was highly integrated despite the mixed population that tended to be Polish in rural areas and German in urban ones. Such an area if treated as a unit, yielded 275,000 votes for Germany and 233,000 for Poland and ought, according to the Foreign Office, to be allocated to Germany on this basis. Such a partition would assign 85% of the current coal output to Germany. But the mines in this area would be worked out in fifty years whereas those falling to Poland held reserves sufficient for centuries to come.

Arguing from an economic point of view, J. I. Craig, the British Director of Food Control for the Plebiscite Commission, pointed out to the Board of Trade that German policy did not envision southward and eastward export of coal. Should Germany come to control Upper Silesian coal, then, her direction of it would prove detrimental to the needs of Central European industry as well as to British foreign trade into whose sphere she would trespass. On these grounds, Craig believed that Upper Silesia's separation from Prussia was imperative, although he did not necessarily advocate cession of the territory to Poland.[18]

Hopes of completing a Plebiscite Commission report in time to be considered at the Supreme Council meeting on April 30 dimmed. Lerond held firm to his recommendation to assign the entire industrial area to Poland; Percival and Marinis refused to concur in the decision. In an attempt to persuade Lerond to moderate his stand, Percival reminded the French Commissioner that allocation of the industrial triangle to Poland would entail heavy liability under Article 256 for that young state. This article of the Treaty of Versailles provided that the beneficiary in any transfer of land from Germany would acquire the former German government property in the ceded territory, but must make a payment to the Allies equal to its value, such payment to be credited to the German reparations account.

---

[17] FO Minute, May 19, 1921, C.P. 2947 in Cab 24, file 18/J/93. In addition see the summary of the views of HMG on the Upper Silesian question prepared for the American ambassador in Curzon to Harvey, May 19, 1921 FO 371/5902, C 10337/92/18.

[18] E. F. Wise (Board of Trade) to Philip Kerr, April 18, 1921 enclosing Craig to Wise, March 30, 1921 in London, Beaverbrook Library, Private Papers of Lloyd George, F/48/3/37.

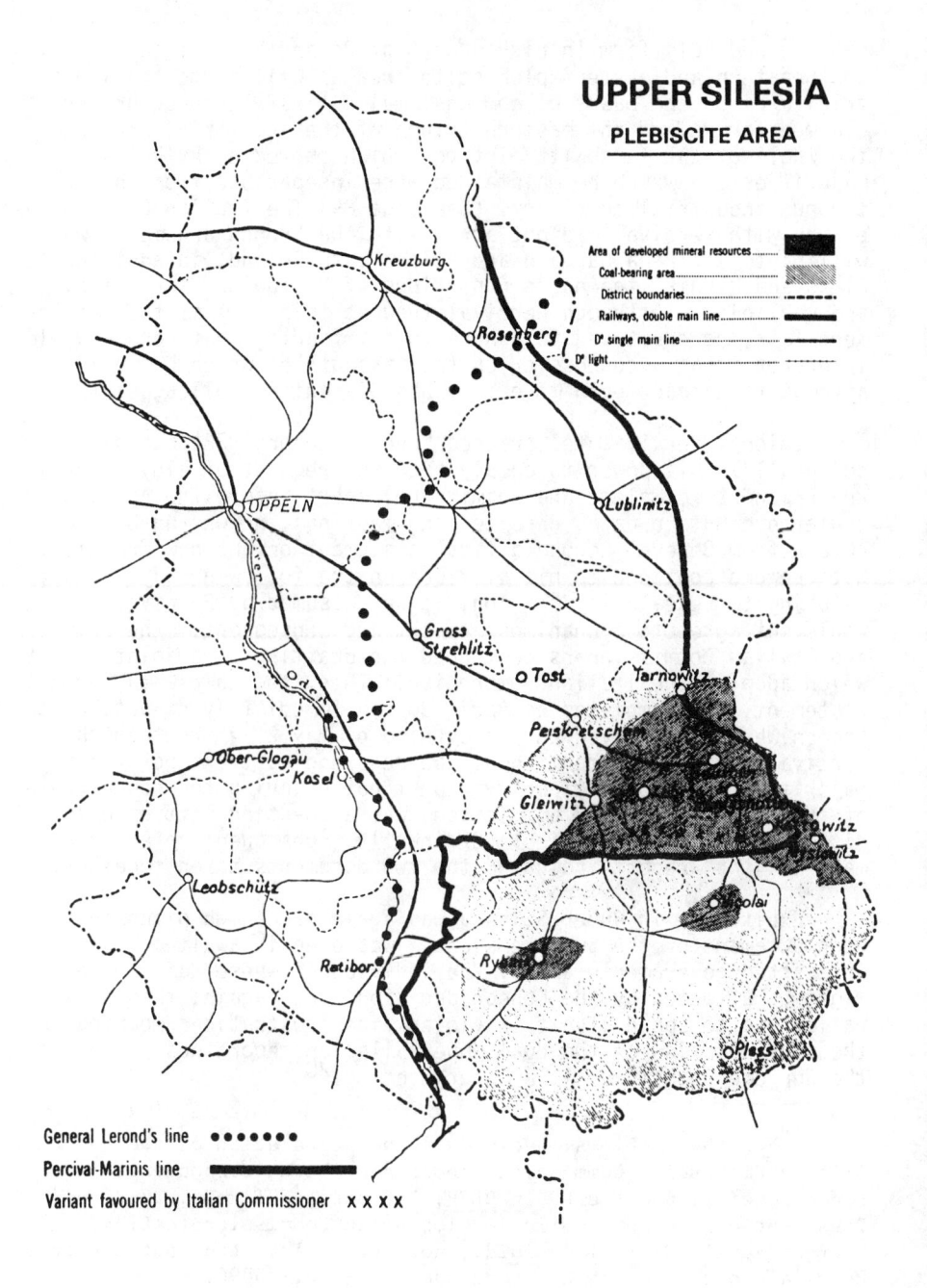

UPPER SILESIA
PLEBISCITE AREA

Area of developed mineral resources
Coal-bearing area
District boundaries
Railways, double main line
D° single main line
D° light

General Lerond's line ● ● ● ● ● ● ●
Percival-Marinis line ▬▬▬▬▬
Variant favoured by Italian Commissioner x x x x

Lerond held firm in his support of Poland's claim to the southeastern and eastern plebiscite area as well as to the industrial area on the basis of communal majorities. Lerond further claimed for Poland the eastern fringe of the industrial area and the whole of the Tarnowitz district which showed heavy Polish majorities and which he maintained were inseparable from the contiguous industrial territory. (See page 89) The Italian Commissioner who with Percival did not agree with the French argument, was willing to strike a bargain and allocate to Poland, in addition to Pless and Rybnik, the eastern portions of Kattowitz, Tarnowitz, and Lublinitz. Although Percival thought this part of the settlement fair, he hesitated to adhere to it, fearing that Lerond would interpret it as a concession on the strength of which he would attempt to extract even more from his dissenting colleagues.

Colonel Percival telegraphed London on April 26 that he was doing all in his power to comply with the request of Lloyd George and Briand to complete and submit the report before the April 30 conference but to date, despite long meetings, he was unable to obtain from General Lerond a final statement on the new frontier. With Lerond confined to his sick bed on the following day and still refusing to reveal his decision, it was assumed by Percival that he would not agree to a unanimous report and consequently the British and Italian Commissioners commenced the drafting of a joint report which adopted the Italian compromise. This, together with Lerond's statement, was completed by April 30 and immediately dispatched to London where it arrived on the evening of May 2.[19] Whether the Percival-Marinis document should be regarded as the report of a majority of two, or a minority report not enjoying the concurrence of the President of the Commission, was a question left open to discussion among the Allies. Ordinarily, subsequent references made to "the" report indicated the two documents taken together.

Excitement in Upper Silesia was again at a high pitch and the pronouncement of the Supreme Council was eagerly awaited by the interested governments and by the individuals whose daily lives might be affected by the London decision. But again, this anticipation was to spend itself in violence as frustrations mounted and the consideration of the dual Upper Silesian report was put off by the Supreme Council until a later meeting.[20]

---

[19] For the problems involved in the preparation of the Upper Silesia Plebiscite Commission report see the correspondence between Percival and the FO in DBFP, 1st ser., XVI, nos. 23-25 and President of the Upper Silesia Plebiscite Commission to Lloyd George, April 30, 1921 in ibid., no. 26. Relevant dispatches from Percival to the FO are also included in FO 371/5896.

[20] British Secretary's Notes of Allied Conference, London, May 4, 1921 in DBFP, 1st ser., XV, no. 85.

A long hot summer of misplaced nationalism, frustrated desires, and abortive revolution would transpire before the report was acted upon and subsequent decisions made.

As submitted to the Supreme Council the Upper Silesian report advanced the Lerond proposals and in a separate recommendation, the Percival-Marinis proposals.[21] The Lerond plan perfectly reflected French policy which during these early post-war years was oriented toward her own security and consequently toward courting the friendship of non-revisionist states in Eastern Europe. Part of the French policy of security demanded not only disarming Germany but also depriving her of her arsenals that might feed the fire of future conflict. Poland, which had only a month prior to the plebiscite concluded negotiations and signed a military alliance with France, was looked upon as a suitable beneficiary of these mineral-rich areas which were of value as the site of potential munitions factories. Lerond proposed that the Upper Silesian frontier should be drawn through the province in such a way as to give Poland the communes which had registered a Polish majority even though this broad area was studded with pockets of German inhabitants, particularly in the industrial cities. More precisely he proposed that Poland receive the two heavily Polish areas and the area linking them, despite its 3 to 2 German majority, including part of rural Ratibor and Gleiwitz, the Gleiwitz industrial area, and the three main towns of the industrial area, Beuthen, Königshütte, and Kattowitz--the "German plums in the Polish pudding." Rural Ratibor to the Oder was claimed for Poland because it contained the water supply for adjoining industrial Rybnik.

On the other hand, the Percival-Marinis proposals sought to maintain intact, so far as possible, an industrial area for transfer to Germany. They agreed with Lerond on the frontier assignment only in the south, but in the central area, considering both the plebiscite returns and the integrity of the network of railways, they preferred to deliver a united industrial area to Germany, although even that section must suffer some unavoidable partition in the east, again owing to attempts to preserve the railway line intact for projected Polish Silesia.

Upon learning details of the report, the Foreign Office agreed that General Lerond's argument adhered closely to the specifications of the Treaty of Versailles. Article 88, annex 4 provided that "the result of the vote . . . be determined by communes ac-

---

[21] For the full Inter-Allied Commission report, April 30, 1921 see FO 371/5897, C 9210/92/18; C.P. 2900, file 18/J/93 in Cab 24; and Sarah Wambaugh, Plebiscites Since the World War, 2 vols. (Washington: Carnegie Endowment for International Peace, 1933), II, 242-61. The summary appears in DBFP, 1st ser., XVI, no. 26.

cording to the majority of votes in each commune" and further, in annex 5, that the recommendation of the Commission should regard the "wishes of the inhabitants as shown by the vote and . . . the geographical and economic conditions of the locality." Foreign Office advisers acknowledged that the Treaty in no way sought to weigh the communes by density of population and that Lerond's regarding of communes simply by the absolute number of their votes was in keeping with the letter of the instrument.

Yet, the British could not espouse his recommendation First, by virtue of the plebiscite results, they deemed the French plan strikingly unfair to Germany, for in the zone awarded to Poland there would be 48½% Poles and in the zone awarded to Germany 86% Germans and only 14% Poles. The British-Italian scheme, on the other hand, admittedly less strictly defensible on the basis of the treaty-text, worked out more justly for both sides and adhered to the Treaty's spirit. Under it Poland would receive territory with a 67% Polish majority and Germany an area with a 64½% German majority. Second, the Foreign Office arguments recalled the fact that on earlier occasions Lerond had contended that Commission decisions must be made by majority vote, a contention which, if accepted, was tantamount to recognition of the Percival-Marinis recommendation as a majority report.

Insurrection and the Breakdown of Allied Authority

When a report was circulated on May 2 in the Upper Silesian press, probably with French prompting, that only Pless, Rybnik, and eastern Kattowitz would likely be assigned to Poland, Polish miners declared a strike in protest and on the following day a general insurrection broke out.[22] Almost immediately the Inter-Allied Commission responded with a proclamation of its intent to use all means at its disposal to put down the disorder. The Polish government disavowed any involvement in the insurrection and dismissed Korfanty who had been acting as the Polish Plebiscite Commissioner and who now assumed formal leadership of the insurgents. British district controllers and adjutants who were present observed that French encouragement repeatedly assisted the insurrectionary movement.

---

[22]Polish sources, even into the period of the Second World War, continued their criticism of Britain when assessing the immediate post-World War I years when Britain was still led by Lloyd George. One such typical evaluation is that by Szuldrzynski which lays much blame for the third Upper Silesian insurrection upon Great Britain for making known her desire that the industrial triangle should go to Germany and that only some rural outlying territory should be assigned to Poland. See Jan Szuldrzynski, Anglia i Polska: w Polityce Europejskiej [England and Poland in European Politics] (Jerusalem: Biblioteka Orla Bialego, 1945), p. 265.

Detailed reports arrived from cities in the south and in the industrial area where the explosion first occurred. From B. Villiers Hemming at Rybnik reports arrived for Percival at Oppeln informing him that the Commission's prestige had so suffered as to embolden the insurgents to fire upon Allied troops, killing 16 Italian soldiers and one officer in the Rybnik attack and in the massacre at Dubenskogrube.[23] Hemming reported the unwillingness of the Italian district controller, Colonel de Bernezzo, to use his troops against the insurgents or to assist Captain Simpson in making some arrests on the ground that in the event of an Italian soldier being killed, General Marinis would protest and have him dismissed.[24]

Martial law was proclaimed and late Wednesday afternoon Italian and French troops began to arrive in Rybnik, the latter openly fraternizing with the insurgents. Repeated conferences were held with Korfanty's men, but the terms were repudiated by them soon after the conclusion of each set of negotiations. Violence alternated with relative calm for a week and on the following Wednesday, May 11, the entire day was taken up with negotiations between the local commandant of the insurgents and the representatives of the Inter-Allied Commission. These talks resulted in an agreement to form a neutral zone between the Allied-occupied town and the insurgent-held nearby villages, the area to be policed by a mixed patrol of Allies and insurgents. The safety and transportation of the APO (*Abstimmungs Polizei*) and of refugees to Ratibor were granted.[25]

By Friday, May 13 there was enough citizen opposition to the disorders that some observers thought that any Allied demonstration of energy might restore the prestige of the Commission and lead to a collapse of the insurrection. So powerless was the Commission, however, that its representatives could not even guarantee safe passage to a wounded woman who was attempting to return to her children and could only issue her a note addressed to the Polish insurgent leader who would make the decision whether she would be

---

[23] Diary entry for Thursday, May 12, 1921 by B. Villiers Hemming in FO 890, part 11, doc. O.

[24] General Marinis was following this policy of not employing Italian troops against the insurrectionaries in view of the overwhelming superiority of insurgents which would in his estimation lead to no military gain but would cause unnecessary bloodshed. See Percival to Curzon, no. 96, May 10, 1921 in DBFP, 1st ser., XVI, no. 49.

[25] Captain A. Michaelson to Major O. J. F. Keatinge, May 20, 1921 in FO 890, part 11, doc. 2.

permitted to return to her village or not.

The death blow to the Commission's prestige in Rybnik came with the announcement of the imminent departure of Colonel Salvioni and the Italian troops, leaving behind only one company of French Chasseurs in a town swarming with insurgents and a populace fearing re-occupation by them. By May 14, the last vestige of Inter-Allied Commission prestige disappeared with the appearance of the new town police. The Commission had agreed to forming the town police force of about 30 men, arming them with pistols and clearly identifying them by issuing special armbands. But those police who appeared had rifles and no identifying badges and their appearance in this form was an eloquent statement of flagrant disregard of the authority of the Plebiscite Commission.

These events describing the insurrection at Rybnik serve merely as an example of the type of activity that also occurred in Pless, Nicolai, Kattowitz, Königshütte, Lublinitz, Rosenberg, and other towns that witnessed disorder. In Pless, for example, the British officer who served as Assistant District Controller refused to sit on a special court which reflected defunct Allied authority there. Another British officer reported from Kattowitz flagrant French fraternization with insurgents and collaboration with them in commandeering of locomotives--all in the face of the Commission's impotence.

In districts where British officers served as district controllers there was little difference. In Lublinitz and Rosenberg, the British district controllers evidenced more initiative than controllers elsewhere, but the difference in the results they achieved was only illusory, for in the end, they too were unable to maintain control of their districts on behalf of the Allies in the face of an insurrection that no one believed any longer to have been spontaneous. The movement was organized and swift in action and despite the fact that its discipline was found wanting, it showed itself to be far more than a rag-tattered, chaotic army of misplaced Polish nationalists.[26]

---

[26] Detailed diaries and reports of the insurrection appear in the Upper Silesia Plebiscite Commission (British Section) Archives. For Pless see FO 890, part 9; Kattowitz, part 6; Königshütte, part 7; Lublinitz, part 8; Rosenberg, part 10. These collections are of varying sizes, each containing usually fewer than a dozen documents. The Archives are incomplete and poorly prepared and preserved. But they provide the basis for an indispensable local study that cannot be made in the Foreign Office General Correspondence.

The chief aim of the insurgents was to occupy the Korfanty Line, i.e., all the territory south of a line through Rosenberg and Groschowitz near Oppeln to the east of the Oder River with the intention of holding it without interfering with the economic and administrative arrangements of the territory. It appeared that their objective included taking no active measures against the Commission providing Commission forces offered no opposition. The aim was not completely achieved since the rebels met Allied opposition. But Allied troops were too few in number to oust the insurgents from Upper Silesian territories which they had occupied.

The degree of success of the insurgent takeover was indicated in the cessation of rail transportation, except for military purposes, and the establishment of road blocks in their territory. Interestingly, British officers were regularly halted at these posts and made to go through all the formalities while French officers were largely permitted free and unhampered passage.[27]

The Commission was reluctant at first to negotiate with Korfanty and thereby to extend a *de facto* recognition of his authority. British representatives both on the Commission at Oppeln and at the British Legation at Warsaw, discouraged such negotiations as productive of self-confidence in the insurgents and consequently an encouragement to Korfanty.[28]

Although the military aspects of the insurrection are not of central interest here, it is important to note the formation of German armed bands at this time in response to the Polish insurgent groups, since in the diplomacy of restoring the Inter-Allied Commission's authority, they and their leader, Lieutenant General Karl Höfer, played one of the major roles. Höfer had come to assume leadership of the German paramilitary groups by secret arrangement with the Wirth government of the Weimar Republic. Under his control the movement became a force to be reckoned with, but one with which the German government, as in the case of the Polish government and Korfanty, denied any connection.[29]

---

[27] Bourdillon to Waterlow, May 13, 1921 in FO 371/5901, C 10193/92/18. Repeated evidence of French partiality, and even complicity in the insurrecion, was supplied by British officers whose revulsion with the situation prompted them to submit resignations. See, for example, Percival to FO, no. 100, Part II, May 12, 1921 in FO 371/5899, C 9848/92/18.

[28] Lord D'Abernon did not agree with this view and believed it a "rather excessive formality to refuse to recognise the existence of a man who had deprived you of half your kingdom, and shot or plundered a large proportion of the people you are charged to protect." See British Museum, D'Abernon MSS, 48953B, May 18, 1921.

[29] For an account of the paramilitary groups during the May 1921 insurrection which is heavily dependent on German sources,

Reports that British officers had participated in the fighting between these self-protection corps and the Polish Silesian insurgents on the side of the former were publicly denied by the German press, but that press confirmed the presence of the British officers in the conflict as "solely directed towards preventing unnecessary bloodshed." Colonel Percival reported that the restraining influence of these officers by months' end was acknowledged on all sides and that, with General Lerond agreeing, they would continue to keep in touch with the self-protection force. It was due largely to British pressure, too, that German railway workers had resumed running food trains to Gleiwitz, but the Commission's authority and prestige remained so low that it continued to be unable to guarantee the protection of these men when insurgents held up the trains.

Percival and the British Section tended to view the German armed groups with more tolerance than the French who looked upon them as no more than German insurgents on a par with Korfanty's men or the free corps in Germany. The British Commissioner reported on May 27

> I need hardly point out that Germany can justly claim that in the past they relied on the Commission for protection against Polish terrorism and that they have shown utmost forbearance. It is now evident to the whole world that the Commission has no power to protect German inhabitants, and to expect the latter to continue to allow their homes and persons to be outraged with impunity without raising a finger in self-defence is to demand the impossible from human nature.[30]

From such variant positions the Allies attempted to restore their authority in Upper Silesia. The history of this task unfolded in negotiations in Oppeln, London, and Paris in which Britain played a leading role. It was she who had most loudly decried the ineffectual role of the Commission in the province and all along had attempted wherever possible to maintain and bolster Allied prestige. Her desire to disengage herself from this Central European commitment was as evident as earlier. But her hopes of disentanglement took the form of a responsible disinterest dedicated

---

see F. Gregory Campbell, "The Struggle for Upper Silesia, 1919-1922," Journal of Modern History, XLII (September 1970), 377-79. A heavily documented presentation describing Upper Silesia during the period of its three insurrections is a compilation by the German commander of the paramilitary groups, Karl Höfer. See his Oberschlesien in der Aufstandzeit, 1918-1921: Erinnerungen und Dokumente (Berlin: 1938)

[30] Percival to FO, no. 155, May 27, 1921 in FO 371/5906, C 11048/92/18.

to tempering France's activities while keeping her as an ally. Britain looked forward to pulling out of a reasonably orderly Silesia, having discharged all the duties which had fallen to her under the Treaty of Versailles.

The Attempt to Restore Order

During the entire month of May, Great Britain took a leading role in attempting to restore order in Upper Silesia, prompted partially by consciousness of her duty there but more so by fear of French unilateral action in Germany and a war between Germany and Poland. Her diplomatic dealings with Poland centered on her repeated attempts to impress upon the Polish government the importance of disavowing the insurrection and closing the frontier. The Polish government categorically condemned the insurrection but otherwise showed itself to be without confidence in its own longevity and it hesitated, out of fear for its own life, to honor Müller's request and follow up with some more overt action, such as a proclamation against Korfanty. When an Allied commission after much British pressure in the Conference of Ambassadors was sent in early June to investigate on the spot, however, it reported that the Polish government had taken serious measures to prevent insurgents and arms from crossing the frontier.

Apart from her dealings with Germany through the Conference of Ambassadors, Great Britain's concerns with that country in May 1921 centered on what posture Britain should assume with respect to the ultimate settlement of the Upper Silesian question and what attitude Germany should take with respect to provisioning the territory occupied by insurgents. The Allies who were dealing with the reparations question at the London Conference from April 30-May 5 issued an ultimatum to Germany on the final day of the conference that within six days she resolve to "carry out without reserve or conditions" obligations as outlined by the Reparation Commission.[31] The Germans hoped either to escape fulfilling the demands or to strike a bargain with the Allies, particularly with the more sympathetic Great Britain. Publicly, the Germans stated that a partition of Upper Silesia favorable to them would equip them to fulfill the economic demands which were being made by the Allies.

A private assurance that the British government would not allow any solution of the Upper Silesian question other than that

---

[31] British Secretary's Notes of Allied Conference in London, May 4, 1921 in DBFP, 1st ser., XV, no. 85. Chapter IV deals with the proceedings of the fourth London Conference and the conversations connected with it. It was decided that the ultimatum itself would be communicated to the German ambassador in London by Lloyd George, the President of the Supreme Council.

based on the report which had been submitted by the British Commissioner was what the Germans sought in exchange for their acceptance of the London ultimatum. No government then in the process of formation at Berlin, they argued, could long survive the double deluge of accepting these Allied reparations terms and losing the industrial area of Upper Silesia as well. Lord D'Abernon held that he could extend no such pledge but he assured a representative of the German Foreign Office that Britain would carry out the Treaty of Versailles in the industrial area--small consolation to the Germans who had seen the Treaty interpreted in many ways since the day they had signed it. He countered their half-threat by reminding the Germans that "there was no golden road to retaining Upper Silesia, but there was a golden road to losing it, and that was non-acceptance of the London conditions."[32]

Sir Eyre Crowe agreed that Britain could not pledge to assign the industrial area to Germany. In fact, he thought it improper to even assure the German government that British policy would remain in favor of Germany's retaining the area. Should the question of Upper Silesia force a confrontation between the Allied powers, its settlement must be subordinated to the necessities of maintaining good Anglo-French relations. Only if the British government were prepared to break with France over this issue could it give the promise Germany sought. And this Britain was not willing to do.[33] But prodding the ally a bit was not objectionable. So, the Cabinet on May 10 agreed to support an official representation to the French government to be conveyed privately by the Prime Minister which called for impartiality on the part of the French in settling the problem.[34]

Lord D'Abernon applied pressure in Berlin to secure official condemnation of paramilitary bands as well as a resumption of railway communications, the provision of food, and the payment of salaries to workers in Upper Silesia. These deliberations were successful in convincing the Germans that their boycott was suicidal and potentially beneficial to the spread of chaos and Bolshevism in the troubled territory.[35] These diplomatic moves were tiny

---

[32] British Museum, D'Abernon MSS, 48953B, entry for May 10, 1921.

[33] See the minutes of Sir Eyre Crowe in FO to Lord D'Abernon, no. 97, May 10, 1921 in FO 371/5970.

[34] Cabinet meeting, May 10, 1921, Cab 23, vol. 25, meeting 37.

[35] Curzon to D'Abernon, no. 530, May 23, 1921 in DBFP, 1st ser., XVI, no. 105. Lord D'Abernon headed a special mission to Poland in 1920 which resulted in his papers related to Warsaw Special Mission 1920 (British Museum, D'Abernon MSS, 48923) and

steps taken in the direction of restoring order. Before serious negotiations to restore the Commission's authority could be considered, the Allies would have to be able to back their words with more troops than were then available. As part of this program of restoration, Great Britain undertook to return to Upper Silesia the troops she had moved to the Rhine during the British domestic crisis earlier in the spring.

From the time of the outbreak of insurrection, the Foreign Office believed it was necessary to send British troops back to Upper Silesia to restore order, but it encountered serious opposition from the military establishment. Repeated Foreign Office asessments of the condition of Upper Silesia focused on the need for a British military presence there, not only to restore the Commission's prestige but also to provide a counterweight to the French. Crowe, with finger on the Entente pulse, recognized that the situation was exceedingly serious and with Germany's acceptance of the Allied ultimatum, which deprived the French of the opportunity to march into the Ruhr, he thought it best to postpone any "acrimonious discussions" with them.[36] When the problem was ameliorated on the Rhine[37] British ability to supply troops for the plebiscite area was restored.

When in early May, Major L. E. Ottley, under Foreign Office instructions went to the War Office about this matter, however, he met consistent opposition. It was well-known at General Sir Henry Wilson, the Chief of the Imperial General Staff, as a policy held that Britain should give priority over European involvement to matters within the Empire. Britain "must withdraw from every

---

his book entitled The Eighteenth Decisive Battle of the World (London: Hodder, 1931) referring to the Battle of Warsaw during the Russo-Polish War. His experience on this mission and his designation of the battle as a Polish service to western civilization which prevented the spilling of Bolshevism into Europe provided him with a theme he never tired of repeating.

[36] See the minute by Sir E. Crowe of May 12, 1921 attached to Hardinge to Curzon, no. 266, May 11, 1921 in FO 371/5899, C 9758/92/18.

[37] On March 8, 1921 as a result of the rejection by the German government of the Allied reparations payment scheme which set a total of 132 billion marks, Foch and his Allied troops moved into the unoccupied German cities of Düsseldorf, Duisberg, and Ruhrort. The situation cooled when in May the German government fell and the new one of Joseph Wirth attempted to fulfill the Allied demands, if only to prove their unrealistic character. See general accounts of German history such as Hajo Holborn, A History of Modern Germany, 1840-1945 (New York: Alfred A. Knopf, 1969), p. 601.

theatre to make sure of the heart."[38] General Sir W. Thwaites largely agreed with the Chief; he told Ottley he believed that from a military point of view home obligations were of greater importance than obligations assumed under the Peace Treaty, that four British infantry battalions would be so few in comparison to the large numbers of Poles in revolt that their positon would be precarious in the event of German military action, and that he personally opposed the dispatch of troops of whose moral influence in Upper Silesia he remained skeptical.[39]

Well into the Cabinet session of May 24 the balking attitude of the military establishment was evident. Both the Secretary of State for War and the Chief of the Imperial General Staff brought to the Cabinet's attention two overriding political considerations: (1) British troops dispatched to Upper Silesia to maintain order might easily clash with the French who had on occasion demonstrated acquiescence in the prevailing conditions in the province; (2) the dispatch of the men would in effect denude the United Kingdom of troops at the very time that the Irish situation might call for them, although there remained the possibility of sending to Central Europe Irish troops who were not suitable for such home duty. After hearing this testimony, however, the Cabinet decided to confirm the Prime Minister's provisional decision to send four battalions to Upper Silesia and supplemented this force with two additional battalions.[40]

Once the decision was made, General Wilson ceased his petulant arguments. The War Office decided to deploy the six battalions, two batteries of artillery, some tanks, and a wireless telegraph section to Upper Silesia. At the Chief's own admission, he was doing what he could to make the small force as "waspish" as possible.[41]

German representatives believed that the Upper Silesian situation could not improve until the return of British troops. There were no similar Polish requests and France, while paying lip service in diplomatic circles to her desire to see Great Britain return to Upper Silesia, sang another tune in the military sphere.

---

[38] Major General Sir Charles E. Caldwell, Field-Marshal Sir Henry Wilson, His Life and Diaries- 2 vols. (London: Cassell, 1927), II, 291. Manchester Guardian, May 12, 1921, p. 7.

[39] FO minute by Major Ottley, May 6, 1921 in FO 371/5899, C 9669/92/18.

[40] Cabinet meeting, May 24, 1921 in Cab 23, vol. 25, meeting 40.

[41] M. P. A. Hankey to Prime Minister, May 25, 1921 in Private Papers of Lloyd George, F/25/1/35.

On May 18, Lord Curzon informed the French Ambassador that because of the serious situation Britain would return the troops which she had recalled in accordance with the promises made at the time of their withdrawal. On the following day, the "serious" situation having hardly abated, Marshal Foch answered that while he had the battalions ready to replace the British units on the Rhine, should the latter be needed for domestic disorder, the Upper Silesian situation had so improved that the British troops were no longer needed there. But the French government came around to accepting the British offer, and the six battalions were dispatched, arriving in Upper Silesia between May 3-June 7 under command of Major General Sir William Heneker. Sir Max Müller from Warsaw reminded Curzon that

> It is important that neither the Polish government nor nation should have any ground for believing that the principal object of the despatch of British reinforcements is the expulsion of the Polish insurgents rather than the re-establishment of the authority of the Inter-Allied Commission throughout the Plebiscite area against Poles and Germans alike. It is I fear all too probable that there may be a certain amount of fighting between the British forces and the Polish insurgents but no efforts should be spared to avoid this so far as is compatible with the restoration of normal conditions in Upper Silesia. At all events it is of vital importance to prevent the German forces from coming to the support of our troops against the Polish insurgents as this would almost inevitably lead to active French cooperation with the latter and we should then have the catastrophe of British and Germans fighting against French and Poles.[42]

With the arrival of British troops during the reign of disorder, the first large step towards restoration of Allied authority was taken. Insurgents were still in control of most of the surrounding countryside but towns in general were held by the Commission. Running concurrently with the debate concerning the dispatch of the troops was the diplomatic drama aimed at putting down the rising. It was characterized by the development of British initiative particularly in proposing schemes to restore the Commission's authority and calling for a Supreme Council meeting to deliver a final decision on the partition of Upper Silesia. Because they saw in Korfanty, a potential Zeligowski,[43] the Foreign Office

---

[42]Müller to Curzon, no. 284, June 1, 1921 in FO 688, box 10, file 50, no. 390.

[43]In the war for her eastern frontiers Poland won Vilna by the coup of General Zeligowski who ostensibly took the city in October

101

devised a plan which was designed to provide practical measures to to quell the insurrection. At the heart of this proposal was a plan to allocate undisputed districts to Germany and Poland. When these governments occupied and administered these respective districts, they would decrease the size of the plebiscite area for which the Inter-Allied Commission would retain responsibility pendint the final settlement. Then the Commission headquarters could move from Oppeln to the central disputed area. Such a plan would go a long way to answer the Germans who had been clamoring to keep order but who had been restrained by the Allies who in turn had proved themselves impotent in the same regard. Such a plan would localize the trouble, enable the Allies to handle it more efficiently and appreciably decrease the expenses involved in administering the plebiscite territory.[44] This was communicated to Lord Hardinge at the Conference of Ambassadors in Paris.[45]

The imprecision of the territorial division notwithstanding, it seems that the unforunate choice of words to describe the proposed German and Polish jurisdiction in these Silesian territories ("to be occupied and administered under their full authority") was difficult to reconcile with the intended temporary nature of the jurisdiction, which was meant in no way to influence the final decision. What was the "full authority" Britain was willing to confer on Germany and Poland? Sovereignty? A mandate granted by the Ambassadors? As it turned out, it was another more practical political consideration that affected France's attitude to the scheme and her outright rejection of it.

On May 7 Lord Hardinge submitted the plan to the Conference which, besides considering it, also referred it to the Inter-Allied

---

1920 on his own initiative but in reality did so with Pilsudski's "blessing." The Allies recognized the Polish *fait accompli*. For fuller explanation of the event see R. L. Buell, Poland, Key to Europe, 2nd ed. revd. (New York: Alfred A. Knopf, 1939), p. 78 and Roman Debicki, Foreign Policy of Poland, 1919-1939 (New York: Frederick A. Praeger, 1962), p. 48.

[44]Percival to FO, no. 82, May 4, 1921 and the attached minute in FO 371/5897, C 9159/92/18.

[45]Curzon to Hardinge, no. 222, May 6, 1921 in DBFP, 1st ser., XVI, no. 36. Footnote 1 to this document notes the May 7 telegram no. 255 from Lord Hardinge in which the ostensibly inconsistent reference to the territory to be occupied in the interim by Poland is clarified. Hardinge assumed Curzon was referring only to Rybnik and Pless and not the strips along the eastern frontier. The FO response which is not printed in DBFP confirms Hardinge's assumption. See FO to Hardinge, no. 238, May 11, 1921 in FO 371/5898, C 9373/92/18.

Military Committee at Versailles for examination from a military viewpoint. Before reading a final decision, the Ambassadors addressed a warning to Warsaw that the Polish government should disavow and assist in suppressing the insurrection.

Monday morning, May 9, the Conference of Ambassadors again took up the question of Upper Silesia. By this time the Versailles Committee report, which recommended rejection of the British proposals, was ready for its perusal. The French government categorically rejected the scheme because General Lerond judged it to be impossible to move headquarters, which would create a power vacuum at Oppeln, and at the same time to prevent chaos in the province.

Not only was Hardinge unable to secure French support but Count Bonin, the Italian ambassador whose orders from Rome were to support the move only in the event of its being accepted by the other ambassadors, refused his concurrence. Hardinge did not press the Ambassadors, but in the absence of their approval, he asked if they could put forward an alternative scheme. France preferred to play a waiting game, all couched in high-sounding rationalizations communicated from Lerond. The more ascerbic nature of Hardinge's personality was conveyed in a private letter to Lord Curzon recounting substantially the same information about his diplomatic failure in the Conference that morning. His only consolations were the Ambassadors' willingness to address a stringent note to the Polish government and his opportunity to say, "I told you so."

> I intended to take a very early opportunity of rubbing into both Briand and Berthelot that however much the Polish government may be responsible for the Polish outbreak, each of them is a *particeps criminis* owing to their opposition to the expulsion of Korfanty from Upper Silesia, and I shall remind them that what has happened is what we have always prophesied from the month of December last. Although it is too late now, nevertheless I think it does the French government good to rub into them their shortcomings.[46]

But at least for the time being Britain could not induce her ally to cooperate.

A murmur arose in the Foreign Office over Hardinge's purported mismanagement of the question. More specifically, it criticized his acquiescence in referring the proposal to the Versailles Committee because it was recognized in Whitehall that Marshal Foch dominated that body.

---

[46]Private letter from Lord Hardinge to Lord Curzon, May 9, 1921 in FO 371/5899, C 9856/92/18, part of which is reproduced in DBFP, 1st ser., XVI, no. 50, footnote 4.

The Foreign Office took a firm stand in instructing Lord Hardinge to urge upon the Conference of Ambassadors acceptance of the interim occupation scheme since apparently no ally was coming forward with an alternate plan and it was becoming increasingly evident that a unanimous report could not be compiled by the Plebiscite Commission. The only alternative to these steps, the instructions continued, was for the Conference to peruse the Commission's report and on the basis of its recommendations, to reach a final decision itself on the Upper Silesian frontier without any further delay. Hardinge tried to impress upon Curzon that the Ambassadors would find it as impossible to make the decision as the Commission had. Moreover, with the final frontier being so much related to other questions of policy, it seemed probable that should a final decision be made in Paris, it would be repudiated by the Supreme Council because the French intended to assign the industrial area to Poland.

Because of the danger of the existing situation, the British government proposed an early discussion between the Prime Minister and Lord Curzon, on one hand, and the French Premier on the other, perhaps as Boulogne. Briand demurred on the Anglo-French rendezvous, claiming that the Upper Silesia settlement was a question to be dealt with not only by these two governments but by the Supreme Council. But Hardinge pressed the issue, pointing out the importance of an informal agreement between the two governments prior to the Supreme Council session. And finally Briand agreed in principle to meet with Lloyd George and Curzon after May 19, the date of his foreign policy address to the Chamber of Deputies.[47]

Before this meeting was held, Korfanty's negotiations with General Brandt of Lerond's staff took place and yielded terms which Lord Hardinge found unacceptable. The insurgent leader agreed to stop the insurrection and effect a cease fire on condition that no attack upon his forces within the Korfanty line was attempted, that no German forces be used in the liquidation of the insurrection, and that Polish officials replace certain German personnel in administrative positions in the insurgent-occupied territory.[48] Not

---

[47]Aide-memoire handed by Lord Hardinge to Briand on May 13, 1921 in FO 371/5905, C 10826/92/18; Hardinge to Curzon, no. 270, May 13, 1921 in DBFP, 1st ser., XVI, no. 60; and Hardinge to Curzon, no. 271, May 13, 1921 in ibid., no. 61. On the following day the French ambassador, Count de Saint-Aulaire, handed Lord Curzon a lengthy statement of French policy respecting the Upper Silesian situation to which Curzon made a lengthy and detailed reply concerning HMG's attitude. See Briand to Lloyd George, May 14, 1921 in ibid., no. 66 and Curzon to French Ambassador, May 20, 1921 in ibid., no. 93.

[48]Hardinge to FO, no. 1401, May 13, 1921 in FO 371/5900, C 9868/92/18.

only was such a course repugnant to the British ambassador as a total capitulation to the insurgents, but there was a stong undercurrent of doubt in the Foreign Office as there had been for some time, that Korfanty actually held control of the insurgents and could wield such power over them. Those of this opinion conjectured that conditions of this extreme nature, which were impossible to accept, were purposely put forward by Korfanty as a ruse to make the Allies believe that he still held sway over the rebels. As long as the Allies did not accept his terms, he and "his" forces would not be called upon to honor any agreement.

At the same time Lloyd George spoke to the House of Commons about the problem of Upper Silesia.[49] Actually he said nothing new, but the Prime Minister's eloquence made a special event of it. Not only would he not tolerate a *fait accompli* by Korfanty, but he refused to sympathize with the Poles who made up "the last country in Europe that has a right to complain" about the Treaty which actually created their state. The bombshell dealt with keeping order in the province:

> Either the Allies ought to insist upon the Treaty being respected, or they ought to allow the Germans to do it. Not merely to disarm Germany, but to say that such troops as she has got are not permitted to take part in restoring order in what, until the decision comes, is their own province--that is not fair.

And Britain, he said, had historically stood for fairness. Korfanty could not be tolerated because permitting defiance would lead to

---

[49] 141 H.C. Deb. 5S. 2380-2388. Typical of the scathing treatment Lloyd George received by Polish writers for this speech is Chapter VIII "Lloyd George Przemówił" [Lloyd George Spoke] in Kazimierz Popiołek, Trzecie Sląskie Powstanie [The Third Silesian Insurrection] (Katowice: Wydawnictwa Instytutu Sląskiego, 1946). On the same day Sir Samuel Hoare (141 H. C. Deb.5S. 2353-2357) also addressed the House of Commons in a similar vein decrying French partiality in Upper Silesia. Such behavior, he said, while "demanding the carrying out of the Treaty of Versailles in the matter of reparations, allows it to be ignored in the matter of Upper Silesia, is doing a great harm" both to France and to the prospective Anglo-French defensive alliance. On that same explosive day in Parliament, Lt. Commander Kenworthy (2357-61) expressed a desire to "let the Germans clean the Poles out if the latter don't listen to reason." Eight years later this scene was recalled by a former member of the Plebiscite Commission, Lieutenant Colonel G. S. Hutchinson, only to register sympathy with these sentiments and to condemn the final partition as contrary to the intent of the peacemakers. See Hutchinson's Silesia Revisited (London: Simpkin Marshall, Ltd., 1929).

"consequences of the most distastrous kind."

The press reaction tended to view his speech as anti-Polish and pro-German and so it was in this light that it attracted or repulsed a following. The French press reacted loudly against it and the Premier, although he claimed no surprise, took consolation from the fact that Lloyd George alone could not summon or deploy German troops to Upper Silesia. It ominously recalled that in the event of German unilateral action anticipating the final Supreme Council decision, French troops would be compelled to tighten the screws by moving into the Ruhr.[50] On the whole, the Polish press, known for its emotional and extreme reactions in matters dealing with Upper Silesia, received the speech with reserve. In Germany, on the other hand, Lloyd George's words had an extraordinarily calming effect.[51]

In her consistent policy of attempting to expedite the final Upper Silesian settlement, Great Britain, besides having proposed the interim occupation plan, repeatedly pressured France to take part in an early meeting of the Supreme Council to consider the question. The British government on May 13 first put forward the suggestion that an Anglo-French top level conversation should precede the anticipated Supreme Council meeting. Hesitantly, the French accepted the invitation in principle. Once scoring this victory the British proposed to open the meeting to American, Italian, and Japanese representatives, thereby practically converting it into a session of the Supreme Council. This was part of Britain's plan to build up a backlog of diplomatic support for her position, but the Americans who were being enlisted for this reason, already having espoused isolationism, consented only to sending an observer rather than an active representative.[52]

---

[50] For French press reaction see Hardinge to Curzon, no. 275, May 14, 1921 in DBFP, 1st ser., XVI, no. 64 and Briand's further statement in Cheetham to FO, no. 278, May 15, 1921 in FO 371/5900, C 9900/92/18. Interestingly, the vituperative attack on the Lloyd George speech had the effect of uniting the British press behind the Prime Minister even those papers which ordinarily attacked him. The Times, e.g., which since the time of the peace conference had consistently attacked Lloyd George's policies, kept its silence immediately following the Prime Minister's speech and merely objectively reported the event of its delivery and the criticism of the French. See Curzon to Cheetham, no. 1388, May 18, 1921 in DBFP, 1st ser., XVI, no. 88.

[51] Müller to Curzon, no. 304, May 18, 1921 in FO 417/10, N 5945/123/55. Percival to Curzon, no. 112, May 17, 1921 in DBFP, 1st ser., XVI, no. 75.

[52] Minutes by Waterlow, Crowe, and Curzon, May 14, 1921 in FO 371/5900, C 9874/92/18.

Time was of the essence and both the Prime Minister and the Foreign Minister expressed their willingness to go to France early in the following week. Italy, the dilatory and unpredictable ally, this time agreed with Britain on the importance of an early Supreme Council meeting in view of the gravity of the situation in Upper Silesia. She had played the role of compromiser before, especially at the time when the Plebiscite Commission report was completed and submitted to the Conference of Ambassadors. Now in mid-May Italy took heart that the softer line of Briand's new government on the assignment of the Upper Silesian industrial area might presage a reasonably satisfactory compromise solution to the problem.

But France kept finding reasons for playing her waiting game. First, she balked at the Prime Minister's statement that the decision should be made by a majority rather than by a unanimous vote in the Supreme Council. Then the French proposed that Britain, France, and Italy each send an engineer who would define the frontier, a lawyer who would interpret the Treaty, and a diplomat who would arrive at an agreement to put before the Powers for their approval.[53] While in the light of the Commission's inability to reach a unanimous decision, the British government admitted the value of such a new independent body's appointment, it maintained, in opposition to the French, that the Supreme Council must first meet to authorize the body and that the experts ought to meet not in Paris but on the spot in Upper Silesia. Only in the second of these contentions was France willing to acquiesce.[54]

Toward the end of the month, Count Sforza, the Italian Foreign Minister, submitted a new scheme designed to settle the question since the Supreme Council meeting by no means appeared imminent. It is unnecessary to consider the details of the proposed scheme except to note that the Foreign Office did not support it because it did not improve upon the Percival-Marinis line. It was an obviously poorly planned attempt, a "Solomon's judgment" drawn up in Rome by those who had not visited the territory in question and

---

[53] Hardinge to FO, no. 340, May 30, 1921 in FO 371/5907, C 11221/92/18. Also see the development of the French scheme for a committee of experts in the following: Cheetham to Curzon, no. 295, May 20, 1921 in DBFP, 1st ser., XVI, no. 92; Hardinge to Curzon, no. 313, May 24, 1921 in ibid., no. 111; Hardinge to Curzon, no. 332, May 27, 1921, in ibid., no. 133 and Hardinge to Curzon, no. 349, May 31, 1921 in ibid., no. 142.

[54] Curzon to Hardinge, no. 294, May 28, 1921 in ibid., no. 136; Hardinge to Curzon, no. 337, May 28, 1921 in ibid., no. 139; Hardinge to Curzon, no. 349, May 31, 1921 cited above.

had no real interest there.[55]

With the failure of the Conference of Ambassadors to adopt the British interim occupation scheme and with no serious attention being given to the Sforza plan, it was evident, especially to those on the scene, that some other expedient would have to be adopted. A proposal first came on May 25 from the British and Italian Plebiscite Commissioners who, acting jointly, advocated achieving a restoration of order by inviting German troops to occupy the Kreuzburg, Namslau, Neustadt, and Leobschütz districts and Polish troops to occupy Pless and Rybnik without prejudicing the final Supreme Council decision. This scheme differed from that proposed by Britain on May 7 in that under it Allied officials would continue their functions in these areas rather than charge Germany and Poland with both the occupation and administration. The proposal came before the special meeting of the Conference of Ambassadors on May 28.[56]

The day before, Korfanty had offered to submit to the Allies on the condition that the Commission make plans for an orderly takeover. The Commission responded by announcing plans to create a neutral zone between the warring groups by interposing Allied troops between the insurgents and the German bands after the arrival of the British battalions. At the Conference of Ambassadors meeting, although conclusive French support could not be won for the Percival-Marinis plan, the Conference approved the establishment of the neutral zone.[57]

Colonel Percival, who had more than once attracted criticism from the Foreign Office for having allowed General Lerond to assume control of the Inter-Allied Plebiscite Commission beyond the intent of the peacemakers at Paris, had several times requested permission to resign. With no one to replace him, even though the Foreign

---

[55] For details of the Sforza scheme see Buchanan to Curzon, no. 184, May 24, 1921 in DBFP, 1st ser., XVI, no. 109 and the lengthy FO minute which serves as a commentary on the plan, May 27, 1921 in FO 371/5905, C 10960/92/18.

[56] Percival to Curzon, no. 143, May 25, 1921 in DBFP, 1st ser., XVI, no. 118. Also see Buchanan to FO, no. 224, May 27, 1921 in FO 371/5905, C 10807/92/18 and Hardinge to FO, no. 328, May 26, 1921 in the same volume, C 10908/92/18.

[57] Percival to Curzon, no. 152, May 27, 1921 in DBFP, 1st ser., XVI, no. 129 and Hardinge to Curzon, no. 335, May 28, 1921 in ibid., no. 137. For the communication from the Conference of Ambassadors to the Plebiscite Commission see Hardinge to FO, no. 1578, May 29, 1921 in FO 371/5907, C 11194/92/18.

Office would have preferred to put a civilian into the post, they repeatedly refused his request. But in the last few months, indications of his own anxieties had become apparent in overlong dispatches to Warsaw which tried the patience of the legation decyphering staff, and in dispatches which dwelt at length on his personal incompatibility with General Lerond. Colonel Hawker telegraphed to Müller on May 30 that from that date he was taking over for Percival owing to the latter's ill health.

Just prior to his illness Colonel Percival had drafted a lengthy reply to the Foreign Office, revealing details of what had transpired that morning in Commission and his own skepticism about the effectiveness of the neutral zone plan.[58] Although it was an ostensibly fair plan, he maintained that it was unfair to the Germans and would bring about effects opposite those desired. After Allied unfulfilled promises of protection to the Germans, the latter had finally formed self-protection corps and succeeded in defending the line of the Oder River and seizing the stronghold at Annaberg. They now were suspicious of the neutral zone plan, seeing it as a prelude to the establishment of a permanent frontier between Poland and Germany on the line here proposed. While Percival believed that the creation of a neutral zone was not impossible, neither did he think that it could become a reality without the exercise of infinite tact. The form his tactful maneuver took was the proposed formation of a close screen of Allied troops behind the insurgent line through which the insurgents would retire. But General Höfer refused to recognize the neutral zone plan which put him in the same category as the rebel Korfanty. Lord D'Abernon, to whom the German refusal was communicated, personally sympathized with the Germans after reading Percival's criticism of the plan which described the psychological value for the Germans of their dominant position at Annaberg.

Lord Hardinge explained that the intention of the Conference of Ambassadors in adopting the plan was to force the withdrawal only of the insurgents whom they regarded as the aggressors. Still the Germans objected because they continued to cling to the principle of indivisibility of Upper Silesia and believed that this would be compromised by acknowledging the neutral zone whose limits might be perpetuated as a frontier.[59]

By June 1 with the arrival of the first of the British battalions, the acting Commissioner reported that the 2nd battalion of

---

[58] A lengthy telegram drafted on the night before his breakdown by Colonel Percival and communicated by Tidbury to the FO on May 30, 1921 is found in FO 371/5908, C 11314/92/18.

[59] D'Abernon to Curzon, no. 279, May 31, 1921 in DBFP, 1st ser., XVI, no. 143.

the Black Watch had been sent as a temporary measure to an area
halfway between Oppeln and Gross Strehlitz, while French troops
had been deployed to the Ujest area. General Heneker's arrival
in Upper Silesia on June 2 was expected to mark the beginning of
the implementation of the Conference of Ambassadors' orders, although he was personally disposed toward the original scheme which
had been proposed by the British on May 7. A new British Commissioner, Sir Harold Stuart, was appointed to relieve Percival. He
had recently terminated a successful term as a member of the
Rhineland High Commission and this capable administrator brought
with him to Oppeln the decisive, efficient leadership that Britain
needed on the Commission. His arrival on the morning of June 4
completed the set of new elements that would operate to boost the
prestige and authority of Great Britain in Upper Silesia and lend
a new impetus to the lingering Allied regime there.

CHAPTER V

BRITISH INITIATIVE: INVESTMENT AND RESTORED PRESTIGE

(June 1921 to October 1921)

Great Britain, never doctrinaire in her formulation of policy, had historically held few basic tenets which guided her course and caused her to pursue specific ends. Her devotion to the lands of Central and Eastern Europe was noticeably and traditionally absent and, in fact, her disinterest in this area had comprised one of the characteristics of her policy. Yet in mid-1921 she found herself assuming a dynamic role and taking an uncharacteristic initiative here, particularly in Danzig and Upper Silesia.

The Free City of Danzig in its newly independent and unique status provided a new field of interest for Britain who consciously and admittedly sought to cultivate maritime contacts for the expansion of her trade. Not only was the Baltic port city attractive as a potential market, but owing to its special relationship with the Republic of Poland, which was bound to result in a customs union between the two states, it provided an open door to new Polish commerce. If in centuries past a port on the Baltic had by others been regarded as a window to the West, Great Britain now sought to reverse that concept and make instead Danzig her window into Central and Eastern Europe, not in order to pursue imperial ambitions as reflected in spheres of interest and political administration, but rather those hopes expressed in British manufactured goods and pounds sterling.

Upper Silesia, on the other hand, had not provided much attraction for British interests. Since the peace conference, it had been regarded in theory as an Allied concern but in practice a predominantly French one. If Britain played any role here, it was one of restraining, but not condemning, her Entente partner who took her relationships in Eastern Europe during the inter-war years very seriously. But as the Upper Silesian problem moved from one stage to another, still wanting the ultimate decision promised in the Treaty of Versailles, Britain found herself, despite her disinterest, and perhaps because of it, assuming the initiative and the inconvenience of an augmented presence in the disputed territory. Two years earlier she had been willing to take the lead in effecting the transfer of power in Danzig, not because she had wished to secure for herself any domination but most simply because she had believed that of all the Allied powers, she could most summarily get the job done. Prompted by this same desire to efficiently dispose of the tiresome problem of Upper Silesia, she now, in mid-1921, increased her involvement and, as a result, her presige as well, by sending six battalions of troops and skilled administrators into the plebiscite area. How Britain assumed the initiative in exploiting investment opportunities in Danzig and the initiative in both restoring Allied authority and also pressing for a settlement in Upper Silesia during the summer and autumn of 1921 are the chief concerns of this chapter.

A Renewed British Interest in Danzig

The spring and summer of 1921 produced a good climate for the improvement of Polish-Danzig relations. With Poland's attention still turned to the disturbed Upper Silesian area she had, in the first instance, less attention to devote to wrangling with the Free City than she would prove to have after Allied withdrawal from the plebiscite area. It was, in fact, the Poles' continuing ability to secure definitive control over Upper Silesia and the coveted city of Vilna, which they had taken in October 1920, that contributed in great part to the weakening of the Witos government. When that government fell in September, because of the resignation of the Finance Minister and because of a grave financial situation, Upper Silesia still absorbed the attention of the Polish government. But a certain degree of good will on the part of Poland was manifested as the successful conclusion to the lengthy negotiations and the signature of the detailed Polish-Danzig treaty which complemented the convention of November 1920 attest.

It will be remembered that when the convention was finally signed in November by Paderewski, Poland's adherence had been made conditional upon her receiving a mandate to protect Danzig. In the midst of much discussion, the High Commissioner had issued his report which stated that Poland should be permitted to use her troops to enforce her right to the use of the port after negotiations with the Danzig government had failed and after a successful appeal had been made to the High Commissioner of the League of Nations. Finally, the Council of the League had assigned to him the task of examining the means of providing a *port d'attache* for Polish warships in Danzig without establishing a naval base there. When these provisions were adopted by the League of Nations on June 18, Poland had other irons in the fire, concerned as she was for her defense and the need for unquestioned control of a port with access to the sea. The Russo-Polish War and the crisis of July-August 1920 had taught her a hard and valuable lesson.

If the Allies intended to restrict her control over Danzig and to forestall her attempt to reduce the "Free City" title to a mere euphemism, Poland hoped to develop another port in her own territory without ever totally abandoning her claims in Danzig for whatever they were worth. Two years earlier a representative from the British shipbuilding firm of Vickers had made a preliminary survey of the proposed site at Gdynia and found that the creation of a port there was quite feasible. Should Poland receive no rights in Danzig, he believed that she could turn to Gdynia and he was eager to have British capital invested in the enterprise.

In the late spring of 1921 as Poland again considered this site, Lieutenant Buchanan of the Royal Navy visited the area and reaffirmed the findings of the Vickers study. While no great depth of water then existed, he noted that the fine sandy bottom could be easily and inexpensively dredged to produce a first-class harbor. Up to then, the only work which Poland had undertaken was the construction of a railway line from Dirschau to the coast and the building of piers and a breakwater.[1] Polish interest in Gdynia fluctuated according to the current state of Polish-Danzig relations and the status of the mandate issue before the League.

On the eve of the June session of the Council of the League, Admiral K. Porebski spoke to Buchanan about the question of basing the Polish fleet at Danzig. He claimed that Poland would drop the question of a mandate to defend the city if Poland's fears were calmed with a satisfactory settlement of the issue of its use by Poland as a naval base. The arrival at Danzig of several reconditioned German destroyers for the Polish navy was expected in mid-June. Buchanan told the Poles that in any case some restrictions on armaments there would be necessary. Müller called upon the High Commissioner to raise the matter in whatever way he thought best but to arrive at the settlement of the naval base question and thereby preclude the kind of Polish excitement over Danzig that was currently being exhibited over insurrection-ridden Upper Silesia.[2]

---

[1] Müller to Curzon, no. 325, May 24, 1921 in FO 688, box 9, file 39, no. 51. British opinion regarding the proposed port was by no means unanimous or positive. A FO minute recorded skepticism: "I would recommend no one to have anything to do with the creation of such a port. Poland is the natural hinterland for Danzig at present and it will be many years before the export trade of that part of the world will be too great for Danzig to deal with. The political complications of having two termini to the corridor are hideous to contemplate. The obvious thing to do is to try and make the Harbour Board workable, before taking up mad schemes of this kind." See the minute by H. F. Crookshank, June 20, 1921 in FO 371/6822, N 7066/283/55.

[2] Müller to Haking, May 13, 1921 in FO 688, box 9, file 39, no. 48. Poland did not envision building a large navy. Her finances in any case would not permit it. By 1924 she had only 2,000 men, 150 officers, and a tonnage less than 4,000 tons--about that of a light cruiser. See J. Didelot, *La Marine de l'aigle blanc* (Paris: Berger-Levrault, 1924), pp. 33-35.

Sir Richard Haking suggested that two alternatives were open to the Poles: (1) to bring the question before the League of Nations and (2) to approach the Danzig authorities directly. The High Commissioner rather favored the second of these, believing that Danzig would offer no great opposition. But Müller, more schooled in the "peculiar temperament" of the country in which he served, sensed that the Poles would prefer to approach the League in search of a "right" rather than to ask a favor of Danzig.[3]

Haking's report on the Danzig question, requested by the Council of the League of Nations in June, was anxiously awaited by the interested parties. But on September 10, he reported that he could issue no decision because of his difficulty in distinguishing between a naval base and a *port d'attache*. As the Poles later interpreted these terms, a naval base was used solely for war purposes while a *port d'attache* supplied the normal peacetime needs of ships.

British policy regarding this issue was best articulated in an Admiralty statement of September 21. In it the Admiralty observed that Poland, being already in possession of Dirschau on the river Vistula, was free to establish a naval base there and should therefore utilize that site for the berthing of those craft which could reach it and exclude those craft from the suggested *port d'attache* at Danzig. Noting, too, that the new Polish port at Gdynia was now under construction, the Admiralty proposed further that any concession given to Poland to use the Free City should be confined only to the period prior to completion of this construction. Finally, since the *port d'attache* would necessitate a lengthier stay than is usual in foreign ports for the Polish ships, regulations were suggested which might direct the use of Danzig's facilities:

> (a) Polish ships of war shall have the right of shelter and of wharfage in the Port of Danzig at any time, subject only to the right of the High Commissioner to demand their withdrawal in the case of circumstances arising which, in his opinion, render this course unavoidable.
> (b) Submarines shall in no case attempt to submerge in the territorial waters of the Free City or to enter territorial water in a submerged condition.
> (c) Polish warships shall be free from all port dues and charges.
> (d) Any stores, fuel, oil, and provisions required may either be brought by river craft from Poland, or may be obtained from local firms without reference to the Danzig authorities.

---

[3]Müller to Curzon, no. 325 cited above and Haking to Müller, May 20, 1921 in FO 688, box 9, file 39, no. 49.

(e) Polish ships shall have the right to get any repairs required executed by local firms, or to embark at Danzig any machinery parts arriving from Poland or elsewhere without reference to the Danzig Authorities.

(f) Ammunition may be embarked at Danzig if brought from Poland by local craft, or if arriving at Danzig direct from foreign firms, after previous notice has been given to the Danzig Harbour Authorities.

(g) The above privileges shall only remain in force until the port of Gdingen [Gdynia] is sufficiently far advanced to provide the necessary accommodation, or for a period of one year. In the event of the Port not being completed in this period the matter will be further considered by the Council.[4]

On September 24 the Naval Sub-Commission of the Permanent Advisory Commission to the Council of the League of Nations issued its report and recommendations[5] after having considered the September 10 report of the High Commissioner as well as the statements of both the Polish delegation and the President of the Danzig Senate on the issue of a *port d'attache*. Its members were unanimous in their decision that "Polish war vessels should be granted facilities for sheltering or storing, and effecting necessary repairs in the Port of Danzig" until Gdynia was available for these purposes.

How to insure these facilities proved to be a point of difference among the representatives on the sub-commission. The British members upheld the genuine independence of the Free City and thought it advisable that Poland should possess no shore establishments there but instead be given the "right of shelter and wharfage" and obtain any necessary stores from either private firms or from Poland via river craft. Repairs should be effected under the same conditions. While the Japanese members supported this view, the French held that since a mandate to defend Danzig in case of aggression had been granted to Poland, it was essential that the latter be granted a permanent establishment ashore where the naval units could effect repairs and replenish stores other than war material. As so often was the case in these inter-allied dealings, Italy found herself *in medias res* between the French and the British, suggesting that the establishments in question should be tem-

---

[4] Original British proposals, September 21, 1921, transmitted in Admiralty to Ovey, December 29, 1921 in FO 371/6826, N 14239/283/55.

[5] Final report of the Naval Sub-Commission of the Permanent Advisory Commission to the Council of the League of Nations, September 24, 1921, transmitted in Admiralty to Ovey, December 29, 1921 cited above.

porarily leased by Danzig to Poland; Italy won a majority to
her point of view. Accordingly, the recommendations in the sub-
commission's report were substantially the same as those of the
British Admiralty seen above except that the (d) and (e) were
replaced by the Italian compromise solution stating

> Polish ships of war shall have the right of shelter
> and of wharfage in the Port of Danzig at any time. For
> this purpose there shall be leased to them on equitable
> conditions by the Free City a definite site which might
> with advantage be situated at the spot intended for the
> unloading of the Polish material in transit.
>
> They shall have freedom of passage on the same foot-
> ing as Polish commercial vessels, in the maritime and
> river waters of the Free City, and use of the locks
> which afford communication between these waters.
>
> Areas, corresponding to their wharves shall be con-
> ceded to them on lease in order that they may establish
> there stores for fuel and material of all sorts--not of
> a military nature--which are necessary for the navigabi-
> lity and upkeep.
>
> These concessions cannot be suspended or withdrawn
> except by decision of the Council, or, in the case of
> emergency, of the High Commissioner.

But the issue did not end at this time and the question of the
port d'attache was to come before the Council of the League of
Nations again the following January for one of its sporadic appearances in that spotlight.[6] This was only the beginning of an
issue that was destined not to be settled until more than a decade
had elapsed and which, after several appearances before the League
of Nations, became the subject of an agreement in 1932 which implied that sovereignty over the port was vested in the Port and
Waterways Board.[7]

Another question between Poland and Danzig that the High Commissioner proposed to bring before the Council was the matter of
the drawn-out negotiations for an economic convention the preparation of which, despite the general improvement in relations between
the two states by mid-year, had not noticeably progressed. This
was destined, too, to remain in a limbo until October 24, 1921

---

[6] Papers related to the *port d'attache* question as it developed in 1921 appear in the collection of League of Nations documents, London, Public Record Office, PRO 30/52, box 8,
C.360.M255.1921.

[7] The Polish Research Centre (ed.), Poland and Danzig (London:
The Cornwall Press Ltd., 1941), p. 17.

when two years of diplomatic dealings finally resulted in a Polish-Danzig treaty. This agreement was intended as a complement to the convention which the same contracting parties had signed in November 1920. At that time, it will be recalled, the question of how authority should be exercised over the port was settled by putting aside the letter of the Treaty of Versailles and taking up the plan of Lord Derby to establish a Harbor Board of five Danzigers and five Poles with a neutral president in which the administration of the port services should be vested. The new agreement which was to come into force on January 1, 1922 established the customs union originally envisioned in the concept of a Free City linked with a special relationship to the new Polish state. Under its terms Danzig became a unit in the Polish Customs Administration. Other major considerations of the agreement included the status of Polish representatives and officials in the Free City, and finally, the working and control of the Danzig railway system.[8]

Related to the question of the control of Danzig's railway systems were the control of the railway workshops and the control of the Danziger Werft in which potential investors in the railway workshops were simultaneously interested. The Werft, formerly known as the Kaiserlicher Werft and later as the Reichswerft, was an important shipbuilding and engineering yard. British firms became interested in investing in Danzig's workshops and Werft as they had already become in the reorganization of the network of the entire Polish railway system.[9]

---

[8] The Times, August 26, 1921, p. 9 and Müller to Curzon, no. 643, October 26, 1921 in FO 688, box 9, file 39, no. 96.

[9] Early in 1921, in response to the Polish government's offer to lease the Polish railway system *en bloc* to a British group, members of the Foreign Office, the Department of Overseas Trade, and the chairmen of Cammell Laird and the Coventry Syndicate met. They proposed to appoint a special railway expert adviser and receive a grant from the Polish government to recondition rolling stock and the railway workshops. The FO favored this scheme. Interest by Cammell Laird remained high until it was found that the British government would not subsidize the venture. Then in March, Colonel E. Graham, the head of the British Railway Mission in Warsaw, learned that the Rothschild firm in Frankfurt am Main had made a definite offer to the Polish Railway Ministry to rebuild some of the repair shops in the environs of Warsaw. The story of Anglo-Polish negotiations related to the question of Polish railways is not central to the present study, but it helps to explain how British commercial interest in Danzig was in part aimed at the extension of British trade into Russia, a development possible only if the intervening chaotic railway network were reorganized. See FO minutes of the meeting of FO, DOT, Cammell Laird, and Coventry Syndicate personnel, January 7, 1921 in

Up to now British firms had been reluctant to exhibit a serious interest in such property at Danzig for various reasons: the uncertainty of ownership of the former German property, until it was settled by the Repartition commission under the terms of Article 107 of the Treaty of Versailles, rendered impossible the making of an attractive and sure offer for purchase or acquisition on lease of the shipbuilding and engineering yards; (2) the views of the Allies toward such an acquisition by British firms were unknown; and (3) it had been impossible at first to obtain adequate information concerning the extent, location, and capacity of the yards as well as of their earlier financial performance records and prognostications. Nothing had come from the feelers sent out in this direction by several British firms. Now the Department of Overseas Trade judged that the time was propitious for such action. The D.O.T. learned that Professor Ludwik Noë, the Director of the Danziger Werft while it was in Danzig hands, proposed not that an outright purchase by a British firm be made, but rather that the Werft should be converted into a limited liability company with capital coming from Danzig, Poland, and foreign, predominantly British, sources. Britain should be guaranteed, too, the right to appoint a British member to the board of directors.

English investment in and trade with Danziq was not a new phenomenon.[10] In the late fourteenth century, approximately 300 English ships visited Danzig annually. Only the remnants of this relationship remained after the Great War in such Danzig placenames as "English House" and "Old Scotland." Should Britain decide to participate in the protected international company here, her action would not be unprecedented.

In the spring of 1921, the D. O. T. found itself in possession of detailed information about the commercial potential for the property and it was in a far better position than at anytime in the past to support a British investment initiative here. Before circulating such information among those firms which would most likely be interested, the Department inquired about the position of the inter-allied Commission for the Repartition of Former German State Property toward the proposal--cognizant of

---

in FO 371/6819, N 462/236/55; J. D. Gregory to Sir H. Llewellyn Smith, January 12, 1921 in the same registry number; and DOT to FO, F. R. 2837, March 1, 1921 in FO 371/6819, N 2782/236/55. The same idea concerning Poland's value as a stepping-stone to Anglo-Russian trade was elaborated upon by Professor Wilden-Hart, "A Paradise for British Merchants," Reprint from The Financial News (September 14, 1921), p. 7.

[10] Polish Economic Bulletin, Vol. I, no. 2 (November 1919) 47-49, and Oscar Halecki, "Anglo-Polish Relations in the Past," Slavonic and East European Review, XII (April 1934) 659-69. See also Leon Litwinski, Business Openings in Poland, 1917, pp. 3-4.

the fact that if the commission's sanction were not given, the scheme for the admission of British financial interest in or control of a yard in Danzig would most certainly fall through.

An opportunity such as this of obtaining for British Trade a firm footing in Danzig which is the key-port to Poland, itself a half-way house towards Western Russia, should not be lost. Moreover, the opening appears to be all the more opportune in view of the fact that the Customs Union involving Unity of Tariff is inevitable between Danzig and Poland, when, as the Tariff on imported manufactures will certainly be high, Danzig will be in the unique position to supply Poland with manufactured articles as there will be no tariff-wall between Danzig and Poland.[11]

E. H. Carr, the British representative on the commission, speaking for that inter-allied body said that for practical reasons the Danziger Werft should be exploited not as a Danzig or Polish state concern but by a private company not directly connected with either state. Foreseeing the likelihood that neither Poland nor Danzig could afford to provide sufficient capital, the commission favored the formation of a company whose capital would come not only from these states but from other Allied or neutral sources as well. Such a company's management, they assumed, would reflect the proportion of subscription of capital.

British firms were simultaneously exhibiting an interest in the railway workshops which had formerly belonged to the German government. Following his visit to several Polish railway workshops, Gilbert Rowe of Cravens Limited, was introduced to Carr whose experience with the problem of Danzig property ownership was considerable. As a result of these and succeeding conversations, Rowe proceeded to Danzig where he also visited the railway workshops, whose ultimate ownership had yet to be determined.

On August 15, Sir Richard Haking, the High Commissioner, issued his decision concerning the control of Danzig railways which sparked a reaction about the disposal of the workshops which served them. Generally, he decreed that broad gauge railways should be administered by the Poles and narrow gauge railways and tramways should go to Danzig. The latter immediately objected on the grounds that he had reached his decision by employing practical and financial considerations rather than by a strict application of the various treaties and conventions then in force which touched upon the matter. On the other hand, the Poles replied to these objections with support for the High Commissioner's views which had

---

[11]DOT to FO, no. 78/U.B., May 2, 1921 in FO 371/6821, N 5297/283/55.

assigned to them the lion's share. It is interesting to note here that when Haking first accepted the League position, he had been looked upon suspiciously by the Poles as dangerously pro-German. By the autumn of 1921 he came to be looked upon by the Danzigers, at least temporarily, as pro-Polish. Intermittently displeasing both sides, he seemed to display the characteristics of an independent League official.

The Polish government consented in principle to Rowe's proposal for the exploitation of the railway workshops. Because of current internal pressures upon the Polish government, however, he agreed to postpone the discussions of financial details until such time that he could take them up again with a strengthened government. Before leaving, he sought the assistance of the British Legation in clarifying the degree to which Cravens was committed to Batignolles, the French firm which he was cooperating in Rumania and which now sought to participate in investment in Danzig. From his communications with London, Müller inferred that French participation should be discouraged because it would inevitably result in friction between French administrators and German employees.[12] He reflected upon the Danzig situation in the same way as many British officers tended to reflect upon the Upper Silesian issue--noting the strong anti-German partiality of the French and attempting to act as a buffer between the two.

Müller strongly supported a dominant British role in these dealings. On September 17, he met the new Polish Foreign Minister, Konstantin Skirmunt, who had replaced Sapieha in June when the latter resigned after failing to secure a vote of confidence from the parliamentary Committee on Foreign Affairs. During these talks he learned that a Geneva decision to reverse the assignment of Danzig railway repair shops to Poland was imminent but he hoped that this would not materialize. Not only did it appear fair and logical to him that the shops should be owned by the same claimant as the railways, but he did not want to witness any complications which would reverse the consent Cravens had already won from the Poles.[13] Three days later he learned from Skirmunt that the Danzig representatives at Geneva had proposed that as compensation for withdrawing their appeal against the railway ownership decision, the railway repair shops should be given to a company in which capital was provided in equal parts by Poland, Danzig, and the Harbor Board. Neither Müller nor Skirmunt liked the new plan but the British representative advised the Pole not to protest so strongly as to

---

[12] Müller to FO, no. 363, August 18, 1921 in FO 371/6819, N 9539/236/55.

[13] Müller to FO, no. 382, September 20, 1921 also enclosing the letter from Müller to Gregory of September 18, 1921 in FO 371/6819, N 10669/236/55.

threaten a rupture in the improved relations that had evolved between Poland and Danzig.

Lengthy Polish-Danzig negotiations ensued and an agreement was signed in Geneva on September 23 by which control of the Danzig railway workshops was divided with 45% going to Polish, 45% to Danzig, and 10% to outside interests. With this signature the Foreign Office took up the cause of Cravens and instructed Müller to determine whether the Polish government was willing to hand over the exploitation of its share to the firm.[14]

One final consideration in this early period of British initiative in Danzig is the role of the Foreign Office in assisting Cravens to gain a foothold in the Werft. The Sheffield firm had both interest in the deal and the necessary capital to recondition the Werft, Danzig's biggest industrial asset, and were eager to begin operations as soon as they could obtain title to the works which would admit Polish, Danzig, and Allied participation upon the condition that the British and Danzig interests together could outvote the rest. No better alternative scheme had been advanced, but it appeared that the fly in the ointment was the cumbersome machinery of the Conference of Ambassadors. In July they recommended a joint Polish-Danzig ownership of the property which should be leased for exploitation to an international company. But the Ambassadors failed to act upon the recommendations as complications and schedule conflicts arose. But British initiative had been taken in Danzig and the next phase of its escalation would reveal no reticence on the part of Great Britain to participate in Central Europe in the commercial role she understood best.

Restoration of Allied Prestige in Upper Silesia

Despite Great Britain's widely-known disinterest in the province of Upper Silesia, her role there, paradoxically, grew in June when General Heneker arrived in command of the forces which Britain had dispatched and when Sir Harold Stuart replaced Colonel Percival as the British Commissioner on the Plebiscite Commission. Not only had France galloped away with the command which was ostensibly Allied because of the aggressive personal qualities of its Commissioner, General Lerond, but also because the other Commissioners had of late shown themselves to be ineffectual in making the positions of their respective governments heard. Max Müller had some time earlier detected that Percival appeared unequal to the responsible task assigned to him, being hampered by

---

[14] FO to Müller, no. 199, October 11, 1921 in FO 371/6825, N 11388/283/55. See also the clarification of the Polish government's point of view by the British Legation in Warsaw in Müller to FO, no. 408, October 12, 1921 in FO 371/6825, N 11472/283/55.

the strained personal relations existing between the British and French officers and officials.[15]

If there is any doubt whether Percival did not fill his post as effectively as he might have, it is confirmed when the immediate capable and activist policy of Stuart is considered. While he appeared rather uncompromising and rigid at first, Stuart represented the new determined mood of Britain in Upper Silesia. Part of this initiative was evidenced in the swift restoration of Allied authority and in his assessment of the measures to be taken which were designed to strengthen that tenuous authority, even if they were not in agreement with French policy. Stuart's inclination to use military force decisively, for example, had won the approval of Lord D'Abernon whom he had met in Berlin while he was still en route to Oppeln. To have an armed force but to be constrained from using it effectively, they agreed was a frustrating situation. The ambassador was greatly heartened by Stuart and the whole British team that was going to the disputed province under the leadership of Generel Heneker. The former team had done their work gallantly, he said, but they appeared now stale and overstrained after a most trying and difficult task. D'Abernon confided in his diary, "A cat may look at a King, but a French Major-General cannot be argued with by any Colonel."[16] Lerond had taken his toll in his own little princedom in Central Europe.

With the arrival of the six promised battalions, Britain unwittingly found herself in an embarrassing position since her disgust with France's flagrant pro-Polish attitude had on the contrary, made her own impartial attitude appear to be sympathetic to Germany. Consequently, the Germans had repeatedly requested a renewed British military presence and General Höfer, leader of the *Selbstschutz*, using an unfortunate choice of words in an interview with a correspondent of the New York Herald, claimed that his bands "hoped to co-operate with British troops in re-establishing the Allies' authority."[17] Again, just two days later at a special meeting of the Plebiscite Commission, Lerond produced a pamphlet which had been distributed by German airplanes welcoming the British forces.[18] In each case, British representatives had tried to dis-

---

[15] Müller to Crowe, Confidential, June 1, 1921 in FO 688, box 10, file 50, no. 400.

[16] British Museum, D'Abernon MSS 48953B, June 3, 1921.

[17] Hardinge to FO, no. 361, June 3, 1921 in FO 371/5909, C 11593/92/18.

[18] Minutes of special meeting of the Upper Silesia Plebiscite Commission, June 5, 1921 in FO 890, part 2, file 2K.

courage such statements and make clear that their troops acted not unilaterally but in conjunction with the Allied forces supplied by France and Italy.

Sir Harold Stuart brought with him to the Commissin a fresh outlook and a dynamism characterized by swift decision and a forceful presence. Almost immediately he criticized the policy by which an Allied ultimatum put pressure on the German self-protection forces while not questioning the advance of the Polish insurgent position. This reaction in the face of the ultimatum to Höfer during the first week of June will be investigated below. He found fault especially with the crippling policy of France which restricted General Lerond's freedom of action and emasculated the Allied armed force which could otherwise restore order in Upper Silesia. Further, he observed with some surprise, that his colleagues on the Commission, besides holding those administrative posts, maintained supreme command of the forces provided in the plebiscite area by their respective governments. To him this was both anomalous and undesirable and he proposed an immediate rectification. The Commission acted as the civil government of the province and it was "unprecedented that any member of a Civil Government should have authority to give orders to military commanders independently of the Government as a whole."[19]

If Stuart had not demonstrated his skill as an administrator, the speed and forcefulness of his action might have opened him to a charge of impulsiveness. Yet, his determination seemed to be a positive influence on both the Allies and the inhabitants of Upper Silesia, whether activists or not. When, for example, it was reported to him only three days after his arrival that a British troop train en route to Gleiwitz from Oppeln had been stopped by insurgents and not permitted to continue until Korfanty's permission was given, he told Heneker that this was intolerable. He contemplated immediate military measures against the insurgents aimed at clearing the Oppeln-Gleiwitz railway line. Accordingly, he advised Heneker to recall the British troops to Oppeln and to withdraw them from French command unless the French agreed to this move. Lerond reluctantly assented and Heneker and the French military commander, General Gratier, worked out a plan which succeeded in clearing the railway line. Stuart had held his position, and his success convinced him that a painful incident had turned to both British and Allied advantage and nicely illustrated to insurgents and other inhabitants in Upper Silesia, that at last something was being done to restore the authority of the Inter-Allied Commission. The Foreign Office applauded his move.[20]

---

[19] Stuart to FO, June 5, 1921 in FO 890, part 2, file 2K.

[20] Stuart to FO, no. 181 June 8, 1921 and FO to Stuart, no. 82, June 10, 1921 both in FO 371/5910, C 11931/92/18.

A serious divergence in policy between the Allies in the plebiscite area was revealed when the ultimatum to Höfer was issued. After Stuart's ceremonial welcome on June 4 by the French and Italian Commissioners, the British military commander, and a guard of honor, he was quickly initiated into the troubles of the area when he was greeted with the serious news that the situation had further deteriorated and that the Germans, despite their promise given on May 21, had advanced, taking two new villages. At once the Commission ordered Höfer to withdraw to a position approximating the one from which he had advanced. A twelve-hour time limit was specified for this movement, non-compliance with which would result in the withdrawal of French troops from the industrial area and their concentration in the Gleiwitz district. The territory thus evacuated by Höfer was to be held by the Allied forces. Berlin protested that the time limit was too short and that it was unfair to force the withdrawal of the *Selbstschutz* to the benefit of the Polish insurgents.[21]

The Foreign Office had repeatedly referred to the ultimatum policy as Lerond's rather than the Allies'. They believed that an Allied withdrawal from the industrial area was unwise and would condemn the German inhabitants to massacre and signal the Germans to advance, in which case the safety of Allied troops could not be guaranteed. Most likely, for instance, hostilities would erupt between the French and the Germans. They feared, too, that such energetic steps taken by the Commission against the German bands would lay the Allied administration open to charges of partiality because they contrasted so markedly with the treatment of Korfanty.[22]

Yet the British government endorsed the policy, although they found it distasteful. Sir Eyre Crowe regarded it as an extraordinary measure but defended it before the German ambassador inasmuch as it represented "fresh and united efforts to reestablish order with the help of the newly-arrived British troops."[23]

---

[21] General account of June 4 by F. B. Bourdillon, June 4, 1921 in FO 890, part 2, file 2K. Stuart to Curzon, no. 173, June 4, 1921 in Documents on British Foreign Policy, 1919-1939 (hereafter DBFP) 1st ser., XVI, no. 154. The text of the ultimatum, the follow-up communication from the Inter-Allied Commission, and the German response appear in FO 371/5910, C 11926/92/18.

[22] FO Minute by Major Ottley, June 7, 1921 in FO 371/5910, C 11914/92/18.

[23] Minute by Sir Eyre Crowe, June 6, 1921 in FO 371/5909, C 11780/92/18.

There was as first some question as to whether Stuart had actually concurred in the decision to send the ultimatum. He had apparently questioned its wisdom and attempted to influence Lerond to refrain from withdrawing troops from the industrial area. From the nebulous references in the Foreign Office correspondence, it appears that Sir Harold Stuart acquiesced in the ultimatum policy upon his arrival in Upper Silesia in order to make it unanimous. Lord Curzon on June 6 recognized it as such when he instructed D'Abernon to act either unilaterally or jointly with the Allied colleagues in Berlin to impress upon the German government the importance of their using their authority to influence Höfer to comply with the "unanimous recommendations of the Allied Commissioners."[24]

When Höfer submitted, it was recognized by the British government that he did so largely because of D'Abernon's representations in Berlin and "in spite, rather than because, of General Lerond's ultimatum."[25] Britain viewed the good news from Höfer as fraught with danger because the ultimatum policy might be regarded by Lerond as a precedent for making the same threat again to achieve some unreasonable demand.

At the same morning meeting on June 4 at which the ultimatum decision was made, Stuart proposed that the three Allied commanders--Gratier, Heneker, and Salvioni--look into the military practicality of forming a neutral zone with the interposition of Allied occupation forces.[26] Although this plan had already been endorsed by the Conference of Ambassadors in May,[27] the Allies had been dragging their feet with it and to date no assessment by

---

[24] Curzon to D'Abernon, no. 144, June 6, 1921 in DBFP, 1st ser., XVI, no. 157. The French Prime Minister also replied to Lord Hardinge's note of June 5 and mentioned appreciatively the participation of the British Commissioner on the issuing of the ultimatum. See Hardinge to Curzon, no. 365, June 7, 1921 in ibid., no. 160.

[25] FO Minute by Ottley, June 8, 1921 in FO 371/5910, C 11925/93/18.

[26] Meeting of the Inter-Allied Commission, June 4, 1921 in Start to Heneker, June 7, 1921 in FO 890, part 1, file 2, doc. 1. Allusion is also made to the consideration of the neutral zone plan in Stuart to Curzon, no. 174, June 5, 1921 in DBFP, 1st ser., XVI, no. 155.

[27] This plan was approved by the Conference of Ambassadors on May 28 only on the assumption that it should be carried out in conjunction with the plan for withdrawal by Korfanty's forces. See Hardinge to Briand, June 11, 1921 in ibid., no. 170.

military men on the spot had been made. What Stuart hoped for was a report which, if it judged the intermediate zone scheme to be unfeasible, would propose an alternate plan. He was a consistent supporter of the application of force and strongly urged his colleagues to obtain from their governments a free hand over the disposal of their troops, the use of which had been considerably restricted as evidenced by Lerond's behavior, despite the denials of the French government.

To restore the authority of the Commission through quick action, initiative, and force was what Stuart and Heneker favored, and the Commissioner was willing to accept the risk of such conduct. But Heneker demurred, believing that such a plan was too slow and that more troops than were on hand should be called up. Stuart considered prompt military action against the insurgents necessary and Heneker considered it feasible. Accordingly, Lord Hardinge was called upon to urge the French government to untie General Lerond's hands so that he could employ the troops in Upper Silesia vigorously.[28] Simultaneously, Müller in Warsaw requested permission to join his colleagues in issuing a joint representation to the Polish government asking it to help quell the insurgents and make clear to them that the Commission was well on the road to restoring its authority.

In order to agree on any military plan, it seemed increasingly important to some British diplomats that civil and military Allied leadership in Upper Silesia be separated. Stuart had complained about the inappropriateness of the situation from the beginning. But neither Hardinge nor Curzon was successful in swaying the French to reconstitute the Commission on a civilian basis and the issue was dropped.[29] Lerond would continue to play the dictatorial president long after the Commission would be formally dissolved.

After several days of consideration the Allied military commanders unanimously reported that it would be possible to occupy

---

[28] Stuart to Curzon, no. 180, June 7, 1921 in ibid., no. 164 and Curzon to Hardinge, no. 308, June 8, 1921 in ibid., no. 166.

[29] Hardinge to Curzon, no. 368, June 9, 1921 and its accompanying note no. 7 in ibid, no. 167. See also Cabinet Meeting 21, June 21, 1921 in Cab 23, XXVI. While Stuart himself would have favored a major change in the Inter-Allied Commission, he considered that since it was not anticipated that the body would function much longer, it did not pay to press for a major overhaul of it. But "I shall never be able to cooperate cordially with a man whose word I cannot trust." Both Lerond and Gratier came in for heavy criticism from the Stuart-Heneker British team. See Stuart to Waterlow, June 12, 1921 in FO 371/5811, C 12502/92/18.

the zone between Polish insurgents and German self-protection
forces and to effectively keep them apart only if a minimum force
of 30,000 men was available. The French, in addition, maintained
that the insurgents were willing to retire progressively in accordance with Allied instructions and that within ten days of putting
such a plan into operation, the Commission could reoccupy the whole
of the insurgent area.

It was decided upon Stuart's proposal at the afternoon meeting of the Commission on June 9, that in the event of insurgent
refusal to honor the agreement for withdrawal, the Allied commander would use such force as was necessary to insure compliance.
Stuart himself found this intermediate zone plan or plan of
progressive withdrawal far from satisfactory, but since it was
the only plan then likely to be put into execution, he acquiesced
on condition that the withdrawals be made rapidly.

Analysis of the Silesian situation in early and mid-June 1921
would indicate three possible alternatives that would pacify the
country, restore order, and settle the frontier question. The first
of these was the French progressive withdrawal scheme already investigated. The second of these was General Heneker's scheme for
utilizing the Commission's troops to drive out the insurgents and
suppress the insurrection by force of arms--a scheme which depended on French cooperation and which it would be difficult, if not
impossible, to obtain. The last alternative was an early decision
on the frontier demarcation. No settlement of the Upper Silesian
question appeared imminent, however, because France and Britain
had conflicting aims here, Britain directing her efforts to quick
settlement and disentanglement and France hoping by delay to
strengthen Poland as part of the grand plan for French security.

Negotiations with the Germans on the progressive withdrawal
plan suffered in French hands until Stuart was successful in getting Lerond to reassign the conduct of the talks to General Heneker
and his chief staff officer, Colonel Dillon. In the course of
these talks, Höfer made it clear at the outset that the moral value
of holding the fortress at Annaberg made it impossible for him to
abandon that position, although he would be willing to gradually
reduce the number of his force as the insurgents on their side
retired. Heneker doubted that the Polish insurgents would regard
this an adequate *quid pro quo* for their successive withdrawals and
he eventually convinced Höfer to give way a little further on actual withdrawal. Hopes of the British Commissioner were not high
that the insurgents would approve the plan, but with the mid-June
weather turning wet and cold and the major fighting having stopped,
there appeared the possibility that less bellicose and ardent insurgents might reach some agreement. At the Commission meeting of
June 16, Stuart was unable to obtain Lerond's agreement that the
Germans should be permitted the whole of their present position if
the insurgents failed to fulfill their bargain under the plan. In-

stead, a compromise resolution was adopted which provided that in the event of either party's breaking faith, the other could return to position held at the stage before the breach took place.[30] But word arrived on June 21 that Höfer refused the new plan.

Höfer then proposed an alternative plan for reciprocal withdrawals, the chief feature of which was that the Poles should withdraw to the eastern boundary of Gleiwitz and the Germans, upon receiving Heneker's assurances that this action had taken place, would themselves evacuate Annaberg and the country behind it. When Stuart brought it before the Commission on the morning of June 22, Lerond categorically condemned it and insisted on the earlier plan. At this juncture, Stuart urged him to reconsider this proposal which involved but little concession on the part of the Allies. It would also provide the Germans with evidence of the good faith of the insurgents who would demonstrate their willingness to leave the industrial area. Lerond eventually agreed; a revised program of withdrawals to commence on June 25 was drawn up; and on June 24 unofficial word was received that the insurgents had relented. Finally, on June 26, Polish insurgents and Höfer's *Selbstschutz* signed the agreement for reciprocal withdrawal which under the revised schedule would be completed by July 5.[31]

There is no question that this was the first major step taken by the Commission which accounted for its restored authority in Upper Silesia. There is likewise no doubt that the British representative's initiative and the skill in reaching compromise which he exhibited, even in the face of his own personal preference for the use of force, were most influential in tempering General Lerond's attitude. Moreover, Heneker's success with Höfer must be credited to the skillful handling of the negotiations by the British commander. The promise at which Britain had hinted in the first days of June with her renewed and strengthened presence in

---

[30] Stuart to FO, no. 203, June 16, 1921 in FO 371/5912, C 12544/92/18.

[31] Correspondence between Stuart and the Foreign Office in DBFP, 1st ser., XVI, nos. 184, 185, 188, 190, 192, 193, and 198; Stuart to FO, no. 201, June 15, 1921 in FO 371/5911, C 12415/92/18; Stuart fo FO, nos. 190 and 198, June 14, 1921 in FO 371/5911, C 12368/92/18 and C 12413/92/18; numerous relevant documents appear in FO 371/5912. The Cologne Post [Upper Silesian Edition], a newspaper published by the British Army of the Rhine, reported that the Inter-Allied Commission had received Höfer's proposals for withdrawal on June 21 and that Stuart and Marinis supported them. The paper anticipated the Commission's acceptance but was unable to confirm this opinion. See The Cologne Post [Upper Silesian Edition], June 23, 1921, p. 1.

the plebiscite territory, she delivered before the month came to an end.

Throughout the course of these negotiations with Höfer and the insurgents, the British representatives continued their program of pressure upon the Warsaw government to close the frontier which Poland shared with Upper Silesia and to allow an Allied inspection at that border. Lieutenant Commander H. B. Rawlings, who represented Great Britain on that inspection team, reported that his observations on both the Silesian and Polish sides of the border convinced him that determined effort had been made by the Polish government to effectively close the frontier, even to the length of inflicting inconvenience and real hardship on Polish inhabitants themselves.[32] Had they acted as vigorously earlier as they had in late June, the Polish government could have helped prevent the decline of the Commission's authority to the depths to which it had plummetted. By July 5 the scheduled completion of the mutual withdrawal movements was complete and the Commission could once more be said to be the authority in Upper Silesia, a position tenuously held, more moral than effective, but nevertheless recognized by belligerents on both sides.

Crisis for the Entente

Even before the withdrawals were complete, Sir Harold Stuart proposed that the Plebiscite Commission return its attention to settling the frontier question. After several abortive attempts at this, the group reported on July 10 that it could not arrive at a unanimous decision and instead, it again called upon the Supreme Council to reach a prompt decision.

In the British War Office, Field Marshal Sir Henry Wilson, the C.I.G.S., who had reluctantly and begrudgingly dispatched his troops to the plebiscite area in early June, immediately speculated on the possibility of troop withdrawal when word arrived that the Commission had regained control of Upper Silesia. But no such notion was entertained in the Foreign Office where it was deemed essential to maintain a military presence until the final result was declared and danger of disorder was past, especially

---

[32] The Rawlings Report is transmitted in Müller to FO, no. 388, June 29, 1921 in FO 688, box 9, file 50, no. 529. His evaluation contrasted with the views expressed by his government earlier when it informed the Dominion Governors General that the Polish government "while dissociating itself from the movement, did not adequately restrain material assistance going from Poland to the insurgents." See Secretary of State for Colonies and Dominions to Governors General of Canada, Australia, New Zealand, Union of South Africa, June 2, 1921 in London, Beaverbrook Library, Private Papers of Lloyd George, F/9/3/49.

since recent irresponsible actions by the French had demonstrated the unsuitability of leaving their troops in complete charge of the area.[33]

Before word of the Plebiscite Commission's inability to reach a unanimous verdict arrived in Paris, the French government intimated that before its August meeting, the Supreme Council should be provided with a report compiled by an Allied committee of experts. Earlier the British government had accepted this proposal in principle only out of deference for Briand's new conciliatory mood, realizing that the divergence in views between the Commissioners was one of fundamental policy rather than of detail and that the consideration of an Upper Silesian settlement by such a group of experts was superfluous until a meeting of the Supreme Council could agree upon the broad principles of policy upon which an ultimate decision should rest. Sentiment in the Foreign Office was strongly directed against the French proposal on the grounds that Allied lawyers and engineers were already attached to the Commission and they could function adequately without the structure of a special committee. And there was little hope that the proposed substitution of diplomats for the members of the Commission would produce French representatives any freer to choose policy than General Lerond was.[34]

With new reports recounting the recrudescence of disorder in the territory and the realization that the Commission's authority was more tenuous, it was agreed that only with further troop reinforcements could the Allies confirm their control in the province. Stuart urged that a full British brigade be furnished. The well-known impartiality of British troops made their presence desirable, in his estimation, in an area where promoters of rebellion stood in need of some sobering. In response to the Commission's request for troops, the French government immediately consented to dispatch a division to Upper Silesia. Britain opposed a strengthening of the already heavy French control of the territory.

Around this issue of whether French or British troops should reinforce the Allied units in the plebiscite area arose a crisis that threatened to rupture the Anglo-French alliance, making Upper Silesia for the first time a primary interest to Britain as the field upon which she could maintain or destroy her relationship

---

[33] Memorandum by the C.I.G.S., July 8, 1921 in DBFP, 1st ser., XVI, no. 214. See also the attached minute by Ottley, July 12, 1921, the complete text of which is not published but appears in FO 371/5915, C 14313/92/18.

[34] FO minute by Ottley, July 12, 1921 in FO 371/5916, C 14365/92/18.

with France. France persisted during the tense days of July and
early August in pursuing the various avenues leading to an Upper
Silesian settlement: the deputation of the committee of experts,
setting a date for the Supreme Council meeting, and the dispatch
of reinforcements. The first two issues provided substance for
concession and *quid pro quo* during the confrontation on the reinforcement question; the last provided the unexpectedly explosive
material whose dismantling could only be achieved by careful
diplomacy.

   The growing abyss between the British and French in Upper
Silesia became increasingly evident as July progressed. The
Krappitz Incident of July 6 was only one event which exemplified
it. On that date General Gratier had employed French and British
troops to clear the area, acting contrary to orders of the Commission in both his treatment of inhabitants and his usurpation of the
authority which was reserved for the police. Only Curzon's caution
prevented the drafting of a "stiff" telegram to Paris at this time
to protest Gratier's action and to hint that recent French activities were seriously straining the Entente.[35]

   It was the opinion of Sir M. Cheetham at the British Embassy
in Paris that it was to France's advantage to delay the Supreme
Council meeting in order to allow her own prestige to grow with
the opening of the Washington Naval Conference in the Fall. Then
she could escape the confrontation with Britain and play off that
ally against the United States, effectively isolating Great Britain
and recapturing for herself the freedom of movement that her ally
had been so intent on tempering. In this matter Sir Eyre Crowe
calculated that the British government had two alternatives: (1)
to accept the procrastinating French position by indefinitely
postponing the Supreme Council session and calling together a committee of experts to deliberate and create the impression for public opinion that something was being done, or (2) to call a halt to
French Fabian tactics and make a serious attempt to persuade the
French government to agree to an early meeting of the Supreme Council. While neither course impressed him unduly, Crowe, the steady
observer of the Anglo-French pulse, preferred the first.

   Meanwhile, France unilaterally issued the fateful note of
July 6 to the German government which demanded among other things
that Germany provide transportation for such Allied reinforcements
as might be sent to Upper Silesia. Lerond in the name of the Plebiscite Commission repeated his request for reinforcements.

   In view of the delay in reaching a final Upper Silesian
settlement the British Commissioner urged his government to adopt

---
   [35]Stuart to Curzon, no. 275, July 20, 1921 in FO 371/5917,
C 14824/92/18 and Stuart to FO, no. 286, July 24, 1921 in FO 371/
5918, C 15000/92/18.

palliative measures. Stuart and Marinis proposed to resurrect the old German-Polish interim occupation scheme which aimed to reduce the size of the plebiscite area for which the Allies were responsible by immediately transferring to the German and Polish governments those portions of Upper Silesia whose final disposition was not in dispute. It was referred to the Conference of Ambassadors on July 24, in the belief that its acceptance could facilitate the work of the approaching Supreme Council meeting. Both interested governments immediately rejected this proposal. The Germans claimed such a tripartite division of Upper Silesia contrary both to the Treaty of Versailles and the economic and social necessities of the province. The Poles, eager for a definitive settlement, were apprehensive about its provisional element.[36]

But palliatives were not what Britain was seeking. What she desired was an early session of the Supreme Council, an immediate decision, one not delayed by prior investigations by committees of experts, as well as a brake on French interventionism in Upper Silesia in the hope that additional Allied troop commitments could be avoided. Numerous exchanges passed between the British and French governments in this regard, further complicated by the Franco-German dealings concerning the French note of July 16. Both of these threads of negotiation led to the same point: France, having publicly committed herself in each question, could not back down from the hard line she had taken vis-à-vis her ally, Great Britain, in the first instance, and Germany, the Behemoth against whom her whole security system was aimed, in the second. In both cases she attempted to extricate herself from the morass into which apparent carelessness had led her. In both cases Britain provided the diplomatic skill and imagination which not only prevented the dispatch of additional French troops to Upper Silesia but saved French face as well.

In the Anglo-French confrontation, Britain would not admit that France could unilaterally deploy troops to Upper Silesia although there was no question that France had assumed a disproportionate share of the burden and responsibility in that province as part of a larger scheme under which predominant roles had been assigned to each major power in the various European plebiscite areas. In the Franco-German confrontation over the July 16 note, which had come to assume such a troublesome character that its authorship was disavowed by individuals at the Quai d'Orsay, the French were dissatisfied with the reply from Berlin which they re-

---

[36] Aide-memoire handed to Briand on July 27, 1921 transmitted in Cheetham to FO, no. 2150, July 27, 1921 in FO 371/5919, C 15317/92/18. For the responses of the Polish and German governments see Roediger to Ottley, A. 2516, July 28, 1921 in FO 371/5920 C 15618/92/18 and Conversation with Polish Minister, July 29, 1921 in same volume, C 15625/92/18.

garded as impertinent. In effect, the German government said it would comply with the demand to arrange for the passage of the reinforcements if the Allies spoke with one mind when dispatching the troops.

The French government demanded either a clear affirmative or negative response. Lloyd George made frequent references to the unyielding French stand and how it was leading to a "rupture" in relations between the allies.[37]

Then the loophole that allowed France to back down gracefully was devised by Lord Hardinge. He suggested that the three Allied ambassadors in Berlin jointly inform the German government that it "must be prepared to facilitate the transport of Allied forces across Germany which the situation in Silesia might render necessary at any moment." Simultaneously, he proposed that the French government should privately assure the British government that no Allied force would be dispatched to Upper Silesia prior to the Supreme Council meeting at which the question of reinforcements would be considered. Briand accepted the plan gratefully and the British government applauded the initiative and the diplomatic victory scored by its ambassador in Paris.[38]

Britain had purchased her success with small concessions. She had acquiesced in the constitution of the committee of experts and sent her own representatives. She had agreed to the transfer of the Supreme Council meeting from Boulogne to Paris and to delay its opening to suit the French. She had exerted herself in removing "all ground of difficulty" in Berlin. But most of all, following an unusually uncompromising policy that tested the strength of the Entente bonds, Britain won the major battle on reinforcements, and the "tug-of-peace" that continued between the two Allies appeared at least for a time destined to proceed on Britain's terms.

Towards a Final Upper Silesian Settlement

When the Supreme Council convened on August 8, it took up the French proposal to send reinforcements to Upper Silesia. Britain had consistently opposed the dispatch of additional Allied troops

---

[37] Charles Hardinge, Lord Hardinge, Old Diplomacy: The Reminiscences of Lord Hardinge of Penshurst (London: Murray, 1947), pp. 257-61.

[38] DBFP, 1st ser., XVI, nos. 221 to 276. See also Lord Hardinge to Briand, July 29, 1921 in ibid., no. 272; FO memorandum by Ottley, July 21, 1921 in FO 371/5917, C 14898/92/18; minutes by Ottley, July 25, 1921 in FO 371/5918, C 14995/92/18; and minute by Ottley, July 26, 1921 in FO 371/5919, C 15479/92/18.

if a frontier decision could be announced before insurrectionary sentiment and unrest again erupted.[39] The French, on the other hand, preferred to have the troops on the spot in anticipation of trouble. If in early August the Allies only held Upper Silesia by moral force rather than by force of arms, disorders increased and the moral value of the Allied troops deteriorated within a fortnight. The Supreme Council returned to the reinforcement question and the British, French, and Italian governments decided to dispatch two battalions each to Upper Silesia. Consequently, a joint communication was made by the Allied representatives at Berlin on August 27 requiring facilities for the transport of these troops.

In addition to its handling the matter of Allied reinforcements, the Supreme Council, when it came into session on August 8, took up the report of the committee of experts regarding the partition of Upper Silesia. That committee had been faced with the conundrum of reconciling those boundaries already proposed by Lerond on one hand and Percival and Marinis on the other (see page 89). During their August 4 deliberations, the British delegation had advanced a new position in an attempt to compromise, but the small French concessions (see page 135) did not go far enough to allow the group to reach a unanimous decision.[40]

Upon receiving this report, the Supreme Council on the suggestion of Lloyd George, resubmitted the document to the experts for their reconsideration. The Prime Minister's action was prompted by the realization that Briand could more easily make concessions on the basis of the committee's recommendations than as a result of pressure in the Supreme Council. He also instructed the British members of the committee to report to him privately if it appeared that an agreement would be unlikely. Under these circumstances, he meant to take up the question again privately with Briand.[41]

---

[39] Briand and Lloyd George dined together on Sunday night and the British Prime Minister reiterated this hope on the part of his government to avert the reinforcement question. See the diary entry for Sunday, August 7, 1921 in George Allardice Riddell, Lord Riddell, *Lord Riddell's Intimate Diary of the Peace Conference and After, 1918-1923* (London: Victor Gollancz, Ltd., 1933), pp. 310-11.

[40] "Report of the Committee of Experts appointed to Study the Frontier to be laid down between Germany and Poland in Upper Silesia as a Result of the Plebiscite," August 6, 1921, confidential print, FO 371/5921, C 16101/92/18.

[41] Lloyd George to Chamberlain, August 10, 1921 in Private Papers of Lloyd George, F/7/4/22.

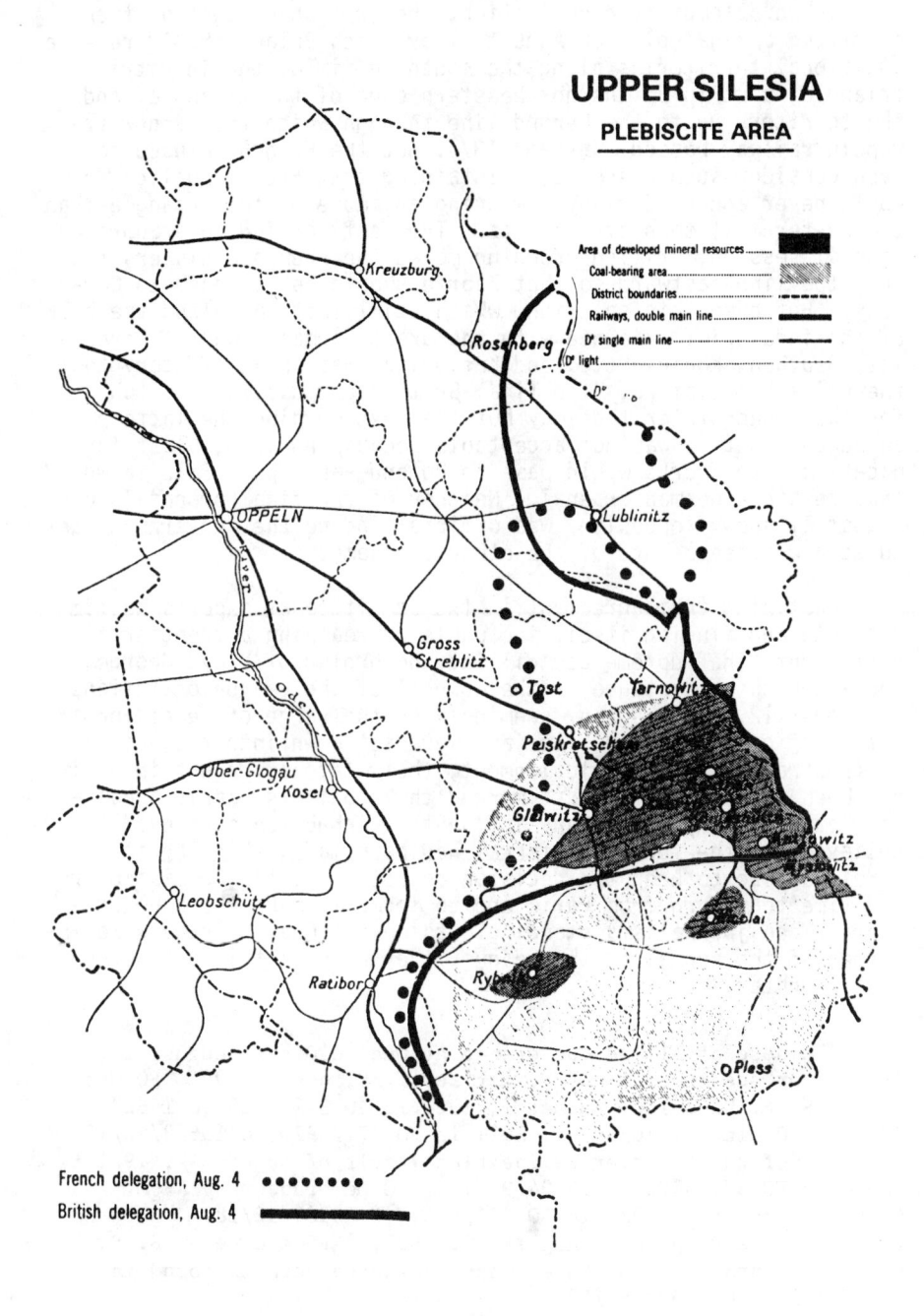

UPPER SILESIA
PLEBISCITE AREA

Area of developed mineral resources
Coal-bearing area
District boundaries
Railways, double main line
D° single main line
D° light

French delegation, Aug. 4 ••••••••
British delegation, Aug. 4 ━━━━━━

In an attempt at conciliation, the British delegation then submitted a final play on August 11 by which Poland should receive additional territories along the southern rim of the industrial triangle, a strip on the northeastern edge of the triangle, and the territory up to the Lerond line through which the Tarnowitz-Oppeln railway passed (see page 137). But the French refused to even consider such a scheme, maintaining that French public opinion would never accept Germany's winning any more of the triangle than the westernmost town of Gleiwitz. The next morning in a Supreme Council session, British prodding moved the French ministers to push the line eastward so that Zabrze should be assigned to Germany. But even this solution, which still left to Poland the bulk of the industrial triangle with the great German towns of Tarnowitz, Beuthen, Königshütte, and Kattowitz, was unsatisfactory to the British ministers. The final British proposal was sketched for the French later that day but the next morning the latter announced that it was not acceptable because no iron, blast furnaces, or steelworks would pass to Poland--and Upper Silesia would thus remain a German arsenal. Neither of the final proposals of August 11 shown opposite was official and neither government secured a written record of the other's scheme.[42]

Realizing that agreement in the committee of experts was impossible and finding itself incapable of reaching a frontier settlement, the Supreme Council, at the urging of Lloyd George, requested the assistance of the Council of the League of Nations on August 12. Once again, seemingly on the verge of receiving satisfaction, the Upper Silesians were let down into the trough of frustration and disillusionment, their fate as uncertain as it had been when they had first marked their ballots nearly a half-year earlier. Actually many influential inhabitants refused to believe that the further referral had been made, thinking it merely a ruse to keep the decision secret until the Commissioners had time to return from Paris and to formally make the announcement. When journalists standing outside the Quai d'Orsay were informed of the appeal to the League, they broke out into "incredulous laughter."

---

[42] Minute of Allied Conference at Quai d'Orsay, August 11, 1921, four sessions, in DBFP, 1st ser., XV, nos. 96-99. FO Minute by S. P. Waterlow, August 1, 1921 in FO 371/5920, C 15622/92/18. FO Minute, August 1, 1921 in FO 371/5920, C 15663/92/18. The text of the frontier delineation itself of August 12, 1921 is found in FO 371/5922, C 16394/92/18. FO Memorandum by A. M. Cadogan, August 5, 1921 in FO 371/5921, C 15980/92/18. "Note on the Frontiers Proposed," August 17, 1921, a FO minute by S. P. Waterlow containing the three maps presented here is found in FO 371/5922, C 16591/92/18.

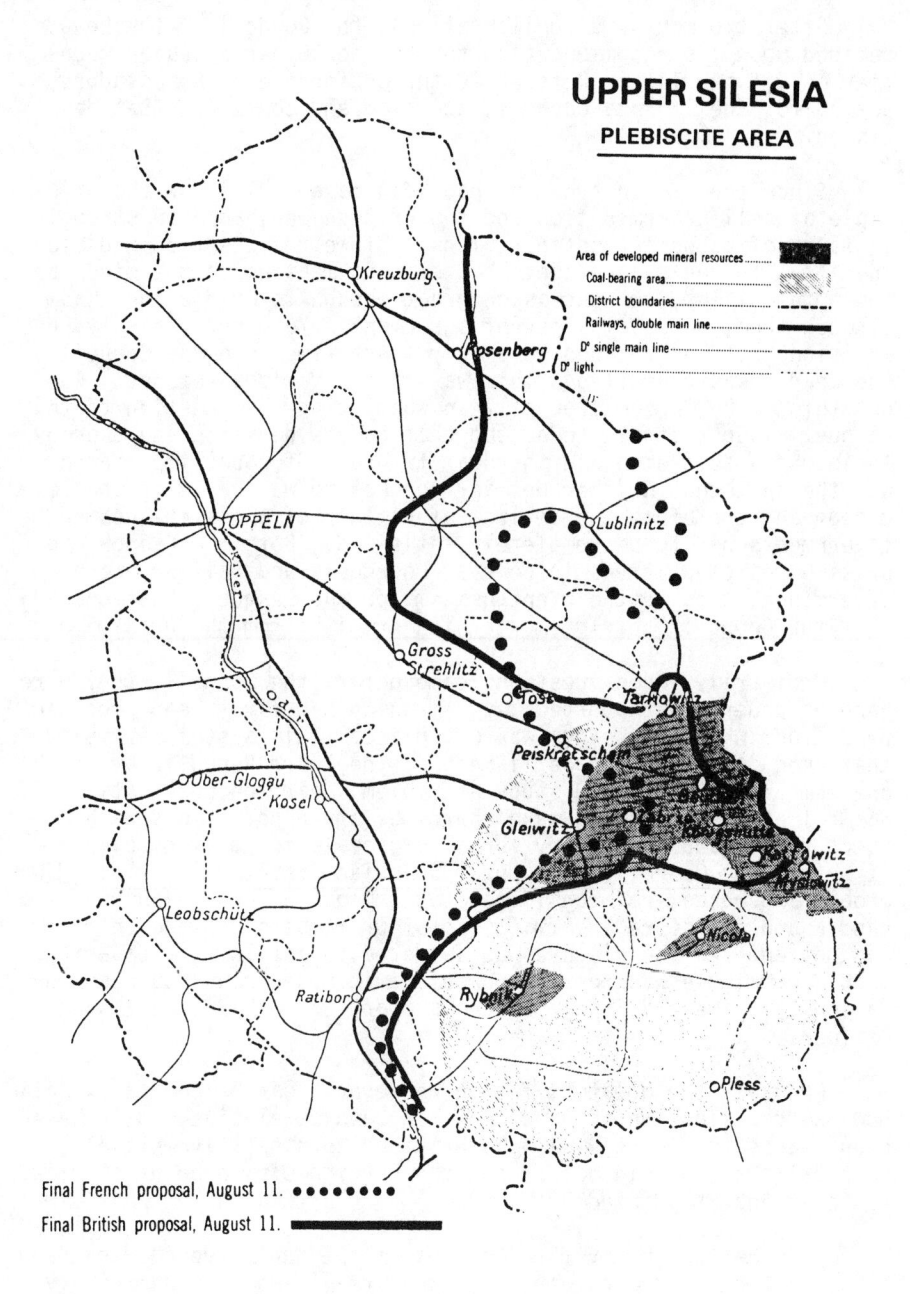

UPPER SILESIA
PLEBISCITE AREA

Area of developed mineral resources
Coal-bearing area
District boundaries
Railways, double main line
D° single main line
D° light

Final French proposal, August 11. ●●●●●●●●
Final British proposal, August 11. ▬▬▬▬▬▬

After two months of deliberations, the Council of the League decided upon its recommendation for the new Upper Silesian frontier on October 14; on October 20 the Conference of Ambassadors, acting for the Supreme Council, accepted and confirmed that decision.

Since the French argument had been based solely on the principle of self-determination and the British one had been strongly in favor of economic considerations, before the question had been submitted to the League there had been no meeting of the minds between the Allies, no concession great enough to bridge the chasm between them, no possibility of agreement. Yet, surprisingly, a decision had been reached in a very short time once the Council of the League was consulted. This was so for various reasons. For one thing, the Supreme Council, in submitting the question to the League, pledged itself to accept that body's decision and thereby to insure a settlement in the near future. Of equal importance was the fact that neither Germany nor Poland was party to the decision and therefore the desires of neither of these interested governments had to be completely satisfied. Both the French and British representatives in Geneva, Bourgeois and Balfour, were determined, too, in their enthusiasm for the League of Nations, that the Council "should emerge with credit" from the great test.[43]

Ordinarily, when questions came before the Council, they were handled under the rapporteur system which had first been proposed by Balfour when the League was organized. This system resembled that used in the French parliament of the Third Republic by which one member was chosen to study a problem, hear the observations of his colleagues on it, to take charge of any negotiations with respect to it, and to lay any formal proposals for action concerning it before the Council. The Upper Silesian issue, unlike most other problems handled, was considered too explosive for a rapporteur to handle and therefore a committee of four members whose countries had not entered the dispute was selected to act in that capacity. Such a committee was formed and before it made known its recommendations, it insured itself of the support of both Bourgeois and Balfour.

Probably the greatest factor, however, that helped to explain how the decision, which up to now had been so elusive, could have been reached so quickly was the British representative himself, Lord Balfour. He did not accept the Foreign Office point of view. As Louis Aubert pointed out

> He thought over the causes of the Anglo-French disagreement, he considered European realities and the relative

---

[43]F. P. Walters, A History of the League of Nations, 2 vols. (London: Oxford University Press, 1952), I, 87 and 146-55.

importance of the political and economic factors in the
indispensable work of reconstruction, and, little by
little, he came closer to the position taken by the
French negotiator, M. Leon Bourgeois, a position which
was intermediate between the first French and English
proposals, that the economic necessities of course must
be taken into account, but that they were not the most
important elements in the question for, in order to arrive at an equitable and lasting solution, one must first
of all give satisfaction to the wishes of the population
as expressed by the plebiscite, even if it was necessary
to cut into two parts that economic unit called the triangle.[44]

It is likely, too, that Balfour was influenced in this course by
Edouard Beneš, the Czechoslovak foreign minister who had been "dis-
creetly advocating the division of the Triangle" using the partitioned Teschen as an example of the success of such action.[45]

The summer of 1921 had witnessed a renewed British commitment
in both Danzig and Upper Silesia. Britain's initiative had put her
in the front row of contenders to profit from the development of
the port and transportation facilities at Danzig.

This initiative had also led her to a deeper involvement in
Upper Silesia whose importance to her until now had been little
more than peripheral. In order to put a quick end to her protracted and undesired involvement, she paradoxically assumed an effective, though unofficial, guidance of Allied policy there by bolstering her own prestige and by playing a major role in taking for the
first time a rather hard line which put her into opposition with
her French ally. She had not planned a confrontation with her
ally, nor had she intended to seriously test the strength of the
Alliance. But when the crisis unexpectedly erupted, even the
cautious Curzon and Crowe held fast to their stand--not because
they were pro-German, although Britain's interest in German economic integrity remained as constant as it had been at the peace
conference in 1919, but because for the first time her own
interests were at stake in Upper Silesia. Acquiescence to French
demands would have caused an irreversible inundation of that province with French influence and control, to the diminution of Brit-

___

[44] Louis Aubert, The Reconstruction of Europe: Its Economic and Political Conditions: Their Relative Importance (New Haven: Yale University Press, 1925), pp. 31-2.

[45] Walters, I, 155. Beneš, a devotee of the League who made himself heard in Geneva, chose a peculiar example. Teschen remained a stumbling-block to good Polish-Czech relations during all the years of his incumbency in the foreign ministry and presidency.

ish prestige and the reduction of Britain to the level of irrelevance and triviality. Yet, playing her historic role of compromiser, Britain extricated France from her difficulties and helped her save face in German eyes. However, it was nearly certain by August 1921 that she would not achieve her original aims of keeping the economically important industrial triangle intact for Germany. Moreover, the honorable disengagement which she sought appeared still a distressingly long way off and her last pence of obligation to the Treaty of Versailles, at least in Upper Silesia, was still left unpaid.

CHAPTER VI

TOWARDS THE RETURN TO A FAMILIAR ROLE

(October 1920 to July 1922)

Great Britain had long lived in a world where central and eastern Europe, unless they brewed problems that directly involved her, might not have existed at all. Her desire to maintain a disinterest in these areas had paradoxically led her to take an increased part in the settlement of their problems, confident as she was that her own efficiency in the carrying out of the provisions of the Treaty of Versailles would put a speedy end to her own unwelcome involvement. Her calculation had proved correct in Danzig where her complete control of the interim civil administration and major participation in the military occupation allowed her to dispose of the Treaty obligations before the year 1920 had come to an end. From that time, her interest in the Free City had been largely confined to making statements which upheld the sovereignty of the new state and to encouraging her investors to develop an interest in Danzig as a new market and also as a door fitted with a convenient customs union to Poland. But Britain's increased zeal to trade with the Free City by early 1922 gave the impression of being an exceptional phenomenon, a short promising interlude just on the eve of a return by Britain to a traditional policy of indifference.

How Britain took the initiative in the summer of 1921 among her Allies in Upper Silesia has already been studied above. As the disputed territory which had often provided the backdrop for Anglo-French tensions suddenly became the field upon which a confrontation between the Allies was enacted, Britain uncharacteristically held her ground and emerged from the difficulty with increased prestige but no less involvement. Her pursuance of a policy to discharge her obligations under the Treaty dutifully and fairly served only to prolong her stay in Upper Silesia. But she always looked forward to the day that she might put "finis" to the implementation of Article 88 and leave the territory. Here, as in Danzig, every indication was that she had worked hard to permit herself the luxury of returning to her historic disinterest and abandoning the inroads she had made with the recent show of initiative and newly-won prestige. By the middle of 1922 it seemed that the end of her dynamism had come and that Britain would return to her traditional policy.

Danzig: The International Company

The British government in mid-1921, as already seen, had eagerly sought a prominent place for its investors in the fertile field of Danzig, particularly in the development of the former German naval dockyard, the Danziger Werft. During the war the

Werft had been renowned for submarine production and late in 1919 it was transferred by the German government into the hands of the city of Danzig which installed as its director the capable engineer and administrator, Professor Ludwik Noë. He transformed the concern, which had heretofore been solely devoted to naval and aeronautical construction, into a civilian industry which by the end of 1921 employed about 4,000 men, built and repaired ships, manufactured machinery, and carried on several subsidiary industries.

The inter-allied commission which was charged with disposing of the former property of the German government in Danzig, proposed that the Polish and Danzig governments should jointly own the Werft and that it should be exploited by an international company formed with Allied capital. Both governments accepted this proposition in principle, and on September 23, 1921 a Polish-Danzig agreement was signed at Geneva which provided that the railway workshops, too, should be run by an international company. Like that designed to run the Werft, 45% of the capital was to come from Poland, 45% from Danzig, and 10% from foreign groups. This obvious parallel with the Werft served to identify these two questions and from the autumn of 1921, the disposition of the Werft and the exploitation of the railway workshops became a single issue.

Carr easily won the serious interest of Cravens, but the French member of the commission who demanded that French participation be equal to British, was unsuccessful in finding substantial backing among the firms in his country. Gilbert Rowe, chief engineer of Cravens who admittedly played along with the French to create the impression that their participation was welcome, made overtures to French firms to induce their cooperation, although that was a distinctly French task. The Société de Construction des Batignolles, already associated with Cravens in investments in Rumania, eventually agreed to subscribe a considerable portion of the French share and to win over other French firms to provide the remainder if Cravens took up the scheme for the British. But French commitments were nebulous: Chantiers Naval Français offered regrets in place of a pledge of francs and Batignolles was vague on the subscription it had been able to secure.

A rough scheme was drawn up during the Paris negotiations in November with Cravens, Batignolles, and Noë, but it became apparent that under this arrangement whenever an important question came before the Board of Directors, Poland and Danzig would in effect cancel each other out by their opposite views and the possibility of a complete deadlock would ensue if the British and French groups did the same. A solution was proposed in the form of Italian participation. Although Italy was a member of the commission with a right to take part, the British group did not particularly welcome her partnership and the French opposed it bitterly. In December, however, the Italian government announced that it proposed to participate in the Werft scheme on an equal basis with the British and French, but otherwise Italy's dilatory attitude for some time contributed nothing more than vague statements of her intended participation.

In early December the British and French groups sent representatives to Danzig to meet the commission for technical and financial conversations. Both sides were apprehensive about making serious commitments because the Werft needed an extremely large capital investment and there was a degree of uncertainty in the financial sphere, particularly in view of the fluctuations in the value of the mark.

They also took up the matter of the railway workshops. While they were technically better equipped than the Werft, the shops possessed two drawbacks from which the Werft was free: they comprised only one industry--locomotive repairs--and they had only one possible customer--Poland. In the talks, the potential investors thought that with some expenditure, locomotives might be manufactured and a wider market envisioned.[1] The talks ended with proposals to combine the Werft and railway workshops, preparations to continue negotiation with the Polish government, and arrangements to reconvene early in the new year with hopes that by that time the Italians would have more clearly defined their intentions. British representatives then returned to Warsaw and received confirmation of earlier assurances from the Polish government that it authorized a consortium of Polish banks to represent Polish interests in the railway workshop scheme and that it guaranteed a number of orders to make the exploitation profitable.[2]

Sir William Ellis of Cravens, at an interview with the British minister in Warsaw, informed Müller that the interested parties had agreed to form one company for the exploitation of both the Werft and the Troyl Workshops, in the interest of reducing overhead charges, and to make use of the services of Professor Noë as managing director of both undertakings because of the exceptional ability he had demonstrated in managing the Werft. The next day Rowe and C. F. Spencer, the chairman of Cravens, held a conference with the Polish bank consortium. It was anticipated that the company would be formed soon after a Polish-Danzig agreement was reached and Danzig's railways were turned over to Poland--probably no later than February 1, 1922. In fairness to the Polish government,

---

[1]"Report on the Proposed Exploitation of the Danziger Werft and Railway Workshops at Danzig by an International Company" transmitted in a letter from Carr to O'Malley, December 27, 1921 in FO 371/6825, N 14200/283/55.

[2]No. D. III, 10260, December 13, 1921 transmitted in Müller to FO, no. 745, December 14, 1921 in FO 371/6825, N 13823/283/55.

Müller believed that it was incumbent upon the British investors to waste as little time as possible in its formation. As Britain's first important venture in Danzig, it was important that this scheme towards which the Polish government had exhibited utmost good will should be brought to successful issue.

British representatives in Warsaw who had not been consulted when Spencer drew up the draft agreement on December 13, were subsequently dismayed when they read the document. One proposal they regarded unreasonable and too sweeping was that which exacted from the Polish government a guarantee to supply the Werft and Troyl workshops with the locomotives, wagons, and carriages for repair adequate in number to keep the existing works, as well as "any extension thereof," fully employed for ten years. British representatives also thought that the price which the Polish government was being asked to pay for the work done in connection with repairs and construction was too high. Not only was this amount to be calculated by covering the actual cost of the material and parts, but also by including salaries and special benefits which Danzig law provided for the workers, exceptionally high overhead charges, the cost of the first running test, as well as a sizeable guaranteed profit for the company. British representatives in Poland wanted to impress upon Cravens the importance of this first attempt on the part of their compatriots to invest in Danzig's industry and convince them that it was necessary to be fair and prevent giving rise to Polish resentment.

In February 1922 the French group formally declared its intention to participate in the venture in response to repeated British inquiries concerning their plans. About the same time as this declaration was made, Cravens' negotiations with the Warsaw government bore fruit and the guarantee from the Polish government to enable and justify the formation of the international company was received in terms approximating the requirements laid down by Spencer in December. This undertaking of the Polish government to Cravens and Batignolles stipulated Polish guarantees for contracts for the construction of locomotives for 15 years and for annual repairs until the year 1931. The company on the other hand was bound to purchase as much suitable material as possible of Polish manufacture and confine the Troyl workshops to repair work for locomotives, tenders, and carriages unless a subsequent agreement was reached to extend their activities. Other precautions were taken to insure the completion of the work pledged and to employ as many Poles as Danzig law allowed.[3]

---

[3]"Undertaking from the Polish Government to Cravens Ltd. and Société de Construction des Batignolles" enclosed in Gilbert Rowe to Commander Maxse, Personal, February 21, 1922 in FO 371/8129, N 1827/129/55.

But in early April 1922 it appeared that the birth of the international company, already long overdue, was destined to again be held up when it was discovered that Cravens were dealing individually with the Polish government through Noë without the knowledge of their French colleagues. Müller strongly objected to Spencer's "double-dealing" on the grounds that Cravens had received a good deal of assistance from the Legation and then attempted without the Legation's knowledge to initiate free-lance negotiations with the Polish government through a third party who, although he was now a Danziger, had until very recently been a German.

Meanwhile, The Times announced that other British plans for investment in Danzig had been completed.[4] British engineers had already reorganized some repair shops at Danzig with a view to reconstructing the railway system of Poland. The Times, which had since 1919 ordinarily pursued a policy favorable to the Poles, reported that the financial community in London had faith in Poland, as evidenced by the £5,000,000 credit it arranged for the Polish State Bank. It was understood that £1,000,000 of this was to be spent in Britain to purchase locomotives and equipment for railway repair shops in addition to raw materials. Such a procedure guaranteed more than a temporary advantage to British manufacturers of railway materials because the use of British standards would be safeguarded and the road to supplying Poland's future railway needs would be opened.

When in mid-May Banca Commerciale Italiana finally advised their government of their inability to participate in the company, one obstruction was cleared from the road. There remained the question of the Polish government's offering adequate collateral to insure a subsidy by the British government. When the Polish offer was judged inadequate by Spencer and the Department of Overseas Trade, it was suggested that "some security such as a lien on the gross railway receipts" should be offered. Such a lien might actually figure in a government budget statement.

If the D.O.T. was as serious about wanting collateral as it claimed to be, it was pushing Poland to play a dangerous game. That country had suffered a major financial crisis the previous autumn and was already in the opening stages of another governmental crisis that led to the forced resignation on June 6 of the entire Ponikowski cabinet which had been in office since September 1921. The price Britain asked was too high for the service she proposed to give. There was, after all, no assurance of the success of the international company and, although it was unlikely that Poland was aware of it, Noë and Spencer would probably have been as pleased to exclude the Poles from the enterprise as they would be to exclude the French.

---

[4]The Times Trade Supplement, April 15, 1922, p. 81.

Opinion in the Warsaw Legation was that Spencer wanted too much: "Both cast iron security and fat profits; a full share of Government support and complete liberty to disregard the advice of the officials on the spot. He wants a good beating."[5] All of this delay was having a bad effect in Poland, reflecting poorly on the British in general. Repeatedly, the Legation called upon London to apply pressure to Cravens at home to conclude the arrangement for the international company.[6]

Finally, the agreement constituting the company was signed on September 22, 1922[7] putting to an end more than a year of volleying between the investors and the Polish government. The text of the agreement made no mention of the Polish government's providing collateral--an issue which had stalled the negotiations for some months. Instead, it appears that the British were content to receive "an acceptable guarantee for the fulfillment of its obligations" on the part of that government. With the conclusion of the agreement, British industry had a valuable financial foothold in the Free City where before long Britain would be called upon to put a critically ill financial house in order.

Danzig, the Allies, and the League of Nations

Since Britain had withdrawn from the civil administration and military occupation of Danzig late in 1920 she had attempted to clear her accounts with the Free City and collect the payments due her for performing these functions. During this period of the growth of her commercial interest there, she periodically submitted

---

[5] Hoare to FO, no. 264, May 26, 1922 in FO 371/8129, N 5238/129/55 and in the same registry a confidential unaddressed and unsigned letter [Hoare to O'Malley], May 26, 1922. Reytiens (D.O.T.) to O'Malley, June 1, 1922 in FO 371/8129, N 5529/129/55.

[6] "Please try to get a move on with the final formation of that wretched international company for the Werft and Danzig Railway shops. The thing is rapidly becoming a scandal. It is quite absurd that the drafting of the articles of association should take all these months. My conviction--not susceptible of proof, is that Noë, who of course does not want the French in the business, is playing for time, probably with the tacit encouragement of Spencer. Not only can we not be parties to this sort of thing but we should resent it vigorously as we are pledged both to the French and to the Poles. . . ." See Hoare to O'Malley, June 9, 1922 in FO 371/8129, N 5703/129/55.

[7] A text of this agreement was transmitted in Consul Fry's dispatch no. 110 to the FO of September 25, 1922 in FO 371/8129, N 9018/129/55.

the claim, several times was convinced to amend her demands, but was destined to keep the debt outstanding until mid-decade.

Early in 1921 the British government assessed the city for the military occupation costs and France also attempted to secure reimbursement for the services of her troops there. Among other reasons, Danzig objected to this charge because under the terms of an arrangement concluded in Paris, she was meant to pay only "an equitable proportion" of the full cost of the Allied occupation. Furthermore, the commander of the occupying force had not been exclusively at her service but had also been in charge of the troops in the East Prussian plebiscite area.

In reply to her arguments, the Foreign Office recalled that earlier in 1922 an inter-departmental meeting had considered this issue and agreed that "equitable proportion" was probably intended to mean a division of costs between Danzig and the plebiscite area of East Prussia. On this basis, the British government felt justified in maintaining its claim that Danzig should pay the full bill because it had already been divided proportionally between her and the Allenstein and Marienwerder plebiscite districts. However, it was willing to accept a scheme of payment by gradual installments if the financial situation in Danzig did not permit immediate reimbursement.[8]

A similar offer was made on the related question of payment for the temporary civil administration of Danzig which involved only Great Britain who had performed this task alone. The British claimed payment of £14,835 12s 3d for this service and, in view of the fact that expenses connected with the High Commissioner's post at Danzig were paid in equal parts by the governments of that city and Poland, it assumed that the costs of the temporary administration should be similarly shared. Poland objected to the assessment on the grounds of the "equitable proportion" clause. If that proportion was intended to be one between Danzig and the plebiscite areas, Poland claimed to be excluded from consideration and the civil administration which was solely Danzig's should be financed by the Free City alone. Poland won her case.[9]

Because of its peculiar status in the family of nations, Danzig was the subject of many questions that never needed to be asked when dealing with other sovereign entities--questions, for example, regarding the function of foreign representatives toward her or the application of the niceties of protocol there. Müller

---

[8] FO to Hardinge, no. 1499, May 17, 1922 in FO 371/8142. See "General Report by the Secretary-General for the 18th Session of the Council," L of N C. 251.M.139.1922.I, May 15, 1922, filed in FO 371/8138, N 4872/1734/55.

[9] FO 688, box 11, file 39.

preferred the French attitude toward dealing with the credentials of a minister who served in Warsaw vis-à-vis the Free City of Danzig to that expressed by his own government. In practice, he maintained, foreign representatives in that capital acted as agents through whom Danzig's foreign relations were conducted; therefore, he strongly favored the French viewpoint that a clause should be inserted in the letters of credence of foreign representatives serving in Warsaw stipulating that their jurisdiction extended to questions of Danzig's foreign relations which were conducted under the terms of the Versailles Treaty and the Danzig-Polish Convention by an intermediary, the Polish Foreign Minister.

His point of view was largely supported in the Foreign Office until legal advisers considered its ramifications. Sir Cecil Hurst, for example, pointed out that since the terms of the Treaty of Versailles made clear that Poland should undertake the conduct of Danzig's foreign affairs, it was impossible after the ratification of that Treaty "for any diplomatic representative to be accredited to Poland without his competence extending to all matters falling properly within the scope of the activities of the Polish government, and therefore, covering the foreign relations of the Free City." Despite Müller's support for the French position, Hurst regarded it otherwise on various grounds: it was superfluous, possibly related to France's desire to see the status of ministers who were accredited to Poland also recognized in Danzig, and potentially embarrassing to Britain should the French try to apply the principle to the British dominions where the mother country directed foreign policy.[10] This question did not much affect the conduct of Anglo-Polish affairs, but it is representative of those questions which continually arose because of Danzig's special and difficult-to-define status.

During the eighteenth session of the Council of the League of Nations held between January and May 1922, ten questions related to Danzig affairs appeared on the agenda, five of which were appeals against decisions of the High Commissioner. None of these need be analyzed here in any detail, but a general observation on the posture assumed by Great Britain respecting them is useful in determining British policy toward the Free City during the first half of 1922. Among the points at issue were the financial situation of Danzig and the question, as already seen, of the city's ability to pay the costs of Allied military occupation. Other items were related to the conduct of foreign affairs, the expulsion of Polish nationals, and other such problems which were by-products of the stipulations of the Treaty of Versailles.

---

[10]Minutes of H. F. Crookshank, L. Collier and G. Mounsey of October 21, 25, and 27, 1921 respectively in FO 371/6825, N 11572/283/55. Müller to Curzon, no. 9, January 6, 1922, FO 688, box 11, file 39, no. 4.

A bone of contention between Poland and Danzig was the interpretation of Article 2 of the Polish-Danzig Treaty of November 9, 1920 which stated that "Poland shall undertake the conduct of the foreign relations of the Free City of Danzig." Poland, in her attempt to reduce the Free City to a satellite in her own orbit, held the view that she could conduct these affairs as she pleased, even to the detriment of her diminutive neighbor. The Danzig government, on the other hand, regarded Poland as a mere agent who should conduct the city's affairs in accordance with the wishes of Danzig, even if they were inconsistent with Poland's policy. To this, the High Commissioner, when asked for a decision, concluded that Poland had a right to refuse to conduct Danzig's affairs according to the Free City's wishes if the matter involved was "clearly to the detriment of the interests of the Polish state." But Danzig must be so informed within thirty days. However, Poland by the same token had no right to initiate and impose upon Danzig a policy clearly opposed to that city's interests. When both parties appealed the decision and the British government took the matter under consideration in order to provide advice for its representative on the Council of the League, it adopted the view of Consul B. F. Fry in Danzig. He was of the opinion that in order to avoid unnecessary friction between the powers in this area of Europe and to secure the stability of the region, it was necessary for Great Britain to "take a firm line against any encroachment on the autonomy of the Free City" as guaranteed by Articles 101 and 105 of the Treaty of Versailles. In line with this, the Foreign Office informed Balfour in Geneva that the decision of the High Commissioner should be upheld.[11] Whenever issues regarding Danzig came before the League, Britain tended to either support the High Commissioner's anticipated decision or, at least, register no objection to it. One is almost left with the impression that in the Foreign Office, after all was said and done, these questions were deemed not important enough to worry about. There was unquestionably no direct British political interest in these Danzig issues and the legal interest expressed was directed at upholding the "Free City" status and at liquidating the Danzig question as a perennial problem to the powers--a point most succinctly captured in a Foreign Office observation that "It is fortunate that there are not more Free Cities under the League."

Expediting the Settlement in Upper Silesia

It has been suggested that while Britain maintained her initiative in Upper Silesia late in 1921 and early in 1922, her efforts were in reality aimed at a settlement which would presage

---

[11] League of Nations document C 116.M.69.1922.I, March 17, 1922 in FO 371/8131, N 2691/279/55. Cabinet Secretary to FO, 38/C/20, April 6, 1922 in FO 371/8131, N 3314/279/55. Fry to FO, no. 7, May 8, 1922 in FO 371/8138, N 4510/1734/55.

the withdrawal of her troops from the area. No sooner had the decision been announced, then, before British speculation began anew regarding those obligations which were still outstanding and in need of fulfillment before the protracted involvement could be terminated.

The settlement, as recommended by the League and as adopted by the Conference of Ambassadors on October 20, 1921,[12] provided for the location of the frontier dividing the Upper Silesian province into German and Polish territory and for the conclusion of a Polish-German convention dealing with specific economic issues. Most of Rybnik and Pless in the industrial basin fell to Poland (See map, page 151) as did Königshütte (Królewska Huta), most of Beuthen Land, and Kattowitz (Katowice). The towns of the industrial triangle that were allocated to Germany were Gleiwitz, Hindenburg, and Beuthen. Farther north most of Tarnowitz and Lublinitz went to Poland.

The intention of this settlement was not only to delineate the frontier that had been so elusive for others who had attempted the task earlier, but also to obviate, in so far as possible, the economic dislocation of the province by providing it with a 15-year interim period for economic readjustment. During this period the German mark would remain the legal unit of currency for the entire plebiscite area until Germany and Poland modified the system; no tariff would be imposed on raw material passing from one side of the frontier to the other; railways would operate as a single system; light, power and water systems were to continue operating without interruption; and Germany was forced to permit the export of the products of its Upper Silesian mines to the Polish zone as laid down by Article 90 of the Treaty of Versailles. All these precautions were to be executed by two new bodies, a Mixed Commission and an Arbitral Tribunal.

Announcement of the award was received calmly in most cases. In the plebiscite area itself there was little disturbance at first. Some rumors still persisted that the entire Upper Silesia would be converted into an independent autonomous state.[13]

---

[12]League of Nations Document C.420.M.301.1921.VII, October 14, 1921 in PRO 30/52, box 9. "The Upper Silesian Award as Confirmed by the Conference of Ambassadors, 20th October 1921" with footnotes indicating the differences between its text and that proposed by the Council of the League of Nations appears in H. W. V. Temperley (ed.) A History of the Peace Conference of Paris, 6 vols. (London: Oxford University Press, 1920), VI, 623-30.

[13]The German-oriented independence movement which fell flat was led by one Stroka who proposed to become president of the new state. Proclamations in all numbering about 10,000 copies, which

ILLUSTRATING UPPER SILESIAN AWARD 1921

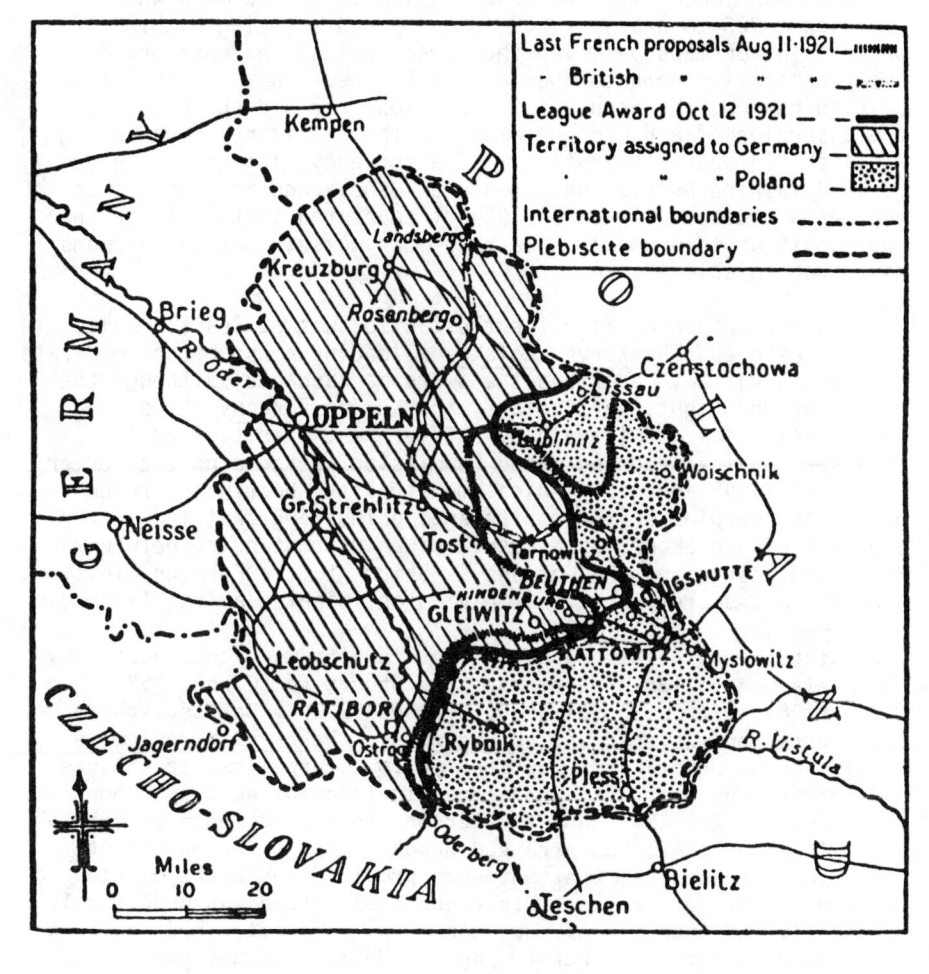

The Germans felt dejected over the loss of virtually the whole of the industrial area of the plebiscite territory. Suffering a grave setback in its foreign policy by the Upper Silesian decision, the Wirth government resigned and a new government, again under Joseph Wirth, was constituted. In addition, the Weimar Republic was faced with the sudden collapse of the mark which fell from about 300 to nearly 1,200 to the pound sterling within a few weeks. The Germans believed that Great Britain had performed a great disservice both to them and to Europe. In their estimation Britain had not obtained a fair decision; nor had she prevented the assertion of a French hegemony on the continent. The Foreign Minister, in what D'Abernon termed a threnody, lamented in exaggerated fashion British negligence at Geneva and abandonment of the German cause. Sir Harold Stuart countered that "but for the English it would probably have been much worse," but the Germans were inconsolable.[14]

Polish response, if not enthusiastic, was at least complacently resigned. The Kuryer Polski, a leading newspaper of moderate opinion in Warsaw, described the award as laudable, although the papers of the right, particularly the Kurjer Poranny--"that uncompromising foe of His Majesty's Government"--criticized the frontier and the proposed Mixed Commission, describing the former as "a political and geographical monstrosity" bearing no resemblance to the plebiscite results and insinuating that the latter's appearance came about "as a result of an understanding between Mr. Lloyd George and the Germans." Skirmunt, the Foreign Minister, however, was secretly content, having anticipated a less favorable

---

were distributed by him appealing for support were confiscated by the Kreis Controller of Beuthen. See Stuart to FO, no. 152, October 28, 1921 in FO 371/5930, C 21001/92/18. Earlier, the Beuthen correspondent in Przegląd Wieczorny (The Evening Review, a local evening paper known for its "yellow journalism" techniques), had carried out energetic propaganda in favor of an autonomous state and alleged that Captain Pearson, an aide-de-camp to General Sir William Heneker, had arranged supper parties for prominent Poles to persuade them that autonomy provided the best solution to the Upper Silesian tangle. Since the publication was notoriously unreliable and sensational, and since the accusation had not been reproduced in the major Warsaw papers, Müller had not considered it worthwhile either to inform the FO or to have Heneker issue an attraction-gaining *dementi*. See Müller to FO, no. 512, September 5, 1921 in FO 688, box 9, file 50, no. 694.

[14]D'Abernon to Curzon, no. 505, October 27, 1921 in Documents on British Foreign Policy, 1919-1939 (hereafter DBFP), 1st ser., XVI, no. 357. Stuart to Crowe, October 28, 1921 in FO 371/5930, C 21066/92/18.

decision. On October 26 the Polish Diet unanimously accepted the decision of the Allied Powers, realizing that whatever of value had remained in the plebiscite area, most of it now would pass under Polish sovereignty even though not all Polish claims had been filled.[15]

Britain's response, as that of a disinterested power who had participated in the making of the settlement, was, on the one hand, one of satisfaction that finally the end of the unexpectedly long issue was in sight and, on the other, of disappointment that the policy she had so long pursued had not been vindicated. She had particularly upheld the economic integrity of the industrial area of Upper Silesia even to the point of subordinating to it the principle of self-determination as expressed in the results of the plebiscite.

Almost immediately from the day of the announcement of the League's decision, Müller began to urge the Polish government to make specific plans and preparations for their takeover of the awarded territory. In the plebiscite area General Heneker issued a special order of the day to impress upon his troops that it was their duty "to refrain from giving expression to any criticisms of the decision" which, once confirmed by the Conference of Ambassadors based upon the recommendation of the League, became the statement "accepted by the Governments of His Majesty and of His Allies."

Sir Maurice Hankey, Secretary of the Cabinet, received the decision less calmly. In a personal letter to Lord D'Abernon which he did not want quoted, he described the Upper Silesia problem as "extraordinarily badly handled at the League of Nations."[16] Before the question had been referred to the League, Hankey had discussed the matter with Sir Eric Drummond, the Secretary-General of the international body, who had assured him that it would almost certainly be referred to an independent tribunal. The irascible Hankey later overreacted when he strongly criticized the League's method of handling the issue and told Drummond that as a result of it, the "official world in Britain" had lost all confidence in the League.[17]

---

[15] Müller to Curzon, no. 412, October 16, 1921 in DBFP, 1st ser., XVI, no. 343. See dispatches of Müller to Curzon, nos. 628 and 646, October 18 and 29, 1921 in FO 688, box 9, file 50.

[16] M. P. A. Hankey to D'Abernon, Private and Personal, October 26, 1921 in British Museum, D'Abernon MSS, fol. 48953B.

[17] M. P. A. Hankey to Prime Minister, October 26, 1921 enclosing Hankey to Drummond, October 21, 1921 in London, Beaverbrook Library, Private Papers of Lloyd George, F/25/2/35.

The development of British policy in late 1921 regarding Upper Silesia did not hinge on the general question of the decision. Rather, having accepted the recommendation of the League and having participated in the Ambassadors' confirmation, Britain exercised her own initiative, not by favoring or deploring the settlement, but by urging the acceptance of a specific method for its implementation.

France, playing her game of delay tactics, represented in the Conference of Ambassadors the point of view that "fixing" the frontier meant literally fixing it on the ground. If this definition were accepted, the fixing could go on indefinitely and therefore the notification which should follow immediately and the thirty day period within which the transfer of authority should be carried out, would all be postponed. Hardinge was unable to dissuade the Ambassadors from accepting the French definition.

The British ambassador was successful, however, in garnering support among his colleagues to override another French proposal and to adopt instead a compromise draft which stipulated that the Economic Council had to be concluded as a prerequisite for the application of the frontier. The French had more than once hinted that the only important part of the Upper Silesian award was the frontier settlement. Once it was carried out, the French believed, no one could force Germany and Poland to implement the Economic Agreement, the "secondary" part of the decision. Hardinge succeeded in winning the Allies to the British point of view that assurances should be given that the Economic Convention would be carried out prior to the notification of the frontier.[18]

In Upper Silesia, British leadership was oriented to as quick a withdrawal as possible after proper safeguards for the conclusion of the Economic Convention had been taken. Sir Harold Stuart deplored the French dallying with their far-fetched definition of "fixing" the frontier.[19] Before this task of the Boundary Commis-

---

[18]Hardinge to FO, no. 2905, October 22, 1922 in FO 371/5929, C 20337/92/18 and Hardinge to Curzon, no. 835, October 31, 1921 in DBFP, 1st ser., XVI, no. 362.

[19]Stuart wrote: "God knows when we shall see an end of the occupation; and even if the decision is left to the Plebiscite Commission I am by no means sure that my two Colleagues will be in a hurry to take a step which will deprive them of their offices and emoluments. They both contemplate with complacency being here until February. That would be a scandal, for the frontier is quite easy to make out on the ground, since it follows the limits of the communes, and once the Convention is concluded there will be no excuse whatever for our delaying the measure which will put an end to our existence." See Stuart to Crowe, October 28, 1921 in FO 371/5930, C 21081/92/18.

sion could commence, the boundary had to be plotted on the map and while many prognostications were made and revised concerning its date of completion, the job was in fact not finished until December 19, 1921.

German and Polish representatives were chosen to negotiate the Economic Convention which was provided for in the Upper Silesian settlement. The Council of the League selected Felix Calonder, a former president of the Swiss Confederation, to preside over the negotiations. The British government supported his appointment and endorsed his desire that the proceedings begin at once. On November 23 the negotiations began in Geneva, and from December 9, 1921 through the following month they continued in Upper Silesia.

The remaining months of 1921 were spent in mutual recrimination on the part of the Poles and Germans over the alleged continued detention of Upper Silesians in German and Polish concentration camps and disturbances caused by armed German bands in Kreis Ratibor. The first of these was solved by the dispatch of Allied inspection commissions and the second was dealt with by the Plebiscite Commission, which was assisted by pressure from Berlin on the leaders of the irregular forces.[20]

The End of the Interlude

If Upper Silesia was the scene of a dispute between Germany and Poland, it was also the field upon which a diplomatic struggle between Britain and France had been, and continued to be, enacted. During the six months of 1922 which preceded the Allied withdrawal, Allied authority had been restored and Great Britain ceased to pursue with such vigor as earlier, the guidance of Allied policy there. However, she did not abandon altogether the role of trying to restrain France in the extremes to which she was given when dealing with Germany, her arch-enemy, and with Poland, her ally and key to her eastern European policy. British conduct in Silesia during the first half of the year implied that Britain was returning to thoughts of withdrawal and disinterest after the passing of the exceptional interlude.

The major episode during these months, in which context the Anglo-French antagonism occurred, grew out of what came to be called the Petersdorf Affair. The French, who sponsored and car-

---

[20]Heneker to FO, no. 262, November 20, 1921 in FO 371/5932, C 22163/92/18. The kidnapping issue is dealt with at length in the Warsaw Legation Archives, FO 688, box 9, file 50. The best single paper of this collection that describes the situation is "Report on Visit to Sosnowice and Neighbourhood" by Colonel Clayton, December 1921 in FO 688, box 9, file 50, no. 823.

ried out a continuing policy of search for arms in Upper Silesia directed against the German population, were themselves attacked in retaliation by a force of local Germans in the early hours of January 31, 1922 when French troops were guarding a cache of such confiscated arms in the school which served as the barracks in Petersdorf, a suburb of Gleiwitz. Two French soldiers died from the wounds sustained in this encounter. As a result, the Inter-Allied Commission declared a state of siege in the Gleiwitz area and, at the request of General Lerond, appointed a court of inquiry.[21] Further, France made unilateral representations to the German government in which she accused the Germans of complicity in the attack and claimed the right to demand compensation. Stuart sympathized with the French in their loss but he deplored their search policy for the same reasons both he and Colonel Percival before him had objected to it. Not the least of his reasons was the belief that its continuation created a serious danger of disturbance in Upper Silesia and of attack on Allied military and civilian personnel in the whole province.

In the Commission's estimation, the practice of searching for arms was due mainly to the secret service which was a branch of the Department of the Interior. It was entirely French in constitution, "grossly partial" in orientation, and illegal in methods. With this in mind and with the realization that the end of the Allied presence in Upper Silesia was not imminent, Stuart proposed a reorganization of the secret service whose activities were totally divorced from that of the police. He successfully pressed for their reconstitution on an inter-allied basis with British direction of the intelligence section.[22]

Sir Harold Stuart, who had never supported the French project of search for arms, urged the Commission to restrict such practices. He proposed that no searches be conducted in the future without the previous sanction of the Commission except in cases of extreme emergency. General Lerond countered with a proposal that would permit the military authorities to conduct unlimited searches on their own responsibility with no restriction other than the approval of the Kreis Controller. Ostensibly, Stuart's persuasive and timely arguments won the day. But the compromise by which Lerond's qualifying phrase *en particulier dans le cas d'une menace imminente contre la sécurité des troupes* was added to the prohibition against the search did little to alter French intentions and conduct.

---

[21] FO 890, part 13.

[22] A strictly confidential draft (508/BC/21) of the proposed reorganization plan of February 1, 1922 appears in FO 890, part 2, file 2K. See also Heneker to Hardinge, no. 9, February 25, 1922, in DBFP, 1st ser., XVI, no. 378.

A court of inquiry which had been constituted to investigate the Petersdorf Affair issued a report of its findings which pointed to the fact that elements of the powerful *Selbstschutz* had directed the attack on the Allied troops at Petersdorf. Moreover, their arms and equipment had come in part from Germany, and the level of their organization was so highly sophisticated as to have been made possible only "with complicity of state officials."[23] Incorporated into the report which was submitted to the Conference of Ambassadors, these conclusions provided the basis for repeated French attempts to initiate an Allied condemnation of Germany and to prepare a case against her in order to exact penalties and reparations.

The Conference decided to instruct the Allied ambassadors at Berlin to request that the German government assist in the search for the individuals whose warrants for arrest had been issued as a result of the inquiry. Two difficulties arose in this respect: Germany did not recognize the authority of the temporary court which issued the warrants, and the Conference of Ambassadors had been led to believe that the warrants charged the individuals with complicity in the Petersdorf Incident whereas in fact they merely charged the individuals with membership in secret societies. Regarding the first of these, Germany's response would probably be negative; regarding the second, it could create a situation in which nearly the entire Upper Silesian population could be liable to arrest for its participation in secret, self-protection groups.

The British government had three possible alternatives to pursue in this "tiresome and dangerous dispute." First, it could instruct Lord D'Abernon to join his colleagues and ask for the assistance of the German government in carrying out the arrests. The drawbacks of this plan did not recommend this course to the Foreign Office. Second, the Foreign Office might explain to Lord Hardinge in Paris and to the French ambassador in London that while it was Britain's desire to bring to justice those guilty of the death of the unfortunate French soldiers, she could not cooperate with her allies in this particular action because it had no connection with that objective. But it was feared that such action would not only damage the prestige of the Commission, but also be misunderstood by the French as a hopelessly pro-German step. A third alternative, adopted by the Foreign Office with some reluctance, was to ask Sir Harold Stuart, who had returned to London, to go back to Upper Silesia and straighten things out, at the same time assuring the French of Britain's desire to help. Although Stuart was soon to undergo serious surgery and could not return to Oppeln, he obliged the Foreign Office by reading the relevant papers, possibly as a preparation for a trip to Paris if necessary. He concluded that the response was generally too

---

[23]Heneker to FO, no. 17, February 17, 1922 in FO 371/7471, C 2393/91/18.

hysterical. Then in the same cool and capable manner he had exhibited upon his arrival in Upper Silesia nearly a year earlier, he recommended a suitable line of action: to make no joint representations at Berlin, but rather to employ the routine arrangement for the mutual arrest and surrender of accused persons wanted for trial in the plebiscite area and in occupied Germany respectively.

Other disorders of a nature similar to that of the Petersdorf Incident followed, like that at a Gleiwitz mortuary where on April 9 an explosion killed several French soldiers while they were carrying out an arms search. Again, the stories were similar, with French at first claiming German guilt, then being persuaded to await a full report of the Inter-Allied Commission, and finally dropping the matter when the investigation proved no German complicity.[24]

In British eyes, all the disturbances in Upper Silesia were either caused or heightened by the presence of the French whose pro-Polish and anti-German attitudes were no secret. One of the major reasons for Britain's repeated call for an early withdrawal from the province was a desire to contribute to calming the embroiled atmosphere by speeding the evacuation of the French troops. Despite Britain's conscious attempts to be impartial, the nonfraternizing and aloof conduct of her representatives in the plebiscite area, when compared to French behavior there, usually took on the coloring of being German-sympathizing and periodic reports or complaints of that nature reached the attention of the British Commissioner at Oppeln or the General commanding British forces in Upper Silesia. These accusations were systematically denied and when it appeared that they might begin to affect Britain's relations with Poland adversely, Commission personnel contemplated the release of propaganda articles to the press to counteract their effects.

During the first half of 1922 besides the Petersdorf Incident and such related disturbances, two other major events occurred which were related to Upper Silesia and in which the British government played only an indirect role--the negotiation and signature of the German-Polish Economic Convention of May 15 and the events surrounding notification of the frontier, transfer of territory, and evacuation of the Allies.

It will be recalled that in accordance with the provisions of the Upper Silesian award, it was necessary to conclude an economic convention between Germany and Poland in order to cushion Upper Silesia's economic adjustment after the date of transfer of

---

[24] Heneker to FO, April 10, 13, 13, and 19, 1922 in FO 371/7472 with the following registry numbers respectively: C 5362/91/18, C 5468/91/18, C 5479/91/18, and C 5714/91/18.

sovereignty. Negotiations to this end which began in November 1921 under the presidency of Calonder, continued into the next year. The only British voice heard throughout these negotiations was one calling for an early settlement, thus giving the impression that any agreement would do as long as it was concluded quickly. Characteristically, the War Office urged a speedy settlement in order to pave the way for the long-awaited British withdrawal from Upper Silesia.

First, the expropriation agreement was signed on April 12, 1922.[25] When the Polish plenipotentiary in the negotiations, Kasimir Olszowski, spoke with the British Commercial Secretary at Warsaw, R. E. Kimens, he explained that the Polish view with respect to expropriation rights for the next 15 years held that all property in German hands on January 20, 1920 was liable to expropriation under Articles 92 and 297 of the Treaty of Versailles whether it was retained under German ownership or was sold to an owner of another nationality. A foreigner, then, who acquired real property in that portion of Upper Silesia assigned to Poland or who purchased shares in such a company might be forced to sell by order of the Polish government upon the expiration of the 15-year term recommended by the League of Nations. He was careful to intimate to Kimens, however, that British companies or individuals who first sought the consent of the Polish government could probably reach a special agreement which would guarantee non-expropriation.

Talks continued as the major economic convention was hammered out. Although the final result of the negotiations differed in some detail from the League of Nations recommendations, it did not clash with the Treaty of Versailles and, on those grounds, the British Commissioner endorsed it, hoping that the Allies would find no reason to object to it. Representatives of Poland and Germany signed it on May 15; the Polish Diet ratified it on May 24 and the German Reichstag on May 30; the Conference of Ambassadors required only minor alterations.

This being completed, it remained only for a permanent Polish-German structure to replace the temporary negotiating body and for a declaration that the frontier had been sufficiently fixed to effect the transfer of authority. The first of these was brought about by the appointment of Felix Calonder as President of the Mixed Commission and Georges Kaeckenbeeck, a member of the League Secretariat and legal expert, as President of the Arbitral Tribunal, both bodies provided for in the League recommendations and both bodies being part of a bold experimental plan for governing Upper Silesia. When he looked back at these groups while writing

---

[25] A confidential print of the full text of the expropriation agreement was transmitted in Müller to FO, no. 223, May 4, 1922 in FO 371/7497, C 6771/123/18.

their history after their 15-year life span had come to an end, Kaeckenbeeck saw them as a success and as a solution that could not have been reached by the League in the war-torn world of the 1940's in which he wrote. Not only had the experiment brought pacification to an area which had been, and threatened to remain, "a scene of chronic terrorism" but also at the end of it "nothing dangerous was left in the Upper Silesian question; no Upper Silesian question was left."[26] Britain's interest in all of these negotiations, as has been shown, was not directed at the substance of the settlement which was rather irrelevant to her. She hoped to secure the mutual satisfaction of Germany and Poland, who would have to live with the decisions which they had written into their economic convention and further, she hoped to assure the speedy acceptance of the agreement which was a necessary precondition of Britain's anticipated withdrawal from the Central European plebiscite area.

The third major event in the province in early 1922 was the action that led to the notification of the frontier and the establishment of the transitional regime. The coming of the new regime was delayed by the unsettled and sensitive question of disposal of prisoners who were serving sentences imposed by the special court in Upper Silesia. Eventually agreement was reached when the German government consented to the French proposal that the prisoners be transferred to the Rhineland to complete their sentences under the control of the Rhineland High Commission.

Accordingly, notification of the frontier was given on June 15, 1922, and on the same day the agreement containing the arrangements for the progressive transfer of the territory to Germany and Poland was signed by the two plenipotentiaries and the three Allied Commissioners. With this notification and the signature of the transfer agreement went the right of the interested governments to take over their respective parts of the country. A progressive schedule of evacuation by the Allies was drawn up and on June 21 the Polish and German plenipotentiaries formally installed Calonder and Kaeckenbeeck at Kattowitz and Beuthen, respectively, to preside over the Mixed Commission and the Arbitral Tribunal which had been newly constituted. Disorders broke out in some areas of Upper Silesia and it was in this atmosphere that the Allies left the province. On June 17 evacuation of the Inter-Allied Commission and its forces was begun and the operation was completed on July 9--a 23-day withdrawal, sometimes among raucous insults, from a thankless task and an uncharacteristically active interlude for Britain.

---

[26] Georges Kaeckenbeeck, The International Experiment of Upper Silesia (London: Oxford University Press, 1942), p. 514.

Many Polish cabinet ministers took part on July 16 in the solemn celebration of the union of Upper Silesia to Poland. However, the Warsaw government, at this long-awaited moment of satisfaction, was at the height of a parliamentary crisis.[27] Marshal Pilsudski had forced the resignation of the Ponikowski Cabinet in June and precipitated a constitutional crisis over the question of where authority to appoint and dissolve governments resided. Finally, by late July the Diet reinterpreted the constitutional clause in question. They recognized Pilsudski's right to select the new government and, therefore, strengthened even further his position in the Polish state. His regime now had the added prestige of extending national sovereignty into the newly-won territory of Upper Silesia.

Investment in Upper Silesia

One last item that might be considered here is the increase in foreign interest toward investing in Upper Silesia. During the months that final negotiations for a Polish-German convention were in progress and preparations for notification of the frontier were being made, British, French, and other European capitalists had expressed a serious interest in investing in Polish Silesia.[28] Britain's participation in Upper Silesian industry in 1922 did not approach the large role she had played there during the early years of the Industrial Revolution. At that time it was her knowhow which had helped to pioneer the enterprise that turned Upper Silesia into a great industrial center.[29] But British activities in the province were less pioneering in 1922.

---

[27] Hugh Gibson, the American Ambassador in Warsaw, in early June 1922 believed that Pilsudski had already emerged from the settlement of the third Upper Silesian insurrection and its aftermath much strengthened. See Zygmunt J. Gasiorowski, "Joseph Pilsudski in the Light of American Reports, 1919-1922," The Slavonic and East European Review, XLIX (July 1971), 425-36.

[28] By the middle of 1922, the zinc and coal mines of the Henckel von Donnersmarck concern and the Vereinigte Königshütte and Laurahütte mines were already controlled by British capital and negotiations for the transfer of more properties in Kattowitz and Laurahütte were proceeding. See The Times Trade Supplement, June 24, 1922, p. 287.

[29] An article tracing British influences in Upper Silesia reported: "By a curious chain of circumstances England, who has been the great teacher of others, found in Upper Silesia her first and most receptive pupil among all the lands of the continent. All the English inventions and discoveries in the field of mining, of smelting, and of technical progress found immediate echo and application there. In every branch Englishmen took an active part,

In view of the fact that the economic convention was not completed until May and the threat of expropriation after 15 years hung over the future of such undertakings, potential investors had often sought out the assistance of the Foreign Office in the hope of extracting guarantees for the property they wished to own. His Majesty's Government encouraged British investment in the area and Kimens at Warsaw, whose commercial knowledge was put at the disposal of the potential investors, proved to be of invaluable assistance. But the types of guarantees that were being sought were impossible for the British government to procure. The convention on expropriation was the final authority in this matter with perhaps whatever concessions Müller could extract on the investors' behalf from the Polish government. Several of these British groups which expressed an interest in investing funds here in the months before Allied withdrawal from the province did not actually seriously follow through on their ambition until after the partition of the province. These interests, particularly in the mines at Radzionkau and Delbrück, will be considered later. It is interesting, however, to note that in early 1922 a British group proposed to work the principal part of the Polish portions of the Upper Silesian industrial triangle. Money was to be promised by Lazards, Lloyds, and British Shareholders Trust Limited who would underwrite the business in the preliminary stages and then become debenture holders when the public issue was made. Despite the description of this project by the spokesman of the group as non-political and purely commercial, a Foreign Office observation was made to the effect that

> It sounds very well to talk of a scheme of this kind being purely commercial, but if it is carried into

directly or indirectly." When Frederick the Great had laid the foundations of modern Prussian industry, he recruited the help of Reden and Heinitz, first-class masters of mining and foundry techniques. Reden, who had been schooled in England, observed how canals and rivers facilitated the growth of industry there. He published Canals and the Regulation of Rivers According to English Practice which influenced Silesian procedures. He was reportedly successful in discovering England's secret for getting sulfur out of coal and using it for smelting iron. John Baildon, a Scottish engineer, built the first and largest blast furnaces on the continent in Upper Silesia. He was the practical organizer of Reden's theories. During a later visit to England, Reden met John Wilkinson, a foundry engineer whom he brought back to Upper Silesia as an advisor regarding experiments being performed with coke and with smelting of different ores. Wilkinson signed himself *Maître de forges d'Angleterre* in Frederick William II's Book of Mines when he had an audience with that sovereign in Berlin on March 9, 1789. See Josef Piernikarczyk, "England's Part in the Creation of Upper Silesian Industry," Baltic and Scandinavian Countries, III (May 1937), 270-73.

effect it cannot help having political consequences, because of the fact that the industrial triangle of Upper Silesia is to central and eastern Europe, what Westphalia and Essen are to western Europe, or what South Wales, Leeds and Sheffield are to England.[30]

Eventually the group withdrew because it was faced with financial difficulties and nothing came of the ambitious scheme. In each approach for assistance from the British government, the groups went away with moral support and the services of the British minister at Warsaw to help win a guarantee against expropriation.

British initiative since the middle of 1921 had been directed toward a settlement of old obligations in order to return to the familiar role of participating in commerce. If her interlude of activism gave the impression of being innovative, it was only because of the new locale in which it operated. Central Europe had not ordinarily provided the setting for the development of her important policy; but the mode of operation she employed was characteristic. She moved in familiar paths when she tried to prevent French hegemony on the continent; she moved in familiar paths when she said she favored a "policy of reconciliation" with Germany; and she moved in familiar paths when she restrained, but refused to throttle, her French ally. Yet, she could do all of these in a setting that was more familiar to her activity away from Central Europe, an area in which she believed that she had involved her officials and troops for too long. So, when Britain achieved her disengagement from Danzig later in 1920 and from Upper Silesia in the summer of 1922, it was not to a splendid isolation that she rushed, nor to a state of denial that the world had changed since 1914, but rather back to her maritime and merchant role which might envelop all these places as well. Under such circumstances, however, it was not she who had to subordinate herself to the Treaty dictates of the Allies to serve these areas, but rather it was they who had to conform to British specifications if they chose to enrich themselves by their relationship with her. She had had at her disposal the opportunity to exploit both Danzig and Upper Silesia for her own benefit and she had not done so. Whether she was prevented by either lack of interest or her proverbial sense of fair play is a moot question. Britain did not build empires in Europe--or at least not those won with infantry and political machination. But she did not abandon plans for those, even in Central Europe, that were measured in sea-going tonnage, gold flow, and flotation markets as the next chapter will show.

---

[30] Interview of Lieutenant Commander Kenworthy, M.P., by Owen O'Malley, March 7, 1922 in FO 371/8139, N 2231/1834/55.

CHAPTER VII

BRITISH PRESENCE IN A TRADITIONAL ROLE

(July 1922 to December 1923)

It was not until late in the summer of 1922 that Britain finally freed herself from the military involvement in Central Europe which had accrued to her as a result of her willingness to take up arms when the lamps of Europe had first gone out. She had now discharged the obligations in that area that had been placed upon her by the Treaty of Versailles. In the course of doing so, she had not wavered from the path of respect for the spirit of that Treaty, even though on occasion she had found it necessary to explain away a rigid and uncompromising observance of its letter.

When Lloyd George's government fell in October 1922 and the Conservatives came to power, Poland claimed that Anglo-Polish relations steadily improved, despite the occasional press attacks in Warsaw against one stand or another taken by the British representative on the Council of the League of Nations in Polish-Danzig questions under discussion. It is this period following political and military extrication from Central Europe, a time of augmented financial and commercial interest there and a time of an ostensible shift in British policy toward Poland itself, that is under consideration in this chapter.

Britain and the Crisis in Polish-Danzig Relations

Polish-Danzig relations traveled an unpredictable, often rocky, road. There had been times, as in the spring and summer of 1921, when an "era of good feeling" was enjoyed between the states, but more often than not there existed an endemic antagonism, either tempered or fanned by the amount of attention given to other issues. Until late 1921 Poland had devoted a good deal of her attention to the coveted Upper Silesia, but with that final award having been made and with her eastern frontiers well on the way to being delimited and agreed upon, Poland had more attention to devote to the neighboring Free City which had been given its unique status by the powers primarily in order to answer Poland's needs for access to the sea.

Minor eruptions in Polish-Danzig relations occurred soon after France had moved into the Ruhr in January 1923 and Lithuania had at the same time seized Memel. Danzigers feared that a *doup de main* in their territory by Poland was imminent. Words flew in either direction but the attack never came.

Danzig's first major political crisis came in the spring of 1923. Late in April and early in May, public statements of Polish officials described their irritation at the "obstructive and unfriendly attitude" of the Danzig authorities. First, the president, Stanisław Wojciechowski, voiced Poland's growing suspicion that Danzig was interested only in milking her special relationship with Poland to her own benefit and threatened to put an end to both his government's policies of reconciliation and to Danzig's misuse of Polish raw materials and labor. Similar outspoken comments of the Marshal of the Polish Senate caused a flurry in the Free City.

Count Alexander Skrzynski, the Foreign Minister, attempted to tone down the President's words. A former minister at Bucharest, he had come to this post after the general election of November 5, 1922 and the subsequent confusing events which were highlighted by the assassination of the newly-elected president and the formation of a new government. He assured Max Müller that Wojciechowski had spoken out of turn and subsequently admitted his error, although Polish demands for unfettered use of Danzig remained undiminished. As a result of the city's ill-will, he claimed, Poland was not enjoying the free use of the port to which she was entitled and the customs union was working in the favor of the Free City but not of Poland. In fact, he alleged, Danzig formed a breach rather than a step in the customs frontier since it could obtain from Poland, at low cost, foodstuffs and raw materials which it needed while goods being imported at Danzig were easily smuggled into Poland to the deteriment of the Polish treasury. If such circumstances continued it might become necessary to abrogate the customs union, although he disavowed the use of violent means to this end.

All the grievances against Danzig gave rise to renewed anxiety in the Free City and rumors of impending Polish invasion of its territory. B. H. Fry, the British Consul still resident at Danzig, however, saw no immediate danger of such intervention.

Aiming to put an end to the stories, the Polish government disclaimed notions for a coup but, embracing the Treaty of Versailles, made known its intention "to secure Poland from dangers to which she is at present exposed." To that end it adressed urgent representations to the League of Nations. The official statement of grievances released by the Polish government was a vague and long-winded pronouncement to the effect that Danzig's legislation undermined Polish treaty-given rights and that Poland was being denied port facilities and postal service rights.

With this, Poland opened the question of whether the Treaty of Versailles or the Polish-Danzig Convention of November 1920 was the definitive agreement between the states. As already seen, the Treaty was intentionally vague in Articles 100-108 devoted to Danzig affairs because of the provision for the adoption of a subsequent detailed agreement which would more carefully define the relationship between the Republic of Poland and the Free City of Danzig. Paderewski had signed the Convention for Poland in November 1920, but as time went on and Poland began to feel its strictures, she began subordinating it to the Treaty of Versailles and claiming the umbrella protection of that prior agreement. After one of her professions of faith in it as the "Bible" of Danzig-Polish relations, she was reminded by Colonel James de Reynier, the president of the Harbor Board, that there were two parts to the Bible--the Old and New Testaments. In this parallel, the Treaty of Versailles was the Old Testament and the Convention the New, being the fulfillment of the Treaty and originally treated as such by the Poles.

Polish assurances that they would not act contrary to the Treaty accompanied the imposition of restrictions upon trade with Danzig. The frontier between Poland and Danzig was closed and from April 20, 1923, goods whose import into or export from the Polish customs area was prohibited could cross the fronter into Danzig only when covered by an import or export license issued by the Polish authorities. Danzig regarded this action as contrary to the Polish-Danzig agreement of October 24, 1921 and protested to the Council of the League of Nations.

With respect to the economic pressures exerted upon Danzig by Poland and the general workability of the agreements which defined the relationship between these two states, the Foreign Office began to favor a mild revisionism tempered by procrastination. Outright revisionism as a doctrine was not tenable in mid-1923 in Britain, but a begrudging, hesitant, nodding acquaintance with it became commonplace. W. H. M. Selby, whose analysis of the issue currently guided the formation of British policy toward Poland's actions in Danzig, after an examination of the question, decided that the difficulties were fundamental and arose out of the provisions of the treaties.[1] The only possible solution in his estimation was the modification of the treaties. But Selby was cognizant of the fact that in the spring of 1923, time was not ripe for such abrupt departures from old policies--there was a difficult juncture in Anglo-French relations stemming from the French occupation of the Ruhr to be considered as well as a trying moment on the European economic scene to be remembered. Therefore, he conceded that the British government should postpone as long as possible the discussion of the Danzig issue in the context of revisionism.

J. D. Gregory also backed away from outright revisionism and decided that the best course appeared to be postponement. "Above all," Britain should manage to avoid taking the initiative or identifying herself with one interest or the other until the High Commissioner's assessment was available. Sir William Tyrrell, a

---

[1] FO Memorandum by Selby, June 5, 1923 in FO 371/9325, N 5088/1064/55. Another similar analysis was discussed in a lengthy minute by Selby which accompanied Drummond to Gregory, June 10, 1923 in FO 371/9326, N 5619/1064/55.

legal advisor, agreed that the League should take up the matter.
But he predicted that the day would come when the question would
be handed back to the Powers whose signatures had given birth to
the Danzig regime.

If the prevalent mood in the Foreign Office was not condemnatory of revisionism, the word of the Permanent Undersecretary of State was. Sir Eyre Crowe put a clamp on all speculations: there could be "no question of altering the treaty merely to confer special benefits on Poland."[2]

But the attitudes expressed by the British representatives on the spot were less scrupulously impartial. Those in Warsaw, recognizing the difficulty of objectivity from their vantage point, generally supported revision of the treaties in Poland's favor while the consul at Danzig sympathized with the city in which he served.

The British minister at Warsaw, now Sir Max Müller, agreed that Poland was not enjoying the unfettered use of the port at Danzig that was her right and if the matter were to be put right "drastic alterations in the constitution of the Free State" were called for. He maintained that practice did not conform to theory and that Poland's control of the port and access to the sea were mere paper fabrications. Specifically he charged that

> The inclusion of the Free City within the Polish Customs frontier is defeated by the absence of unity of control in the customs administration; theft and smuggling flourish; there is untold delay in the forwarding through Danzig of food arriving from abroad in transit for Warsaw as I know by repeated personal experience; as to export, shippers tell me that they encounter such insuperable difficulties at Danzig that they prefer to forward their goods via Riga, Königsberg or Stettin.[3]

But Müller did not pretend that the Poles were innocent either. He cited their unfortunate choice of officials and the practice of their politicians to, irrelevantly, demand "sovereign rights in Danzig" instead of concentrating on defending their treaty rights there as factors contributing to the hysteria of the spring and summer of 1923. His repeated support for a British policy of revision was echoed in his Legation staff.

---

[2] FO Memorandum by Selby, June 5, 1923 cited above.

[3] Müller to Curzon, no. 260, June 7, 1923 in FO 371/9326, N 5222/1064/55. See also Leeper (Warsaw) to Selby, June 7, 1923 in FO 371/9326, N 5413/1064/55.

Consul Fry in Danzig, on the other hand, viewed the Polish grievances against the Free City in a most unsympathetic manner.[4] When the Polish government charged that in response to their own demonstrations of good will the Danzig Senate had exhibited only a contrasting hostility, he attempted to put the city's "hostility" into proper proportion by noting the volatile nature of the Polish Commissioner, Leon Plucinski, and by showing how Poland, despite her protestations, had failed to live up to her obligations in assuming the conduct of Danzig's foreign affairs, in providing funds for the Harbor Board, and in other such omissions. When the Polish government claimed that the Danzig Customs Administration[5] performed its duties unsatisfactorily and thus made the city a virtual breach in the Polish customs frontier, Fry again came to the smaller state's defense, claiming that by and large, Polish tariffs and restrictions were actually more rigidly applied in Danzig than in Poland. When the Poles charged that they had been barred from legitimate access to the sea, he said he found no ground in fact for the assertion since goods bound for Poland passed in bond duty-free through the port and since Polish vessels enjoyed the same rights as those of Danzigers. But Fry's assertions were based more on theoretical agreements than on real operation. On paper, Polish needs were satisfied in Danzig, but in practice, this appeared not to be completely true.

If one assesses the validity of Polish claims through the eyes of one who sought self-determination for the Free City, then certainly Danzig had a right to curtail or "contain" Polish exploitation and control. If, on the other hand, the judgment is made through Polish eyes seeing Danzig as having received her unique status for the sole purpose of servicing the needs of Poland as she stretched to the sea, then certainly the Senate's actions were pure obstructionism and Danzig's jealous defense of her independence had the tone of insolence. It was from the first vantage point that Britain had viewed the Danzig question since the Paris peace conference. But by the summer of 1923, slight evidences of revisionism, characterized by disinclination to take up a policy of activism in this regard, began to be entertained in official circles.

---

[4] Fry to Curzon, no. 33, June 16, 1923 in FO 371/9326, N 5661/1064/55.

[5] This was an independent body under the Danzig Senate which received technical instructions directly from Warsaw. It grew out of Article 104 of the Treaty of Versailles, the Danzig-Polish Convention of November 1920, and the amplifying agreement of October 24, 1921.

Danzig before the League

The real confrontation between Poland and Danzig took place in Geneva in July in an atmosphere of strained relations further complicated by a concurrent pursuance on the part of the Polish government of a policy of unilateral action in expelling sixteen Danzig citizens from Poland in retaliation for a similar Danzig move. Owing to the fact that most important points were dealt with in private negotiation and therefore did not find their way into official records of the Council's session, the records are necessarily scanty and incomplete on the quelling of the crisis. J. W. Headlam-Morley was present and supplemented these official papers with records of his personal impressions in an attempt to fill as many of the gaps as possible.[6]

Wishing to nullify the "constraining" agreements dealing with her relationship to Danzig that had been signed since the Treaty of Versailles, Poland attempted to eliminate the Harbor Board, to challenge the competence of the High Commissioner in questions not specifically related to the Treaty of Versailles, and to continue her exercise of retaliatory measures. These measures took the form of imposing disabilities on Danzigers who came within the Polish frontiers and maintaining that it was beyond the competence of the High Commissioner to inquire into such "internal" matters.

While one of the many issues involving Danzig was being discussed before the Council of the League in early July, a telegram arrived from the Free City informing Heinrich Sahm, President of the Danzig Senate, that the Poles had closed their frontier, thus preventing Danzigers who were in that country from returning home, and had stopped supplies of food. The dearth of information from the Free City made the response difficult to formulate, yet Sahm hoped to make a prompt reply in order to prevent rash retaliation by the Danzigers. A meeting between him and Mervyn MacDonnell, the new High Commissioner who earlier in the year had replaced Haking, was arranged and the Council decided to issue a conciliatory report which, according to Headlam-Morley, was typically evasive, indecisive, and "not as strongly worded in its condemnation of Polish action and repudiation of Polish arguments as strict justice would have required."

Almost as quickly as the crisis in Polish-Danzig relations had erupted, in the spring, it now disintegrated, with the Poles incongruously acting self-satisfied. While it was one of the sporadic eruptions of the endemic antagonism, it was an explosion that occurred suddenly for no apparent reason. It seemed all too easily settled for it to have been a genuine crisis, and British

───────────
[6]Headlam-Morley to Selby, July 11, 1923 in FO 371/9326, N 6195/1064/55.

representatives in Geneva and Warsaw suspected it had been merely a Polish ploy that had to be abandoned mid-way as unsuccessful.

In March 1923 Poland had won two satisfying victories: the Conference of Ambassadors had recognized the eastern frontiers and Poland had incorporated Vilna into the republic. Whether these victories gave courage to the Polish chauvinists to look hungrily at Danzig in order to satisfy their appetite for a true outlet to the sea cannot be proved. There is no evidence that the Polish government was so motivated. As the year progressed, Poland adopted a more conciliatory attitude toward Danzig and the stormy interlude was left behind.

During the late summer and fall of 1923 another crisis confronted the Free City. This time it was a combination of shortages of food and ready money that led to a general strike. Given the more balanced outlook of the Warsaw government and the acting Polish commissioner at Danzig, no exploitation was attempted by Poland, and the Danzig Senate was permitted to solve the problem in its own way. How the economic crisis developed and the role played by Britain in its alleviation will be investigated below.

The fact that Poland had met defeat in seeking solutions for her major grievances before the League of Nations in July did not mean that she ceased to pursue her own interests in Danzig. At the twenty-fifth session of the League Council in September she put forward two general contentions: (1) that she could place any Danzig issue she chose immediately before the Council and by-pass the High Commissioner and (2) that her relations with Danzig depended only on the Treaty of Versailles, and thus any subsequent agreements which might prove inconsistent with it were to be disregarded.[7] The first was rejected by the Council, thereby preserving the authority of the High Commissioner, and the second, which had been Poland's cry at several recent League sessions, was only in part honored. Where the construction of the later agreements was doubtful, the Council decided the Treaty of Versailles could help in its "elucidation."

Some outstanding issues continued to trouble the Polish Foreign Minister, Maryan Seyda, who served in the short-lived second Witos cabinet from May to October. He told Müller that his fears concerned the decisions to employ a separate police force for the Harbor Board and to directly subordinate the Danzig customs officials to Polish authority. Concerning these matters of a rather technical nature, the British minister could offer no opinion. Before their meeting came to an end, Seyda assured Sir Max that his

---

[7] Great Britain. Parliamentary Papers. Misc. No. 4 (1923), Twenty-fifth Session of the Council of the League of Nations (Lord Robert Cecil), Cmd. 1921. London: HMSO, 1923.

government regarded Britain "as more directly interested in Danzig than any other Power," on account of both the nationality of the High Commissioner and the interests created by British trade with Poland. Therefore, he hoped that a settlement could be reached which would prove practical and at the same time assure the commercial rights promised to Poland by the Treaty of Versailles.[8]

Many minor or detailed questions continued to arise during the year between Poland and Danzig. In these cases, the British government, with no direct interest in the questions, tended to follow a policy of supporting the decision of the High Commissioner in technical and local matters. By the end of 1923, thirty-two decisions had been given by the High Commissioner regarding Danzig problems. Only five of these had been accepted without appeal. At the same time twenty-one of them were accepted in their original or modified form and twenty-one of the thirty-two were settled directly between the two parties either with or without the assistance of the High Commissioner or the Secretariat.

Various critical periods which blew the Danzig issue out of proportion as well as hints of revisionism in the face of unworkable treaty provisions gave rise to the notion that Danzig was a troublesome and/or troubled step-child of the League involved in endless controversy, never finding satisfaction. But this generalization is not borne out when the statistical summary is considered. What emerged, in fact, by the end of 1923, was a unique entity--the Free City--repeatedly defending its rights against foreign encroachment and evolving more into a settled condition and less into an issue.

The Financial and Economic Crisis of 1923

Ever since Great Britain had withdrawn her troops and civil administration from Danzig in 1920, she had made intermittent attempts to collect from the Free City the costs for her services there. Although it was recognized in 1921 that the extremely difficult economic situation in Danzig precluded immediate payment, Britain was not averse to allowing Danzig to draw up a scheme of payments which would not weigh too heavily upon the city's budget. By the end of 1922 no reimbursement had been made and the outstanding debt to Britain stood at £243,444 7s 0d.[9]

---

[8] Müller to FO, no. 390, September 11, 1923 in FO 688, box 13, file 39, no. 75.

[9] Of this total, civil administration costs were assessed at £14,862 15s 10d. The largest amount was for military occupation at £227,755 11s 9d and Britain's half-share of the costs for boundary delimitation stood at £825 19s 5d. See FO minute attached to Reparation Commission to FO, Annex 1621, d and e, December 20, 1922 in FO 371/9322, N 840/533/55.

Danzig, which had retained the German paper mark, was faced with the same serious inflation as Germany. When the French and Belgians occupied the Ruhr in January 1923, charging the Berlin government with default in reparations payments, the mark sank catastrophically, the German government trying to pay the civil servants and workers in the Ruhr to maintain a policy of passive resistance. With the German mark heading towards collapse, the economy of Danzig appeared doomed.

But the crisis had been in the making for some time. The year 1922 had already seen a sudden depreciation of the currency in the wake of Germany's receiving the London ultimatum in May 1921 and losing the industrial triangle of Upper Silesia in October. In September 1922 the Council of the League of Nations recommended that Danzig should meet the growing crisis with a temporary expedient--issue Treasury notes in some stable currency rather than the German mark. This the government of the Free City regarded as impracticable. In order to bolster the economy of the city, however, the government issued municipal emergency money (*stadtnotgeld*) in the amount of 360,000,000 marks. Although this amount proved insufficient for the task of keeping the government running efficiently, a further issue was deemed unfeasible in view of the fact that local banks feared that such an increase in the notes would place the emergency money as a discount. There still remained 400,000,000 marks to be raised by the Danzig government to meet the amount required for quarterly payments at the end of 1922 to the Allies, and Danzig did not know from where this amount would come.[10] The Free City was expected to pay its share of the reparations debt in addition to its share of the Allied adminis-

---

[10]Danzig authorities sought assistance from Germany in an attempt to save the city from either bankruptcy or from a reorientation toward Poland. Poland would probably have negotiated the loan with harsh terms for Danzig. The German government which was facing its own financial difficulties realized that to refuse Danzig assistance was tantamount to abandoning the city to Poland. Since the sum involved was great (a 500 million mark discount of Danzig treasury bonds) and the transaction one of political implication, the Reichsbank insisted that a secret guarantee of the loan be given by the German government. Eventually, the German authorities acceded to Danzig's wishes, but cut the amount to 250 million marks. Further assistance was given throughout 1922 but none was sufficient to prevent Danzig from eventually being forced to adopt a new currency. See Christoph M. Kimmich, The Free City: Danzig and German Foreign Policy, 1919-1934 (New Haven: Yale University Press, 1968), pp. 49-50. This secret activity on the part of Danzig to keep herself in the German orbit was contrary to the Convention of November 9, 1920 whose Article 7 forbade the Free City to contract any foreign loans without previous consultation with the Polish government.

tration and occupation costs, the German and Prussian public debts, and the purchase price of the former German government properties allocated to Danzig that were located in that city.

At the September 9, 1922 meeting of the Council of the League of Nations, the Polish government offered to provide some assistance in the form of taking over the real estate in Danzig which had formerly belonged to the German state but had subsequently been allocated to Danzig. Poland intended to take over the payments to the Reparation Commission which ownership of the property entailed. In January, however, the Senate stated that such a transfer would not solve the financial problem and the matter was not pursued further.

It was at the same meeting that the Financial Committee of the League urged Danzig to take up immediately the question of introducing a new currency, a matter which will be investigated below, and urged the Reparation Commission to consider granting some postponement of those liabilities placed upon Danzig as a result of the peace settlement. In response to the League's recommendation, the Reparation Commission on January 6, 1923 decided to grant a moratorium of twelve months on Danzig's liabilities respecting former German and Prussian government properties (Treaty of Versailles, Articles 107, 256) and their share of the German and Prussian public debts (Articles 108, 254), reserving the right to charge an interest of 5%. Because the Council considered them within the jurisdiction of the Conference of Ambassadors, it made no decision regarding the outstanding debts for inter-allied occupation and administration.[11]

Generally, members of the British Foreign Office in early 1923 agreed it was desirable that there be further investigations of potential sources of the revenue which Danzig required before any further concessions were granted by either the Reparation Commission or the Conference of Ambassadors. Further, any concession which was granted should be made conditional on Danzig's fulfillment of certain obligations to either introduce a more stable currency or grant a first charge on available assets. Selby regarded the moratorium as an absolute necessity if the collapse of the Free City was to be averted.

Throughout March the crisis in Danzig showed no signs of abating and the serious need for funds to meet current expenses of internal administration prompted the Finance Committee of the League to recommend that the Council ask both the Reparation Commission and the Ambassadors' Conference to allow Danzig to raise a credit with a ceiling of 500,000 gold marks "in priority over the

---

[11] League of Nations paper C.103/1923, January 1923.

obligations arising out of the treaties of peace, and in respect of the costs of the Allied occupation." General Haking, who until the previous month had served as the League's High Commissioner at Danzig, suggested a solution in the form of Allied financing and control of state expenditures through the agency of the League of Nations. While the Danzig Senate objected to this proposal it did nothing to act on the Financial Committee's recommendation to introduce a stable currency. The runaway inflation of the German mark, which was also the currency of Danzig, prevented an alleviation of the critical situation in the Free City and yet the Senate persisted in making no serious effort to effect the change. Under these circumstances the Foreign Office favored granting permission to Danzig to raise the loan. It will be recalled that Poland envisioned the day when she and Danzig, joined in the customs union, would have the same currency. But abandoning of the German standard and espousing of the Polish one was still regarded as an unwelcome form of polonization in the German-speaking city. Considerations of national consciousness perhaps were not decisive in determining practical financial solutions, but nonetheless, they do in great part help to explain the Senate's dilatoriness in the matter.

The responsibility for granting a moratorium on her payments and thus opening the door to a new loan for Danzig laid heavily upon Britain who was the chief creditor as regards Danzig's liabilities under the Treaty of Versailles. The British Treasury tended to view the financial crisis of 1923 in the larger context of Danzig's over-all prosperity. In so doing, it believed that the Conference of Ambassadors should inform Danzig "that subject to the final decision on the question of reparations loans, and provided claims of other powers are similarly dealt with," there was no objection to allowing a ten-year loan for a sum not exceeding 500,000 gold marks whose repayment would rank prior to the Allied claims for civil administration and military occupation. Further, the Treasury urged a moratorium of a year on the civilian administration debt, one of three years on the military occupation debt, but the immediate payment of the charge made by the Boundary Commission which was almost negligible. All these concessions should be granted on the condition that Danzig formally admit her obligation to pay the sums being claimed.[12] Lord Crewe, who had replaced Hardinge as the British ambassador at Paris in late 1922, so in-

---

[12] In a private letter to B. W. Kemball Cook, the British representative on the Reparation Commission, Niemeyer from the Treasury wrote that "the essence of the position is that no one will lend a penny to Danzig while the present ridiculous charges on her rank first. If the loan ranks first they don't much matter." To ruin a place for so small a sum he regarded as "absurd." See O. E. Niemeyer to Kemball Cook, March 29, 1923 in FO 371/9322, N 3351/533/55.

structed the British delegate on the Financial Committee of the Ambassadors. Similar instructions were sent to the British delegate to the Reparation Commission.

Thanks primarily to French resistance, the Ambassadors on June 13 decided that existing evidence was insufficient to justify their endorsement of the British proposal as delineated by the Treasury. Instead, the slow-moving wheels of the inter-allied bureaucracy turned and the Financial Committee of the Conference was asked to look into the matter. Lord Crewe sought further weighty arguments in support of the British position which the Treasury provided.[13] It was not until the first week in August that the Conference of Ambassadors' financial experts, an advisory group, agreed to the British proposals allowing Danzig to float a loan of 500,000 gold marks, but the Ambassadors themselves as a body adhered to their former claims.

Later in the month the French government finally agreed to adopt the report of the Financial Committee on the proposed loan and moratorium, but it insisted on making the loan conditional upon exclusion of German banks from participation. Instead of withdrawing this condition as requested by the British, the French offered an alternative--that in communicating the authorization of the Conference of Ambassadors to the League of Nations, they make it understood that the proposed loan was subject to the stipulation of Article 7 of the Convention of November 9, 1920 which provided that Danzig could raise foreign loans only after prior consultation with the Polish government.

Recognizing that the French alternative would serve merely as an encouragement to the Poles to play the obstructionist game, British diplomats in Paris and Geneva objected. For lack of any

---

[13] Esmond Ovey to Secretary to the Treasury, June 26, 1923 in FO 371/9322, N 5286/533/55. This request, emanating from the Conference of Ambassadors, elicited a tactfully indignant response from the Treasury. Niemeyer thought it inconceivable--in view of the support for the moratorium by Britain, the chief creditor in the question--that the French government should place obstacles in the way of Danzig over a matter of some £50,000 which would in all likelihood not be collectible if no moratorium were granted. He likewise recalled that the financial advisers of the Ambassadors could not be placed on the same level with the members of the Financial Committee of the League of Nations who on other occasions had supported Danzig's claim to this "very small indulgence." See Niemeyer to FO, F. 6046/2, June 29, 1923 in FO 371/9322, N 5842/533/55. The minutes to the Conference of Ambassadors meetings of June 13 and June 20 were transmitted by Lord Crewe in dispatch no. 1762, July 26, 1923 in FO 371/8599, C 12907/569/62.

other practical solution, the Foreign Office proposed to authorize its representatives in Paris to agree to the first French condition if the Treasury concurred. This the Treasury did with the understanding that the restriction on German banks be regarded simply as an expedient in a period of crisis but not as a precedent. With this acceptance, the Conference of Ambassadors adopted a resolution on August 25 which, except for the French-inspired qualification barring German banks from participation in the loan, substantially represented the position taken earlier that summer by the British government. They decided not to oppose the priority ten-year loan whose maximum was set at 500,000 gold marks, to grant a year's moratorium on the civil administration payment and a three year moratorium on the military occupation payment, to dispose of the payment for boundary delimitation at the time of the loan, and not to demand any formal guarantees from Danzig concerning the future payment of outstanding debts.

Danzig's problems were not immediately alleviated with the assistance from the Conference of Ambassadors: Poland was still nearby assessing the situation of her troubled, diminutive neighbor. Müller reported from Warsaw that news of the food and money shortage in Danzig was being closely monitored in Poland but that he detected no desire there to exploit the difficulties of the Danzig government. The Polish Commissioner in Danzig assured British representatives that the present crisis was being regarded on both sides as purely economic and one that the Senate would have to settle itself without any threat of intervention by the Poles. Müller sympathized with the Polish concern that internal strife in Danzig might cause interruption to their communication with the sea, but in his dispatches to London, he reiterated both official and unofficial Polish attitudes of non-interference in the financial crisis in the Free City. This understanding attitude toward Danzig's plight was not characteristic of the Witos government whose policies were oriented to good relations with neighbors to the South and East but whose attitude toward Danzig was generally truculent.

A week later, Müller in a personal conversation with Henryk Strasburger, a Polish undersecretary who was destined to succeed Plucinski as Commissioner at Danzig, learned that two alternatives concerning the proposed introduction of new currency into the Free City were being considered. The first involved the creation of a Danzig bank supported by Berlin to facilitate the issue of the currency. The second involved raising a loan in England to make possible the issuance of the new currency and establishing the currency on a gold basis in connection with the British pound.[14] It was improbable that French support could be secured on the first

---

[14] Müller to Gregory, August 22, 1923 and the reply of September 6, 1923 both found in FO 688, box 13, file 39, no. 72.

177

issue in view of the French stand regarding the loan to Danzig earlier in the month; the second later proved to be incorrect in detail but the basis for things as they materialized. In a conversation on September 11, Müller discussed Danzig with Seyda, who favored immediate currency reform, although he did not surrender hopes that Poland and the Free City would one day have the same monetary system as contemplated in the Convention of November 1920. Further, the Foreign Minister expressed the desire of his government to participate in the new bank of issue, an objective Müller thought not unreasonable.

Later in the month, the British Treasury revealed more precise details about the proposed currency from the Geneva talks and it was learned that the gulden, or unit of the Danzig monetary system, would equal 1/25 of the pound sterling, that the bank would be a private institution, and, that since no question of a foreign loan arose and Article 7 of the Convention would not come into play, no Polish permission was necessary for the adoption of the measures. This Treasury statement that no foreign loan was involved is difficult to reconcile with the facts. Shortly, it was contradicted by a statement of Sir Otto Niemeyer from the Treasury itself.[15] As early as December 1923, an unassuming half-inch of column space buried inside The Times was devoted to an announcement from Danzig that the Bank of England was supplying £200,000 to, and pledging to cooperate closely with, the new bank.[16]

When the Senator of Finance, Dr. Ernst Volkmann, returned to Danzig from Geneva and London, he reported to a Danzig parliamentary committee on the result of his activities. The negotiations with London financiers had gone satisfactorily for Danzig and made possible genuine financial reform. Nevertheless, he said, even with "the greatest expedition" it would be impossible to introduce the new currency completely until January 1924. He announced that a transitional gulden would be introduced as a unit of reckoning, not legal currency, as a fractional part of the pound sterling. In about four months time, it would be convertible at par into definitive currency. At the end of October with the introduction of the provisional currency, Consul Fry reported that confidence had increased and that it was becoming more likely that the issue of the final currency would lead to a reversal of inflation and an increase of trade with Britain. Danzig broke with the German paper mark when introducing the provisional gulden. She had developed a brisk trade with the United States after winning status as a Free City. Since then, as the German mark fell in value, the American dollar began to displace the unstable currency as a favored medium

---

[15] Niemeyer to FO, F 6703/2, February 27, 1924 in FO 371/10451, N 1787/1410/55.

[16] The Times, December 21, 1923, p. 17.

of exchange. The new provisional gulden was now expected to complete the work of the American dollar and drive the German mark out of general use. The Danzig *Central Kassenactiengesellschaft*, a temporary bank which was to be liquidated when the state issue bank was ready to assume the duties of providing currency for the Free City, issued the transitional scrip.[17]

Occupying the former premises of the German Reichsbank, the new Bank of Danzig was duly founded on February 5, 1924. Coinage was issued and the notes then being printed in Great Britain were awaited. Provisional gulden were beginning to be withdrawn as the new currency, tied to that of Britain, replaced them, and legislation was introduced which was designed to reform currency practices and curb inflation.

Although there had been provision for foreign participation, the British Treasury claimed to have no knowledge of capital having been subscribed in Britain. But the Bank of England proposed to cooperate with the Danzig bank as it did with the other central banks of the world. The Treasury, however, refused to make public the precise arrangements of this cooperation which it deemed to be "of a purely private nature." Although it spoke guardedly of the British role, it revealed that in order to facilitate the exchange transactions involving payment in sterling for gulden notes, the Bank of England had undertaken if necessary to give the Bank of Danzig an open credit of £200,000.[18] Moreover, Volkmann and Dr. Meissner, the new governor of the bank, had been in close touch with the Treasury throughout; in fact, the British Controller of Finance was responsible together with two colleagues from the League of Nations Financial Committee for advising on the actual statutes of the bank. Expectedly, the British Treasury looked upon a new currency on a sterling standard "as a most promising experiment in currency reform" which was likely to greatly benefit both Danzig and Britain's commercial and financial dealings with her.

---

[17] *The Times*, October 25, 1923, p. 11. Within a month, paper marks had virtually disappeared from Danzig and while they still remained legal tender, it became difficult to get merchants to accept them. With the new money, however, the cost of living rose and the problem was compounded by serious unemployment. The Danziger Werft was working only a three-day week. See *The Times*, November 12, 1923, p. 11.

[18] Consul Fry was told about the £200,000 open credit and instructed to keep the knowledge confidential if it had not been made public in the Free City. With this document the file ends abruptly and the involvement of the Bank of England in the Bank of Danzig is not pursued further in the Foreign Office correspondence. See Niemeyer to FO, F 6703/2, February 27, 1924 in FO 371/10451, N 1787/1410/55.

Montagu Norman, who had been governor of the Bank of England since 1920, embarked on a policy in 1923 aimed at assisting the stabilization of the European currencies which were then under great pressure. He regarded the 1923 election, which had turned out the Conservatives and their plans for protectionism, as a mandate from the electorate to pursue a policy with broader compass than merely national development. Ordinarily, he cooperated with the League of Nations in selecting the beneficiaries of his financial reconstruction.

Because the first such clients were Germany, Austria, Hungary, Bulgaria, and Danzig, Norman faced the criticisms that he was helping former enemies at the expense of former allies and that his assistance was motivated not so much by questions of economics as by politics. He denied both these charges.[19] Occasionally, he participated in schemes for stabilization even without the recommendation of the League of Nations or the full approval of the British authorities. Such was the case with Poland when he helped work out a scheme of assistance without the backing of the British government or Geneva in which an international banking group arranged a loan. His effectiveness was made possible by his collaboration with Benjamin Strong, the governor of the Federal Reserve Bank of New York.

It was known generally that the Bank of Danzig was "largely supported" by the Bank of England, especially during the first years of its existence, but both Foreign Office and Treasury sources are silent about the nature and extent of this support. Sir Otto Niemeyer, who together with H. A. Siepmann assisted Norman in his policy, left no indications in his papers that he had in any way helped establish the Bank of Danzig. Besides the unofficial claim from the Free City which appeared in The Times on December 21, there was no contemporary newspaper coverage or awareness in Britain of the degree of the involvement of the Bank of England in the establishment of Danzig's new bank and currency.

---

[19] Norman was asked by the FO in 1929 why British firms were losing business in Eastern Europe. He believed that Britain's non-political policy was largely responsible. Countries like France made their loans to governments on condition that the firms of the creditor country be hired. It was not customary for Britain to do so. Norman agreed with Austen Chamberlain that "League" loans, i.e., loans recommended by the international body, should take priority. For Britain to protest against the French government's persistence in political loans, both regarded as useless and dangerous. But they were willing to consider the merits of each case separately and were prepared to lend diplomatic support "to any respectable British house." See the most scholarly biography of Norman by Sir Henry Clay, Lord Norman (London: Macmillan and Co. Ltd., 1957), pp. 286-88.

Upper Silesia after Allied Withdrawal

A tinderbox of mixed nationalism and militancy, Upper Silesia had finally been partitioned and, as a result, Poland had incorporated into her territory the richest portion of the plebiscite area on June 18, 1922. The following weeks saw a withdrawal of the Allies and their Commission which had administered the area since the Treaty of Versailles had come into force at the beginning of 1920. Polish Upper Silesia, which had been the historic scene of seething political controversy and conflicting loyalties, seemed overnight to lose a good deal of her patriotic ardor. When the Polish Chief of State, Marshal Pilsudski, toured the region in August 1922, he found a population among whom Polish prestige had declined and whose violent nationalism appeared to have in great part spent itself. Since the territory came under Polish sovereignty during a time of political difficulty in Poland, it seemed that the party discussions raging as a result of the cabinet crisis were transplanted there, throwing the province immediately into a partisan political fever involving coming elections and distracting it from its former more simplistic Polish nationalist sympathies. Reports of the strength of Korfanty's autonomy movement, however, and the difficulties of disposing of irregular military formations which had grown up over the years persisted.

During these first months of Polish control over the area, there was much anxiety over its economic dislocation. In all likelihood the problems related to railway transport were the most serious owing to the grave technical difficulties with which the new Polish railway administration had been confronted, the obstructionism of the Germans, and the comparative inefficiency of many of the personnel involved. With a majority of railway officials having come in from greater Poland to operate an unfamiliar system, and with the unanticipated departure of many German employees who had promised to stay, the condition of the railways, as well as that of the other means of communication, offered little hope for political and social stabilization and economic development of the territory.

Another grave factor contributing to Silesian difficulty was the food shortage caused by the activities of speculators. When the transfer of the plebiscite area had been effected, prices of food in Polish Upper Silesia were lower than in the rest of the country. Speculators flocked in from the east and bought out available stocks of provisions, creating a shortage and forcing prices up. If the parallel situation in Posnania was any indication, the speculation would be remedied only after the imposition of price controls.

Then, finally, there was the shortage of currency which gave rise to serious discontent. Like Danzig which had found herself without the necessary money to continue operating properly owing to her bond with the German mark and its critical condition, Polish Upper Silesia found herself stifled. Under the terms of the Polish-German Economic Convention of June 15, 1922, the German mark was to remain the unit of currency in all of Upper Silesia for the 15-year readjustment period. But the Polish government sent billions of Polish marks there to compensate for the deficit that could not be filled with German notes. Whatever dissatisfied response was evidenced in the beginning on the part of those who were paid in the new currency is not important in explaining the eventual alleviation of the situation. Rather, there is no question that the wild inflationary crisis in Germany brought about a quicker Silesian stabilization since it invited the influx of Polish marks to meet the emergency long before normal evolution would have accomplished this.

In an attempt to solve the problems connected with their newly-awarded province, the Polish government by the end of 1922 announced the intended construction of a new railway line in order to improve the transport in Upper Silesia and reduce the congestion of existing traffic. The projected growth of the railway, the desire to maintain friendly commercial relations with Germany, the averting of financial disaster by introducing Polish currency, and the reasonable policy adopted by the Polish government respecting their rights of expropriation in Upper Silesia all prophesied the successful conclusion to a long and complicated problem. What is more, generally speaking, incorporation of the wealthy portion of the plebiscite area into Poland had a favorable influence on that country's economic structure. It contributed to her economic independence, to the improvement of her trade balance, and to her wealth, especially when as a result of the occupation of the Ruhr by the French and Belgians, demands from Germany for coal and iron greatly increased. It is ironic that Poland, in her long struggle with Germany over Upper Silesia, despite her exaggerated claims at the peace conference and her questionable behavior during the period of Allied occupation, not only deprived Germany of the bulk of the spoils as a result of the League's award but also profited from the two major crises that Germany was forced to face in 1923--the occupation of the Ruhr and the financial chaos.

Because the transfer of territory and sovereignty had been completed, it did not mean that the work of the Inter-Allied Commission had entirely come to an end in the summer of 1922. There were still financial questions to be considered, costs of occupation to be assessed and collected, and disorders accompanying Allied evacuation to be investigated.

By and large, the French, notably General Lerond, attempted to extend the life of the Commission and take up these matters at a leisurely pace. The British government, however, pressed for a prompt dissolution of the body. In August 1921 the Supreme Council had decided that upon evacuation of the Plebiscite area, the Commission should base itself in Paris, draw up a report of its activities, and settle outstanding financial questions in collaboration with financial experts. With the completion of the evacuation in July, both the British and Italian ambassadors hoped to prevent the resurrection of the Commission in Paris with a large staff to do work which could better be completed by the existing financial committee of the Conference of Ambassadors. General Lerond later that month addressed the Ambassadors, pointing out the difficulties of curtailing the life of his Commission. Although the Conference would not reconsider its decision to dissolve the Commission, it agreed on July 26 to attach that body's financial officials to its own financial committee and rather vaguely gave each of the former commissioners "new and personal powers" for a limited period in order to authorize them to handle any unfinished business

Lerond, claiming authority by virtue of this decision, revived the plebiscite governing commission and he and General Marinis, without the presence of the British Commissioner, met and took up various as yet unsettled financial questions. They invited Sir Harold Stuart to join them, but he and the Foreign Office maintained that until the financial experts had taken up the matters and prepared them for the consideration of the group, it was superfluous to attend. In the meantime, the British government assumed no responsibility for the decisions taken during Lerond's sessions. Hardinge had learned in confidence that the accommodations Lerond had taken up in Rue d'Ulm for his group had been granted by the French government as a concession in order to forestall his insistence upon offices in the Quai d'Orsay itself. He was hardly on speaking terms with the ministry, and he was being permitted to play out his game away from the center of the stage.

Finally, on October 4, the Conference of Ambassadors decided to formally convene a meeting of the commissioners. Sir Harold Stuart, owing to ill health, was prevented from attending the meeting which was scheduled to begin on October 9 and instead, his deputy F. B. Bourdillon, went to Paris.

Recognizing that there were questions of German and Polish claims against the Allies as well as matters of internal administrative accounts to be completed, the British government agreed to the convocation of the Inter-Allied Commission. However, it wanted the Commission's powers to be renewed only for a limited period after which time any outstanding questions should be entirely handed over to the Conference of Ambassadors. The Conference then renewed its powers for a ten-day period, October 9-19, and the British position on the issue appeared to have been successful.

During the tenure of the Plebiscite Commission, revenues had been received from the area, as stipulated by the Treaty of Versailles, but they had done little more than cover the costs of the civil administration. Accordingly, the Conference of Ambassadors decided to retain the money left in the Commission's treasury after the dissolution of the body and allocate it to the Allies in partial payment for the military occupation. Finally, they also decided to fix the proportion for payment of the costs of occupation at 58% from Poland and 42% from Germany.[20]

Throughout most of the following year, the accounts of the late Commission continued to be a matter of discussion, but the costs of occupation remained unpaid.[21] But with the serious financial crisis in Germany, the Allies found it difficult to demand in 1923 payment for a 1920 debt in coin of pre-inflationary value. Like the Danzig debt owed to the Allies, the one in Upper Silesia appeared to be destined to a long and lingering life.

France had always been much more interested in Upper Silesian developments than Great Britain, but once military occupation duties were over and the prospect of confining her activities to investment in that territory was imminent, Britain's interest and willingness to assist her capitalists was augmented. The Poles, despite their being allies of France, had more than once hinted to British representatives that they had no intention of making their country into a French satellite. They extended invitations to British investors. Even before the Allied evacuation, they intimated that the British were welcome and that it was not their intention to turn the Polish industrial area into a French monopoly. A representative of the Economic Department of the Ministry of Foreign Affairs told Kimens that his government would welcome British capital in Upper Silesia and assured the Commercial Secretary that no difficulties would be encountered by British groups in obtaining concessions for the lease of land and mines, drawing special attention to the exceptional riches of coal deposits in the as yet unexploited districts of Rybnik and Pless. The latter invitation was again proffered to British interests in the spring of 1923 when Italy took up negotiations with the Polish government for the exploitation of undeveloped coalfields in Rybnik.

---

[20] Hardinge to FO, no. 604, November 15, 1922 in FO 371/7469, C 15714/33/18.

[21] F. W. Leith-Ross (Reparation Commission) to Treasury, October 19, 1923 communicated from the Treasury to Wigram, F. 3925/2, October 22, 1923 in FO 371/8809, C 18244/3961/18. The claims amounted to 148,074,984 francs by France; £1,210,330 15s 1d by Great Britain; 70,725,386 lire by Italy.

While more and more British firms began to contemplate the profitability of investing in Upper Silesia, the trials of one important concern provide an enlightening look at the attitudes and actions of British representatives. This was Henckel von Donnersmarck Beuthen Estates, Limited in which the British Bewick, Moreing, and Company participated, and whose Radzionkau area colliery lay in the frontier area. Their properties had been severed by the new frontier drawn up by the League of Nations and they called for rectification of the line by the Boundary Commission.

The Donnersmarck story is an example of official British cooperation with the investors and the successful and skillful use of fair argument. Just after the frontier in Upper Silesia had been notified in July 1922, representatives from Moreing's approached the Foreign Office to point out what disastrous effects accrued from that boundary which cut off the pit shafts and placed them into Polish territory. They told Sir William Tyrrell that a sound argument demonstrating the unreasonable nature of the decision would have been honored when first made except for the ill-judged and ill-fated interview that a Moreing spokesman, Lord Cozens Hardy, and held with Colonel Boger, the British Commissioner on the Inter-Allied Boundary Commission. When the former attempted to pressure Boger into altering the decision, the Commissioner understandably took offense and declared himself unwilling to damage the excellent relations between him and the French representative over such a matter. Colonel Clarke, the mining expert who was then present, had studied the matter and informed Boger that the boundary ought to have been altered so as to allot the small area with the pit shaft to Germany in a similar manner as the allocation further down the line had been made where German pit shafts of a Polish mine were transferred to Poland. The Foreign Office decided that the most tactful course to follow would be to have Lord D'Abernon ask Boger to come to Berlin and put the situation before him. In their resulting conversation of July 25, Boger agreed with D'Abernon that on economic grounds the German case was strong at Radzionkau.

In the meantime, Lord Cozens Hardy again began carrying on vigorous propaganda in Upper Silesia in favor of Radzionkau's assignment to Germany; the Poles, attaching great importance to the possession of the rich deposits of coal in the district, objected. Their protests addressed to Müller were forwarded to the Foreign Office.

An interesting turn of events occurred when Moreing put its case before Boger with the backing of the Foreign Office and won a favorable decision. But the German government expressed alarm at the favorable settlement which would include Radzionkau in Germany, fearing that in consequence the Poles would press for compensation in other directions more important to German national interest than the loss of Radzionkau. So serious were its fears about this that it proposed Moreing withdraw the application from the Boundary Commission and agree to the Radzionkau pits remaining in Poland. In compensation, the German government offered to pay for the construction of a new pit on the German side of the frontier. Accordingly, the company withdrew its original demand for the incorporation of the whole Radzionkau mine into Germany and requested only that the ventilating shaft be attributed in order to allow for the future development of the western mine field. The proposition was made in an unbiased, business-like manner, the British representatives creating a favorable atmosphere for the negotiations, and before long Polish assent to the proposal was received and the Donnersmarck interests won their case, thus putting an end to the question.[22]

An Improved State of Anglo-Polish Relations

Questions related to neither Danzig nor Upper Silesia were ever in the first instance regarded by the British government as issues to be considered with either pro-Polish or anti-Polish bias. For the two years ending in 1921, Anglo-Polish relations were not in a good state. The British attitude toward the Russo-Polish War and toward Poland's seizure of Vilna contributed to the poor understanding between them. There were also always near the top of a Polish list of grievances against Britain, the policies of Lloyd George at the peace conference which had prevented an outright cession to that country of the coveted port city of Danzig and the mineral-rich province of Upper Silesia. The year 1922 saw an improvement in the relations between the two countries, and with the passing of these two controversial areas out of the spotlight of contention, less stress was laid in Poland upon the role the British had played in their original settlement.

With the breakdown of Lloyd George's coalition with the Conservatives in October 1922 and his consequent resignation, the new Conservative government under first, Bonar Law and then, Stanley Baldwin was looked upon with great favor in Poland, simply because it was not Lloyd George's government. Warsaw press evaluation of the farewells to the war leader were more restrained than might have been expected, the most chivalrous statement recalling the words of a Polish statesman that "we cannot forget that Mr. Lloyd George's signature is on the Treaty of Versailles which brought Poland back to life." As 1923 progressed and especially when a

---

[22]D'Abernon to Crowe, October 5, 1922 in FO 371/7497, C 14018/123/18 and the enclosed letter from Moreing to D'Abernon. See also Boger's monthly report no. 42, No. 1903/36 of December 17, 1922 recording the settlement of the Radzionkau question in FO 371/7498, C 17486/123/18. Dzieje Pracy: Górnego Sląska, 1922-1927 [Labor News: Upper Silesia] (Katowice: Strazy, 1927), p. 141.

favorable decision was reached by the Conference of Ambassadors regarding Poland's eastern frontiers, the Warsaw press went so far as to indulge in a few laudatory remarks about Great Britain. The Rzeczpospolita [The Republic] put it well when it surveyed recent relations with Britain and attributed the friction not only to the "prejudices" of Lloyd George but also to the "inability of the Poles to win the respect of England owing to the various 'absurdities' of which they had been guilty" during the first four years of their country's existence. It was recognized that the Franco-Polish alliance was not inconsistent with an Anglo-Polish rapprochement but that Britain, pursuing a broader world policy than France, stood in no need of Polish assistance and consequently she would be less disposed to afford assistance to Poland on a scale similar to that of France.[23]

Representatives of the Polish government as well as of the Polish press maintained that the new government in Britain, pursuing a new policy regarding the methods of participation in Europe, had diminished, even banished, any apprehension in Poland about British designs in Central Europe. Even on the touchy question of Danzig, the two did not conflict as they had previously, although strong efforts were still needed to remove remaining obstacles.

Müller more than once had tried to impress upon the Poles that his government had no intention of attempting to curry favor in Warsaw or to compete with France--or any other nation--"for Polish smiles." He stressed that the political party in power in Westminster in no way should concern the Poles, that no British party could ever be described as having an orientation that was either pro-Polish or anti-Polish. It was, in fact, a diplomatic way of saying that the very existence of Poland seemed irrelevant to London.

In the past, Poland, despite her pretentions to being a great nation and her denials of those prophecies which said she would prove to be only a seasonal state, paradoxically, in asserting her status in the family of nations, sought guidance from the powers on what course she should take. Her ally France had always been easy to understand; their continental policies of defense were parallel. But Britain was inscrutable to the Poles, a sphinx conveying no hint of where Britain considered that Polish interests lay. With the improved trade relations between them and the progress of current negotiations for a commercial treaty in late 1923, Britain's objectives were more clearly revealed to Poland. A dispatch from the Warsaw Legation summarized Britain's aims:

---

[23] Müller to FO, no. 234, May 24, 1923 in FO 688, box 14, file 47, no. 3.

> Once we can succeed effectively in convincing them that our main interest in Poland is to do what we can to promote Poland's own internal resources, because in so doing we provide a profitable and reliable market for ourselves and because the stability of Poland, apart from any ulterior political considerations, is in itself a British interest, confidence in and understanding of our motives will increase proportionately and the effect in Poland itself will be of a steadying character.[24]

Britain was historically a nation in the habit of relying on her own resources and as such, her first thought was always to develop those resources to the utmost before looking outward. How natural it was, then, that she should apply the same test to other nations. As interest grew and relations improved between the two countries in 1922-23, Britain came to believe that she was as important to Poland as France was--not, however, in the role of "flashy champion," but rather in that of "staid adviser."

---

[24] Leeper to FO, no. 537, December 11, 1923 in FO 688, box 14, file 49, no. 2.

CHAPTER VIII

BRITAIN AND THE CHANGES IN THE STATUS QUO

(1924-1925)

The fact that Germany was learning to remain silent, with the exception of a few public utterances, in the matter of the Danzig and Upper Silesian settlements did not mean that she had reconciled herself to an ostensibly independent Danzig or a partitioned Upper Silesia. Instead, she was settling down to a policy of revisionism unvocalized for diplomatic reasons. Poland, on the other hand, never ceased announcing to anyone who would listen, and even to those who tired of hearing it, that she pursued a policy of uncompromising non-revisionism, at least toward the territories that had been transferred to her sovereignty as a result of the Treaty of Versailles and its consequent agreements and developments. Toward those, like Danzig, to which her dominion did not legally extend but where she was given specific rights and guarantees, she consistently sought to stretch the letter of the Treaty in order to win for herself greater control than the peacemakers had intended she should exercise.

Those who questioned the wisdom of the Versailles settlement or who commented on its inadequacy, Poland immediately regarded as threats to her existence. When Great Britain was heard to voice such thoughts about the unfairness of the Upper Silesian award or the "impossibility" of the Danzig corridor, Poland began to fear her or her party in power as an anti-Polish danger, despite assurances to the contrary. She had come to realize that British policy was much wider and universal in scope as compared with that of her French ally, but she did not understand that neither Danzig nor Upper Silesia--not even Poland herself--was a matter of primary concern to Britain. It was only the way in which these fitted into the context of a greater British policy that gave them any real part in determining the policy pursued by Great Britain. British revisionist voices that were beginning to be heard more often in 1924-25 were not then anti-Polish expressions, but expressions of a broader policy--to perpetuate a peace settlement in Europe that was reasonable, practicable, and conducive to economic regrowth and commercial success. Never doctrinaire in her orientation, Britain understandably refused to commit herself to categorical support for an unmodifiable Treaty of Versailles. Her loyalty to its spirit had been evident since the days her Prime Minister had helped fashion the document, and public utterances of her representatives well into the 1920's claimed unflinching devotion to the Treaty which was the masterplan for the inter-war European condition. Yet her more frequent statements on revisionism remained nothing more than words down to mid-decade and while she paid lip service to revisionism, her actions remained as orthodox as before, consigning the contemplated changes to some far-distant, purposely undefined future. How Britain's relations with Poland suffered because of Poland's failure to comprehend the intent of British policy and how Britain's commercial endeavors reached a point short of success in Danzig and Upper Silesia, two foci of Polish interest, will be investigated here.

Danzig and Anglo-Polish Relations

Britain was on good terms with Danzig during 1924-1925. The new bank had come into operation and Britain's part in its design had not been inconsiderable. She had consistently upheld the independence of the Free City and had seen in Danzig a door to trade with Central and Eastern Europe. Yet, the Convention of 1920 prevented Britain or any other state from dealing directly with Danzig since it provided that Poland should conduct the city's foreign affairs as well as her own. Aside from questions dealt with in the League of Nations, the major Danzig issues that concerned Britain were outstanding debts, the progress of the International Engineering and Shipbuilding Company, and various trade agreements.

When, during the height of the financial crisis of 1923 the Free City had found itself unable to pay its debts owed to the Allies for their civil administration and military occupation, the Conference of Ambassadors had agreed to grant to Danzig a moratorium of one year on the payments for civil administration and one of three years on the payments for military occupation. In August 1924 the first of these installments came due but no payment was forthcoming. Negotiations with the Reparation Commission aimed at drawing up a scheme for a consolidated annuity payment yielded nothing material and the issue dragged on unchanged until the following June when the Conference of Ambassadors decided to arrange a schedule of repayment for that debt to be liquidated within a maximum period of five years, to earmark for military occupation expenses 50% of any payments made by Danzig, and to again invite the Free City through the agency of the Polish government to expedite payment to the Allies of the already well-overdue debt. As a result of this action, the Polish Embassy in November finally forwarded a check to the British government in the amount of £15,688 15s 3d. This closed the door on the long outstanding issue of payment for the boundary delimitation and the Allied civil administration.

Another issue related to Danzig that much interested Britain was the progress made by the International Engineering and Shipbuilding Company. Throughout the summer and fall of 1921 and most of 1922, negotiations for combining the Danziger Werft and the Troyl Workshops and for the establishment of the company had been held and prolonged. Finally, in September 1922 the agreement constituting the company had been signed and Britain, thereby, not only gained a valuable foothold in the Free City but she also came to enjoy a position of prestige in the tiny state.

Over a year passed and little was done, however, about fulfilling the pledges of investment made by the participants at the time of the company's formation. Danzig had in the first instance suggested foreign, especially British, participation in the venture primarily to attract the working capital that she herself was unable to provide. During the negotiations of early 1922 the British group had pledged to furnish up to £100,000 to the combination and to double that amount in the event of non-participation by the Italians. There had been opposition within the Danzig government to setting up the company along the proposed lines and finally, owing to President Sahm's tact and the modifications proposed by C. F. Spencer, the Chairman of Cravens, the contract was agreed to with the understanding that the British group would provide working capital, material, world-wide orders, and assistance in sales abroad.

By the spring 1924 apart from a £26,000 loan by the British group upon which interest and amortization were being paid, no working capital or material had been provided and no orders had been brought to the company. The indefiniteness of the functions of some personnel was beginning to raise suspicion in various circles concerning the health of the company and the competence of the management and the Danzig directors.

President Sahm voiced his concern when he discussed the issue with Fry. The consul privately informed him that Spencer did not have full confidence in the management abilities of Professor Noë and the general operation of the company, which might go a long way to explain his hesitation in providing the working capital. Despite his attempt to rationalize British behavior for Sahm, Fry reported to the Foreign Office how the entire venture must have appeared in Danzig's eyes--with one of her greatest potential assets of a probable standing value of some £5,000,000 being handed over to foreign industrial groups for 50 years for a fraction of the sum agreed upon in the September 1922 contract. He did not try to deny the fact that the Polish government had likewise, up to this time, failed to act after making the agreement to submit orders for locomotives for 15 years at the rate of 6 per annum provided the company set up the necessary installations. The company had not taken these steps; nor had money been provided for the purpose. Fry favored using diplomatic channels in the interest of British prestige to urge Cravens to provide the working capital and to more clearly define the description of each managerial position held in the Company.

This proved unnecessary when Sir William Ellis, one of the British directors of the company, came to speak with both Sahm and the Polish Commissioner in Danzig, Henryk Strasburger, while en route from a board meeting in Berlin. He announced to them and later to Consul Fry that it had been decided to furnish the £100,000 for working expenses and that the amount would, if necessary, be increased. Further, the general question of organization and control was undergoing reform as well. So, after a long bout with growing pains, it appeared that the project which had so excited the potential investors in 1921 was finally about to live up to the anticipations of the Danzigers.

Britain had, of course, not lost interest in trade with a Danzig that provided access to an entire new sector for her commercial endeavors. A manifestation of this interest was the negotiation of an Anglo-Polish commercial agreement. The text of the Treaty of Commerce and Navigation of November 26, 1923 did not explicitly mention the accession of the Free City, but since it was the intention of both contracting parties that the agreement should embrace the Free City, the Danzig Senate accepted it and the smaller state's accession was effected in the form of a note from the Polish Foreign Minister to the British Minster at Warsaw which was annexed to the treaty. Both the treaty and the note were subsequently registered with the League of Nations.[1]

It has already been noted elsewhere that the current degree of Polish dissatisfacton with the extent of rights allowed in Danzig usually determined the degree of interest exhibited in a purely Polish port like the one proposed but only partially developed at Gdynia. Polish grievances, as well as Polish claims that they needed a second port, again provided the impetus for plans for the improvement of Gdynia in 1923 and early 1924 in the presence of naval representatives. They decided to award the contract for developing the harbor on a long term credit basis to a private concern. Their statements seemed to be all cut from a "Poland first" pattern and tended to discourage any further investment in Danzig until the Poles received in actuality the rights given them theoretically in the Treaty of Versailles. They envisioned good rail communications between the new port and the other parts of Poland and discouraged the use of foreign ports by their nationals, whether merchants or immigrants.

The German port of Stettin responded by offering its services but not its sovereignty to Poland. But it was not merely an efficient outlet to the sea that the Poles sought. It was the psychologically reassuring fact that they owned their own port which concerned them. A British observer had once noted that the Poles were not true businessmen; they would sooner consent to losing a million pounds than to sacrificing a square mile of their territory. So none of Stettin's cooperativeness could satisfy the

---

[1] For the documents dealing with the negotiations for the commercial treaty in early 1924 see FO 371/10442, file 74.

desires of the Polish government.

Müller regarded the undertaking at Gdynia as a political and financial error on Poland's part which demanded vast expenditures at the very time when retrenchment was called for; nevertheless, if the Polish government undertook the work, he desired that British firms be placed on equal footing with other competitors. He protested the discrimination shown toward British industry.

In April 1923 President Wojciechowski and other Polish officials had viewed the rudimentary construction which had taken place at Gdynia. Later in the spring, the Polish government suffered another of its crises and the problems of cabinet-making temporarily replaced any preoccupation with the construction of a port which the late government had entertained. Count Maurice Zamoyski became the Foreign Minister when the Grabski government, devoted to financial reform, took control in December. In the past, Zamoyski had been singled out by British diplomats as affable, cooperative, and friendly. But he was no more cooperative in attracting British investors in Gdynia than his predecessor.

Instead, in early April 1924 the Polish government signed a contract with the Polski Bank Przemysłowy for the construction of a port at Gdynia located in the extreme western corner of Danzig Bay. The bank had already negotiated an agreement with the French Société de Construction des Batignolles, who were to put up the greatest part of the capital--the same firm which, with Cravens, had taken a major part in the establishment and operation of the international company in Danzig. Another major participant was the French Schneider-Creusot and Hersant firm. Included in the new port would be an outer port, a smaller outer dock, and large inner harbor to be connected by a double gauge railway passing through exclusively Polish territory.

The scheme, of course, was an old one, having been in existence since 1919 and, in fact, partially implemented in 1923 before being nearly abandoned for lack of funds. But the new strain in Polish-Danzig relations and Poland's claims that she could not afford to have a replay of 1920 when the Free City prohibited the unloading of Poland-bound ammunition in the port probably more than any other factor prompted the decision to construct the port at this time, despite the need for economy in state expenditure. When the work of construction began in earnest in 1924, French capital made it possible, but the Polish engineers and technicians were assisted in their planning not only by French but also Belgian, Dutch, and British experts.[2]

---

[2] A. Haus and A. Bauer, Gdynia: From Fishing Village to International Port (London: [n.d.] c. 1940), p. 13.

Later Müller learned that the Polish government had not desired British interests to become involved because it feared that Britain would obstruct the port project on political and financial grounds. He smugly recorded that nothing would come of the typically "grandiose" Polish scheme. Every time talk about an alternate port had been revived by Poland, it had met with the same negative and incredulous attitude in the Foreign Office. There was no anticipation that the project would be carried out, much less that it would be successful.

Danzig and the League of Nations

If Britain had consistently supported a Danzig free in more than name, Poland consistently tried to chip away at that status and, in effect, to make Danzig wholly dependent upon her. Talk of a crass *coup de main* by Poland had not been heard in a long time in Danzig. Instead, Poland had begun using more refined methods of intrigue and "nibbling around the edge of her legal position" to the same purpose. One such case was the Polish attempt to interpret overly-strictly the Treaty article which charged her with carrying on the Free City's external affairs. She insisted that even private societies or associations in Danzig were not competent to send invitations to foreign guests and that this must be done through Polish channels and under Polish control. Recognition of this right by the High Commissioner would in effect make the Polish diplomatic representative in Danzig the city's ruler, but MacDonnell struck down this interpretation.

In late 1924 he had ruled in another case that Danzig had a right to maintain consular attachés at the expense of Poland in those foreign cities where she had important economic interests. A disagreement arose over how differing opinions of Danzig and Poland on the need for these representatives could be reconciled. The Danzig Senate appealed MacDonnell's ruling to employ compulsory arbitration for this purpose on the ground that it deprived them of the right of appeal to the High Commissioner which was guaranteed in the Polish-Danzig Convention. The British government, following its consistent policy of preserving the city's free status, considered that Danzig's request in this matter should be granted, and the Foreign Office instructed the British representative on the Council of the League of Nations to follow this line of argument.[3]

The administration of railways was another question which Poland attempted to use in various forms in order to increase Danzig's dependence upon her. Her claims in 1922 to unilaterally establish an administration within Danzig territory which would

---

[3]Memorandum to League Representative, December 4, 1924 in FO 371/10462, N 8813/8813/55.

control railways in Danzig and portions of Poland were disallowed by the High Commissioner. Then in 1924 new Polish claims were made aimed conversely at transferring to Poland the administration of the railways which were located in the Danzig territory. In all these matters, the British representative on the Council of the League was authorized to support a solution of the problem on a realistic basis and to follow a clearly-recognizable British policy that was based more on practicality than on legalism, more on the preservation of Danzig's sovereignty than on the extension of Poland's, and more on a consistent agreement with the decisions of the High Commissioner than in the formulation of uniquely British policy.

One of the more serious points of contention between the same states in 1924 dealt with the expulsion of Danzig nationals from Poland. Two Danzigers had been expelled by the Polish government without any apparent cause, and this action was followed by representations on the part of the High Commissioner. The Senate did not deny the Polish right to expel undesirable aliens, but it complained that it had no way to protect its nationals while they were in Poland except by requesting that the Polish commissioner in Danzig make the necessary representations to Warsaw--an ordinarily valueless exercise. Danzigers, unlike the Poles, did not have a representative in the other state to look after them, and while they were in Poland, they found themselves to be "nobody's children." Failing this protection for her nationals, Danzig sought the protection of the League of Nations.

A committee of jurists looked into the matter and agreed with the High Commissioner's decision to uphold Poland's right to expel foreign nationals and to put the obligation upon Danzig of proving that the reason for the action was purely arbitrary. To this the British government adhered, and the Foreign Office instructed the British representative on the Council to endorse the report of the jurists. By this opinion, Britain upheld the rights of a sovereign Poland and the policies of High Commissioner MacDonnell, but also the justice of Danzig's desire for protection.[4]

While these controversies are not exhaustive of the Polish-Danzig problems before the League, they are sufficiently representative to illustrate how, with the passage of time, Poland came to try and dominate Danzig by a non-violent, "acceptable" method of getting her rights in the Free City recognized by the family of nations. By mid-decade, however, there was an attempt by various powers to move these interminable bickerings from the spotlight in Geneva and settle them by other means or simply to eliminate the most trivial of them.

---

[4]FO memorandum by G. Forbes, November 28, 1924 in FO 371/10458, N 8714/2245/55.

Speculation in the Foreign Office was directed toward finding any acceptable method of thus limiting the Polish-Danzig questions that came before the High Commissioner and the Council, particularly those under appeal. Out of conversations held between MacDonnell and members of the British Foreign Office grew the scheme that embodied the new position.[5]

The plan provided that in the case of general questions, appeals from the High Commissioner's decision should be referred at once by the President of the Council to the rapporteur on Danzig questions, in this case the Spanish representative J. M. Quiñones de Leon, who would consider the matter, obtain the assistance of experts from within the technical advisory bodies attached to the Secretariat, and give a report on the rendered decision. If both parties accepted his report, the matter would be settled; if either party declined to accept, the matter would go through regular channels to the Council which would consider the rapporteur's statement along with the other usual relevant documents. Obviously, it was hoped that the adoption of such a procedure would dispose of a considerable number of appeals before they ever reached the Council.

For matters of a more technical nature dealing with customs, railways and such, the British plan proposed a procedure like the one used between Poland and Germany under their transit treaty whereby the Council appointed an arbitral tribunal of three members which dealt with the technical question unless the High Commissioner considered the matter one he would deal with himself, subject to appeal to the Council.

On May 11, 1925 a modification of this plan was submitted to the Council by Quiñones de Leon. Under its provisions, it became the responsibility of the High Commissioner to insure that any dispute in which he became involved could not be settled by direct negotiation. Should such a settlement be impossible and an independent technical or legal opinion prove necessary, he would apply to the Secretary General for assistance and with it he would issue his decision. Appeals against it would be taken to the Council of the League of Nations. In view of the fact that no existing treaties were modified by this plan and that it would most likely, as the rapporteur claimed, obviate frequent appeals to the Council, thereby preventing technical or legal disputes from assuming a political character, Britain supported it.[6]

---

[5] A record of this conversation and the seven points MacDonnell suggested was recorded in a FO minute by Ogilvie-Forbes, February 24, 1925 in FO 371/11003, N 1248/968/55.

[6] FO Memorandum, February 1925 in FO 371/11003, N 1333/968/55; Cadogan (Geneva) to FO, March 11, 1925 in the same volume,

In the spring of 1923, it will be recalled, Danzig-Polish relations had suffered a setback with the sudden crisis in which silent antagonism exploded into hostile verbal confrontation and fear of violence. Since then, those relations had been on the mend, but even with the passage of nearly two years, there was little love lost between the neighbors. Their bickerings irritated all Europe until some means of muzzling them began to be sought, but a hostility of nearly critical proportions again erupted in January 1925 in what has come to be known as the Post Box Incident.

Poland's postal rights in Danzig were recognized under Article 29 of the Polish-Danzig Convention of November 1920 which provided that

> Poland shall have the right to establish in the port of Danzig, a post, telegraph and telephone service communicating directly with Poland. Postal and telegraphic communications via the port of Danzig between Poland and foreign countries, as also communications between Poland and the port of Danzig, shall be dealt with by this service.

But on the night of January 4-5, 1925, without warning of an attempted extension of rights in Danzig, the Polish government erected outside the Helviusplatz premises, where legitimate Polish postal activities were carried on, letter boxes for material intended to be sent to Poland. In addition, Poland claimed to be able to deliver outside these regular premises postal matter which had been brought from Poland by the Polish postal service. Danzigers responded with vandalism against the new receptacles and there was renewed fear that Poland was again flexing her muscles and attempting to dilute, or even to completely obviate, the Free City's sovereignty.

They appealed to the High Commissioner who ruled on February 2 that the Polish action was illegal. The issue then moved first to the Council of the League of Nations and from there to the Permanent Court of International Justice. This court's advisory opinion declared that the Polish postal authorities were entitled to offer their services to the public by setting up post boxes and collecting and delivering postal matter outside the Helviusplatz premises, but only within the confines of the port of Danzig.

In view of the fact that the decision was the result of a definite appeal by the Council of the League and that it was in accord with the extant documentary evidence, the Foreign Office

---

N 1430/968/55; and the memorandum to the British representative on the Council of the League of Nations, June 4, 1925 in the same volume, N 2799/968/55.

urged the British representative to accept it. With her support of the court opinion, Britain ranged herself with the Council which had, in effect, betrayed its own High Commissioner by disavowing his decision and referring the matter to the high court, the first time an official in this position had been dealt such a blow. Although Britain had not taken the initiative in the matter, her passive acceptance of the situation turned into a *de facto* recognition of the extension of Polish rights and the diminution of those of the fearful, ostensibly free, city of Danzig.

Of course, the decision aroused great satisfaction in all Polish circles. But J. W. Headlam-Morley was distressed. Because the decision had been handed down, he acknowledged that it must be carried out,

> but I will confess that it seems to me to be a wrong decision and I am not surprised at the feeling aroused in Danzig. It is to be hoped that the Poles will not press the advantage they have gained in any offensive way and that the change in the constitution of the Senate will make a mutual spirit of conciliation easier.[7]

In fact, once Poland's right to have the post boxes in Danzig was established and the haggling came to an end, most of the boxes in the port remained unused and unnoticed.

By mid-decade, Great Britain found that her relations with Poland had suffered to some extent because, among other things, their attitudes concerning Danzig were divergent. By upholding an independent Free City, Britain was, by the very nature of her policy, on record against the encroachment of Polish control there. Because of this political attitude, Britain was deliberately bypassed, and even consciously ignored, by the Poles when the question of developing the port at Gdynia came up. Where several years earlier, it had appeared that British investment would have priority in the construction of the new harbor, more recent events proved that the Poles preferred to seek the economic cooperation of their French allies who held a foreign policy discernibly similar to their own and who would be sure to present no political opposition to the project. Pursuing a policy in the League of Nations on Danzig questions consistent with that which she had followed since the formation of the international organization, Britain ostensibly upheld in principle the genuine free status of the city. But by her disinterestedness, her lack of initiative,

---

[7] Muller to FO, no. 451, September 24, 1925 in FO 371/10098, N 5576/115/55 and the minute attached by J. W. Headlam-Morley of October 12, 1925.

and her usual concurrence with the decisions of the High Commissioner, she contributed in part to the creation of the situation which became evident in 1925--that in practice, if not in theory, Poland was being permitted to eat away at Danzig's sovereign status.

Economic Deterioration in Upper Silesia

In early 1924, conditions in the metal, mining, and engineering industries in Polish Upper Silesia began to deteriorate. The promise of the rich paradise did not come to fruition. When the League of Nations had decided on the award of the province in 1921, there was no question that the Poles had won the better part of the mineral-rich province and its vital industrial area. Then, when Germany was faced with almost insurmountable crises in 1923, Poland had benefitted from her plight. With the astronomical inflation of the German mark, Poland more easily injected her own currency into her newly-won province. With the French occupation of the Ruhr, Poland found a rich market for her Upper Silesian industries in coal-starved Germany. But the crises passed and 1924 began a story of industrial and commercial decline for the province.

By the end of June, the Polish government was alarmed at the critical situation brought on by the falling off of the home demand for resources resulting from the general economic depression which Poland had been experiencing and by the reduction of exports owing to the high, non-competitive cost of Polish production. It looked as though a Foreign Office commentary on an economic survey written by the British Commercial Secretary in 1922 was prophetic: "The League's award allotted a lion's share to Poland and she will have great difficulty in digesting it."[8] A commission of inquiry was set up by the Polish government in conjunction with employers and trade unions, but its inadequate findings showed merely that the decline in exports was due to the high cost of production which in turn resulted from high wages and excessive overhead charges. With the current high cost of living, a reduction in wages would have been impossible. As an alternative, the committee recommended the introduction of the ten-hour day in the iron, lead, and zinc industries. The Polish government, acting upon this recommendation, authorized this temporary measure which was accepted by both labor and management. Later it was extended as the result of an employer-employee agreement in these industries.

R. E. Kimens paid a visit to Katowice, the capital of Polish Upper Silesia, in the autumn of 1924, and his observations corroborated the story of a change for the worse there in both the poli-

---

[8] A General Survey by Mr. Kimens on the economic situation in Upper Silesia, undated, [1922], in Documents on British Foreign Policy 1919-1939 (hereafter DBFP) 1st ser., XVI, no. 387, note 2 by S. P. Waterlow.

tical and economic spheres.[9] First, he noted that there had been a lesser decline of chauvinism in Upper Silesia than in the rest of Poland. After the reconstitution of the Polish state, the early years had been characterized by extreme Polish nationalism and class feeling, the latter being directed against Germans, mainly in their role as employers of labor.

Germany, realizing that she was in a strong position because she was the chief market for Upper Silesia, was encouraged further in her overweening attitude by reports that the British government did not favor the award made by the League of Nations which had led to the partition of Upper Silesia. In view of this, Kimens believed that the proper policy for the Poles to follow at this point was one of conciliation and reasonableness towards Germany. While he assigned to the Poles the greater part of the blame for the poor relations which led to economic impasse, he did not attempt to whitewash the Germans who constantly stirred up matters by repeatedly declaring that they did not regard the political settlement in the province as final.

Kimens's findings were in some cases similar to those of the commission of inquiry. His observations on the economic situation indicated that he saw its deterioration as an adjunct of the poor political climate as well as the result of rising production costs and the reduced purchasing power that accompanied tight money and general depression. Based on these evaluations, Kimens saw that Upper Silesian prosperity was dependent upon three major factors: (1) maintenance of the interdependence between German and Polish Upper Silesia, (2) cooperation between the ethnically German and Polish populations in the Polish province, and (3) fair administration of the district. With these in mind, he advocated the extension of those privileges of the economic convention which were due to expire on June 15, 1925 because they reinforced this natural interdependence. If cooperation were to be evidenced in the population, it must begin with the Poles recognizing the rights and privileges of former Germans who were not their countrymen and with these former Germans understanding that the duties of loyalty accompanied their new Polish citizenship. And finally, good administration did not mean substituting Poles for Germans or Polish expropriation of German property, for both of these practices led not to good administration but to ill-feeling and friction that inevitably were reflected in poor production.

The Polish-German Economic Convention of 1922 had been designed to provide for a 15-year period of economic readjustment.

---

[9] Memorandum by R. E. Kimens, undated, transmitted in Leeper to MacDonald, no. 489, October 22, 1924 in FO 417/17, no. 10.

However, portions of it had a three-year enforcement period and were subject to renegotiation and renewal. It was the extension of these arrangements that Kimens advocated in 1925. When Germany made their renewal subject to such strict conditions that Poland rejected the demands, Germany imposed an embargo on the importation of Polish coal, and a commercial war was begun.

In May, Poland had taken the first steps in a general revision of her tariffs. High duties on German articles were part of the scheme and after June 15, Germany also set up tariff barriers. By this time, her currency had been stabilized and industry sufficiently revived to enable her to penalize Poland in this way without huring herself. The confrontation would probably have come earlier had not the Ruhr occupation crisis in 1923 intervened and forced Germany to turn to Polish Upper Silesia for her coal supply. Events, however, again turned to the good of Poland when in 1926 Great Britain was paralyzed by the general strike which permitted Upper Silesia to displace her exports and gain almost the whole of the northern European coal market.[10]

Polish Upper Silesia seemed to have closed in on itself. The anachronistic chauvinism displayed there again was evidence that local affairs comprised the chief interest. Whether the slow decline of this sentiment in the province, which did not keep pace with that in the rest of Poland, resulted from the delayed settlement of the plebiscite question or from the emergence of old and latent insurrectionary attitudes is immaterial. The fact that Upper Silesia did not yet consider herself Polish, that she expressed total disinterest in the matter of the Polish-Danzig crisis in early 1925, and that she sustained the shocks of economic dislocation resulting from partition as well as from external factors, all combine to illustrate a province in the midst of an identity crisis that was crippling her economically. She was no longer a territory under the control of the Allies who could judge, prescribe, and then administer the palliative or the curative which they regarded as the correct one for her. Rather, she was an integral part of the Republic of Poland and, aside from general commercial observations and economic recommendations, there was little which outside powers like Great Birtain could do for her.

One service which Britain had been able to perform was to send the financial expert, Hilton Young, to Poland to help that country overcome its financial problems. He advised the Polish government about how it might balance the budget and he blamed the inflation of the currency for the inability of the government to achieve this end. The Polish mark, like the German one, became

---

[10] Great Britain, Department of Overseas Trade, Report on the Industrial, Commercial and Financial Situation in Poland, (London: His Majesty's Stationery Office, 1927), p. 24.

dangerously inflated in 1923. Even the currency which had been injected into Upper Silesia by the Warsaw government to save the province from the collapsing German mark was itself already falling in value. A new currency proved to be as unsuccessful in balancing the budget as increased taxation and retrenchment had. Finally, in early 1924, the Bank of Poland was established and the new zloty, fixed at the value of one Swiss franc, was established as Poland's sole monetary unit.

Since 1922, when Poland had taken over her portion of Upper Silesia, she had suffered, in addition to her financial problems, a decline in industrial production. Coal production, for example, declined steadily:[11]

1913	32,000,000 tons
1922	25,000,000 tons
1925	21,500,000 tons

But with the circumstances of 1926 and the consequent expansion of Polish markets, the output increased and the province appeared to recover from its setback.

The results of an attempt to discover whether Upper Silesia contributed to the growth of Polish trade with Britain are inconclusive, but the answer to the broader question of Anglo-Polish commercial growth is very clear. Poland was not a very significant factor in British commercial growth in the early 1920s.[12]

---

[11] William John Rose, *The Drama of Upper Silesia: A Regional Study* (Brattlesboro, Vermont: Stephen Daye Press, 1935), p. 210.

[12] Statistics concerning imports and exports of Britain, Poland, and Danzig are from *Almanach de Gotha, 1919-1927*. In the annual reports submitted by R. E. Kimens to the Department of Overseas Trade, he provided statistical information bolstering the argument that British trade was important to Danzig, although the reverse was not necessarily true. A compilation of his information for the year 1921-24 indicates that Britain retained third place behind Germany and Denmark among Danzig's trading partners in the amount of her tonnage which entered and cleared the port of the Free City. This is inconclusive, however, because there is no indication whether any portion of this tonnage was involved in Anglo-Polish rather than Anglo-Danzig trade. Kimens, likewise, recorded no growth in the early years of the decade in the interest of British merchants concerning the Polish market into which Polish Upper Silesia was incorporated. Probably the depreciation of the Polish currency dampened any such potential interest, but Britain did not seem enthusiastic about producing goods according to local Polish requirements, relinquishing British standards of size, or advertising in any but its own language. By 1924, some British

Origins of British Revisionism

It was not only internal financial problems that troubled the Polish government with the coming of 1924, but also recent events in foreign affairs. As a result of the British general election in December 1923, the first Labor government under J. Ramsay MacDonald came to power in January 1924. Rumors of an impending change in British foreign policy disturbed Poland.

At the same time, France, Poland's first and most steadfast ally, entered into a political agreement with Czechoslovakia, Poland's neighbor and long-time antagonist. French interest in that country stemmed from the desire of the Paris government to associate itself with the non-revisionist eastern European bloc known as the Little Entente, which had been established in 1920 and 1921 by alliances among Czechoslovakia, Yugoslavia, and Rumania. It was a part of the French policy of security that her Polish ally should likewise improve relations with these countries. Already allied to Rumania since 1921, Poland, with French support, eventually did sign treaties of arbitration and commerce with Czechoslovakia in March 1925.

Although the Poles increasingly looked to Great Britain for guidance, their sense of apprehension grew upon hearing stories like those purportedly from "official British sources" which contended that the partition of Upper Silesia and the establishment of the Danzig corridor had been "a great mistake" and that the arrangements "could not last." Assurances of official British support for arrangements deriving from the Treaty of Versailles did not allay Polish fears. Yet, by the end of 1924, the Polish government was trying desperately to assure Britain in return that they were not "tied to the chariot wheels of the policy of France" and that, in fact, they were eager to act in accord with British policies. If their recent performance in Geneva belied this assertion, they claimed it was only because they had feared the position taken by some British delegates which seemed to intimate the possibility of treaty revisionism which the Polish government could never admit.[13]

---

capital found its way to Poland, but even the Anglo-Polish commercial treaty of July 1, 1924 did not appear to increase significantly the contacts between the two states. See Report on the Industrial, Commercial and Economic Situation in Poland, 1925 cited above, pp. 16-17 and Appendix No. XV on p. 40. See also the Report on the Industrial, Commercial and Economic Situation in Poland, 1923, p. 18 and Appendix XIV on p. 46.

[13] Leeper to FO, no. 477, October 15, 1925 in FO 688/15, file 114, no. 7A and Müller to Chamberlain, no. 529, November 18, 1925 in the same box, file 49, no. 16.

Polish fears grew with the "sinister" implications of the speeches made by Lord Parmoor, the new British representative at Geneva, in early 1924. Although Parmoor, who had been invited by MacDonald to join the Labor government, was a capable and eminent lawyer, his views of foreign affairs were based on little more than religious pacifism. In conjunction with the problem of German minorities in Polish Upper Silesia and their difficulties in acquiring Polish nationality, Parmoor hinted that if Germany entered the League of Nations, she would be in a better position to defend those Germans living in her former territories. His idea was not a new one. Lord Cecil had suggested a similar one more than two years earlier when he noted that the "grossly unjust" Upper Silesian settlement might be altered more to Germany's advantate if she were to become a member of the League and have her opinion heard.[14] But the outspoken views of Lord Parmoor were attacked by the Polish-sympathizing Times, and the British government in general made no secret of its dissatisfaction with his attitude of overt partiality. Parmoor made the unforgivable mistake of saying in an interview what more schooled diplomats confined only to memoranda and minutes in the Foreign Office files.

It is true that publicly the British government continued to uphold the status quo as delineated in the Treaty of Versailles and its consequent agreements. But privately among the members of the government--in their speculations and proposals--variations of a new revisionism arose. Britain, whose foreign policies historically developed pragmatially not dogmatically, could by mid-decade be called revisionist--but only in the most practical of senses. She repeatedly tried to avoid committing herself to the principle that the European frontiers were fixed forever, that the Treaty of Versailles was a legacy in perpetuity. But she was not prepared to assist in its early alteration if it meant substituting new problems for old ones. She was, likewise, not prepared to assume the image of champion of revisionism and thereby contribute to the alarm of such nations as Poland whose entire policies were rooted in the maintenance of the Treaty.

Nevile Henderson, who in the next decade would be known as a firm believer in the policy of appeasement, delivered a speech at Burnley in early 1925 in which he declared that the Treaty of Versailles "had failed in its purpose" and that "immediate revision was essential." This statement in no way represented the official views of the British government, but it was symptomaatic of a growing body of opinion inside Great Britain and other places, a fact which the Poles recognized.

Since its announcement, the Upper Silesian settlement had never been greatly loved by Britain, and any notions there of

---

[14]British Museum, Cecil MSS, fol. 51125, memorandum of June 6, 1922.

change in the status quo of Europe would probably be directed at least in part at it. Foreign Office memoranda speculating on the necessity for modification in that area proliferated. One of these was a statement on British security written by Harold Nicolson in early 1925.[15]

Schemes to alter either the regime or the function of the Free City of Danzig were also forthcoming. Headlam-Morley, who had been most influential in drawing up the articles of the Treaty of Versailles which defined the city's status, saw no need for change. Strangely, it was from Philippe Berthelot in the French Ministry of Foreign Affairs, that the suggestion for the solution to the Polish-Danzig antagonism came, when he advocated the retrocession of Danzig to Germany with compensation for Poland in the form of Lithuania.[16] Such a settlement, which was perhaps not consistent with existing Polish sentiment, was not without historical precedent. And Sir William Max Müller believed that Poland's access to the sea under the guarantee of the Treaty should have been implemented with the cession of the port of Memel, a corridor, or even the incorporation of Lithuania as an autonomous Polish province. Such a settlement, be believed, would have obviated the four years of Polish-Lithuanian bickerings that had so many times endangered the peace of Eastern Europe. This solution would have created a less intransigent Germany which would have been willing to allow commercial rights to Poland in a German Danzig. "Now it is too late for all this," he noted in 1925.[17]

He oversimplified Central and Eastern European affairs in this assessment, overlooking the Vilna question which had probably been more injurious to Polish-Lithuanian relations than the question of Memel. It was most unlikely, too, that Germany would have happily acquiesced in Poland's taking over Memel--a German-speaking city which she had been forced to surrender by the Treaty of Versailles-- any more than she accepted Lithuania's incorporation of it. He may not have been right in assessing the creation of the Danzig corridor as a blunder, but his regret over a lost opportunity to compensate Poland with Lithuania was superfluous. Danzig had an historical and psychological attraction for Poland and the evidence seems to indicate that in 1919 Poland would not have been willing to settle for the more practical but less romantic solution.

---

[15]Memorandum by Nicolson in FO 371/10729, C 4049/459/18.

[16]Berthelot's comments were made in the course of a conversation with Ernest Remnant, the editor of the English Review. Remnant, a friend of Gregory's, passed on the information about the two-hour meeting to the FO. See FO minute (Gregory), May 20, 1925 in FO 371/10097, N 3028/43/55.

[17]Müller to Chamberlain, no. 106, February 28, 1925 in FO 688/16, file 59, no. 11.

But the direction of British policy toward the disposal of the city of Memel was not affected by these expressions. The Foreign Office, in fact, instructed Lord Crewe in Paris in June 1925 to press the Conference of Ambassadors for a prompt transfer of sovereignty over the city to Lithuania and not to defer this transfer as France and Poland advocated. A Lithuanian *coup d'état* had taken the city, which at the time of the peace conference the Allies had reserved for future disposal, and Britain now recognized this *fait accompli*. Her acquiescence in the Memel question, like her acceptance of growing Polish control over Danzig, was not so much an expression of revisionism as acquiescence in the normal evolution that might be expected in any political situation. Austen Chamberlain, who came to the foreign ministry with the rise of the Conservatives at the end of 1924, observed that once this territory passed under Lithuanian sovereignty, nothing short of war by Poland was likely to bring Memel under Polish control. As Chamberlain wrote:

> The principle underlying the Memel solution is the replacement of the present arrangement by some entirely new arrangement. This principle I believe to be both wrong and harmful. We are in some danger of working on a tacit assumption that a change in the conditions laid down by the peace treaties is inevitable, and that it is the business of His Majesty's Government to initiate such alteration. With barely six years elapsed since the treaties were signed, it is early to talk of the inevitability of change. Our object should rather be to change as little as possible unless and until existing arrangements prove unworkable.[18]

But the coming months would see him taking Britain into a new era of European international relations with the signature of the Locarno agreements and showing his country to be a state bound but not strangled by the provisions of the Treaty of Versailles.

In order to provide the new state of Poland with the unquestionably Polish-speaking territories and with the access to the sea which the Fourteen Points had promised, the Allies found that they generated not only the infamous "corridor" problem but also the controversy and feeling of intense nationalism that went with it. In providing Poland with the corridor, they perpetrated what they regarded to be the lesser of two evils--the severing of the province of East Prussia from the body of Germany. By 1925 Müller was volunteering that his years in Warsaw had shown him the difficulties and even the dangers presented by the Versailles settlement with respect to Poland's access to the sea. He sought a de-

---

[18] Chamberlain to Müller, no. 470, June 16, 1925 in FO 371/10733, C 8063/459/18.

vice to insure the permanence of the frontier perhaps by the neutralization of East Prussia under German sovereignty and the retention of the corridor as Polish. Some foreign diplomats hoped to preclude future difficulties by an outright Polish cession of the corridor to Germany. Neither Lord D'Abernon nor Foreign Office officials gave much attention to these musings. There was no question of Britain's seriously sponsoring such major revisionism in 1925 and the speculations, like most of the others in this vein, died in the Foreign Office files by either neglect or wrist-slapping by superiors.

As the decade progressed, several important attempts were made to reinforce the cause of peace. One of these which failed was the proposal for the Geneva Protocol in March 1924. It would have outlawed all aggressive war, imposed compulsory arbitration upon the potential belligerents, and provided for disarmament and mutual support in cases of unprovoked aggression.

More important among the diplomatic attempts aimed at reinforcing peace, because it was successful, was the German initiative in February 1925 to emerge from subordination to the *diktat* of Versailles and to voluntarily espouse some of its major territorial provisions--a policy which culminated in the signature of the Locarno agreements.

Stresemann and his People's Party in Germany followed this policy simply as a compromise. He wanted to assure France that Germany respected their common frontier as laid down by the Treaty of Versailles, and he proposed a security pact to that end in February 1925. He hoped to placate occasionally the Nationalists whose interest was directed at the eastern frontiers. He had no interest in the Russo-Polish frontier farther east and when the question of Germany's entry into the League of Nations became acute in April, he hastened to assure the Russians that Germany had no intention of recognizing that frontier as the Council of the League had already done. From time to time, he paid lip service to eastern issues merely to "avoid giving campaign material" to the Nationalists. The agreements which comprised the Locarno pacts represented an ingenious compromise of all these objectives. He bound Germany to permanently honor the western frontiers; but in the east he renounced only forceful means to achieve the adjustments for which the Nationalists clamored.

First, the Poles were disappointed by the rejection of the Geneva Protocol by the League of Nations because of British objections. Then, they were gripped by fear when Stresemann proposed his combination of security pacts and arbitration treaties which they believed endangered Polish interests by not placing a value on the Vistula frontier equal to that of the Rhine frontier. Alexander Skrzynski, the Polish Foreign Minister, regarded the proposed agreement, which sought to prevent aggression and insure the use of arbitration in altering the Polish-German frontier, as tantamount to a surrender to Germany of Polish territories in the west.

Polish press response to the German overtures was negative and violent. According to the Warszawianka:

> Wherever the future security of Europe is debated one fact stands out with ever-growing clearness, and that is that the question of world security is closely bound up with the question of the security of Poland. Germany's plans are evident. It has been shown by the Inter-allied Commission of Control that Germany is not disarmed. If she is arming it is for a war of revenge, and the Germans cynically admit that they are plotting an attack on Silesia, Danzig, and Poland generally.[19]

The Messager Polonais, which was directly inspired by the Ministry of Foreign Affairs, saw the German proposals as an attempt to create a breach in the Treaty of Versailles with the hope that with this, the entire Treaty would collapse. This press campaign continued with undiminished vehemence. Even the flattering references to Poland made before the House of Commons by Austen Chamberlain were insufficient to quell the fears of a Poland who was grateful that she still could count on her French ally.

Count Skrzynski delivered a speech to the Diet Commission for Foreign Affairs on March 24 upon his return from Geneva and Paris in which he emphasized the pacific means to which Germany, under the proposed Locarno agreements, promised to confine herself in attempting to alter any portion of her eastern frontier which bordered on Poland. When several days later he discussed the matter with Müller, Skrzynski appeared to have sharpened his anti-German sense during his recent Paris visit and he told Müller that he believed that Stresemann's scheme was motivated by the German desire to drive a wedge between Poland and France "and to lull to sleep the suspicions of the Allies while they, the Germans, make ready to recapture Upper Silesia and the Corridor including Danzig."[20] Skrzynski was mistakenly taking Stresemann's sabre rattlings literally. While Stresemann's policy was unquestionably revisionist in intent, he plans did not include changes on the eastern frontier in the near future.

From time to time public opinion in Poland, as reflected in the press, launched out against Great Britain and her inability or

---

[19] Warszawianka, March 2, 1925.

[20] Müller to Chamberlain, no. 156, March 28, 1925 in FO 688/16, file 59, no. 38.

unwillingness to recognize how vital border areas like Upper Silesia were to Poland. By autumn Poland had accustomed herself to the fact that negotiations for the pact would open soon, and Skrzynski took much consolation from Chamberlain's promise that conversations between Germany and her eastern neighbors would begin in the same place and in the same week as those between Germany and the western powers. Skrzynski hoped that the east would not be compromised by the whim of the west.

Great Britain, on the other hand, favored the conclusion of the pacts. Although the British government did not propose to take part in the eastern agreements, it was far from disinterested in them since they might significantly diminish the need for France to exercise her obligations in the east, which in turn, might involve the British guarantee in the west. However, the British government refused Skrzynski's request to commit itself to a policy of total non-revision of Poland's frontiers which had been established by the Treaty of Versailles and subsequent arrangements. This would necessarily have ruled out any modification, even that achieved by peaceful means. The British government consistently attempted to maintain this elbow room and not bind itself uncompromisingly to the terms of the Treaty.

After months of speculation, the conference convened at Locarno on October 5. From the beginning, Chamberlain tried to avoid having Britain drawn into the position of sponsor for eastern arrangements, maintaining a position consistent with his prior public declarations.[21] But in a conversation he held with the Polish Foreign Minister, Chamberlain assured Skrzynski that the policy followed by the British delegation should not be construed as disinterestedness in the settlement of eastern Europe. If the far right in Poland hoped that Skrzynski would discredit himself at Locarno and, by his obstructionism cause the breakdown of the conference, they were disappointed. He bore himself well, making both the arbitration agreement with Germany and the mutual assistance pact with France. After initialing the agreements at Locarno in October, Skrzynski, like the French Foreign Minster, Aristide Briand, was faced with opposition from the right upon his return home. But after hot debate, he won the support of the Polish Diet before the final signature of the pacts took place in London in December.

Polish press response swung between criticism of the wisdom of Britain's policy of conciliation toward Germany and exultation at a diplomatic victory over the Germans. *Le Messager Polonais* carried a daily feature during the sessions of the Locarno Con-

---

[21] Memorandum by M. Lampson, October 7, 1925 in the Papers of the Locarno Conference, FO 840/1, LOC/56/B.D., file 4, paper 1.

ference and remained factual and unbiased in its reports. Once the Locarno accords were initialed, the newspaper endorsed them and applauded Poland's participation and her solidarity with the Allies in the cause of peace. The British, on the other hand, tried hard to regard the Locarno proceedings and their products not as a victory of one side over another, but as a fair and dignified agreement reached between nations in a benevolent "spirit of Locarno" that heralded a new era for European peace and security.

When only a month later the German Foreign Minister complained to Lord D'Abernon that the existing boundaries of Poland gave rise to "almost insuperable difficulty," referring to the corridor and the Upper Silesian frontier, the British ambassador proposed that the most practical policy for the German government to pursue would be to improve its diplomatic and commercial relations with Poland. Having created this more congenial atmosphere recently, the Germans should find it easier to negotiate the revisions in which they were interested, he suggested.[22]

Because the Locarno Conference had been successful and Germany had voluntarily pledged herself to guarantee her western frontiers and to renounce force in trying to alter her eastern ones, this did not mean that the voices of revisionism were silenced. Proposals within the Foreign Office to neutralize Danzig and transform the corridor into two autonomous German states raised a few eyebrows and were summarily dropped by Sir William Tyrrell, who had replaced Crowe as Permanent Undersecretary upon the latter's death in the spring of 1925. Talk of other schemes which in effect would create a German corridor through the Polish corridor was also terminated in view of the fact that the time was not yet right to take up revisionism.[23] The British government did not choose--before, during, or after Locarno--to be bound by a forever unalterable Treaty of Versailles, but it did shrink from initiating any revision which time, evolution, or a *fait accompli* might more conveniently impose. Briand had once said that when he was called upon to form a ministry, he always reserved one portfolio for time. It was this that Britain proposed to do in 1925 when she steadfastly stood in the twilight zone between the eternal Treaty of Versailles and outright revisionism.

---

[22] D'Abernon to Chamberlain, November 26, 1925 in DBFP, 1A ser., I, no. 118.

[23] Memorandum by M. H. Huxley, December 17, 1925 in DBFP, 1A ser., I, no. 151 and Minute by L. Collier, December 24, 1925 in ibid., no. 159.

CHAPTER IX

CONCLUSION

Most characteristic of British attitudes involving her participation in East Central Europe during the years immediately following the First World War was her desire to withdraw from the area as quickly as possible. This desire prompted her to press for control of the Allied occupation in Danzig in 1920 and to increase her troop commitment in Upper Silesia in 1921. Both these actions were directly bound up with Britain's attempt to dispose of the responsibility she had incurred as one of the Allied powers under the terms of the Treaty of Versailles--a tolerable but unwelcome postscript to victory.

In this extrication, however, she was wise enough not to return to the old policies of maintaining splendid isolation in an old world that no longer existed. Instead, she returned to her old paths of commerce, inviting these areas of the world into her orbit. In so doing, she returned to a traditional role in an expanded sphere. But neither Danzig nor Upper Silesia played as important a role in British commerce as Britain came to play in theirs.

Britain's involvement with Danzig and Upper Silesia necessarily affected her relations with Poland who had at one time made claim to both areas and who had lost them, at least in part, owing to the British Prime Minister's activities at the Paris peace conference. By 1921, after the beginnings of repair, Anglo-Polish relations suffered another setback with the announcement of British attitudes toward the partition of Upper Silesia which in Poland were interpreted as pro-German. With the withdrawal of the Allied presence from the plebiscite area in the summer of 1922, relations generally improved, although from time to time in the next years they met reverses when the two nations found themselves at loggerheads over Danzig in the theatre of the League of Nations.

Poland proceeded to court British friendship and British investment all the while she tried, by various methods, to tighten her control over the Free City of Danzig, which Britain seemed determined to keep free in more than name. But in the League debates, British representatives usually took the line of least resistance and supported the decisions arrived at by the High Commissioners and in so doing they found themselves by the mid-1920s in the anomalous position of defending Danzig's independence in word but seeing the city's sovereignty slowly eroded by Poland in fact. Britain had acquiesced in this evolution of events without any conscious intention toward this end. By 1924-25, she found that either the effect of her policy, the strength of propaganda, or the necessities of the situation had spawned a plethora of

revisionists among her officials. That Britain in 1925 rejected
revisionism as untimely, rather than impossible, was an indication
that she might be more amenable to it later when the time for it
became more auspicious.

Of the British statesmen who had been involved with these
matters of foreign policy, there were three who sustained a degree
of popularity or notoriety in Poland based, in part, on their
attitudes toward the troublesome Danzig or Upper Silesia issues:
the Prime Minister, David Lloyd George; his Foreign Minister, Lord
Curzon of Kedleston; and the Conservative Foreign Minister in
1924-25, Austen Chamberlain.

Sir William Max Müller found it impossible to convince the
Poles that Lloyd George had not deliberately set out to pursue
a policy which was discriminatory against them. A *leitmotif*
running through a large body of Polish historical studies is the
assertion that the Prime Minister had an anti-Polish bias and
consistently pursued it in his policies and public statements.
Such works accept literally the uncomplimentary and informal statements Lloyd George made about Poland and assign to them a value
equivalent to that of his official statements and policy decisions.
The Polish press, on the whole, spoke warily or critically of him
during the period of his incumbency, wrongly making Lloyd George
seem to be the sole reason for Poland's failure to win Danzig
and Upper Silesia from the Allies at the peace conference.

Probably the best assessment of the man and his policies is
that by Harold Nicolson who saw him as maintaining three major
principles of British foreign policy: control of the seas, the
balance of power in Europe, and imperial defense. It is primarily
in upholding the second of these that he has been revealed in this
study--insuring that Germany should not be abandoned to "the mercy
of a Franco-Polish Alliance."[1] To that end, he not only tried to
withhold both Danzig and Upper Silesia from Polish control but he
also, by his own admission, tried to "save" what he could of the
industrial triangle of the plebiscite area for Germany.[2]

What Lloyd George had in personal magnitude and eloquence,
Lord Curzon, his Foreign Minister, could not duplicate. Lloyd
George stole the stage from him, and it was not until he served
under Baldwin that Curzon came to conduct his own calm and
conciliatory policy. Perhaps those historians who strongly

---

[1] Harold Nicolson, Curzon: The Last Phase, 1919-1925: A Study in Post War Diplomacy (New York: Houghton Mifflin Co., 1934), p. 55.

[2] British Museum, D'Abernon MSS, fol. 48953B, in the diary account for June 21, 1921.

attack him are unfair in their assessment, but only because stricture is usually invited by very positive and active means. Curzon, with respect to the questions studied here, did literally nothing to earn it. His policy was wary and cautious to the point of frustration and ennui. His opinions on both the Danzig and Upper Silesia issues were usually in the form of concurrence with cautious Foreign Office statements, refusal to take a harder line against French interference and partiality, and unwillingness to countenance any hint of revisionism in post-war Europe--even as time went on and revisionism would have meant little more than recognizing a *fait accompli*. On only two occasions within the scope of this study did Curzon propose to take an uncompromising stand. On the expulsion of Korfanty, he soon gave way; on Allied reinforcement of troops in Upper Silesia in 1921, Lord Hardinge was called upon to negotiate a face-saving escape.

According to Nicolson, the Prime Minister and his Foreign Minister offered "intermittent support and encouragement" to Germany in matters like Upper Silesia where British interests were not involved. Where commerce and reparations were involved, however, they treated her like a conquered victim and by their dual policy drove France to "isolated action" and Germany to "suicidal despair." For all his faults and want of skill, it is difficult to assign blame to Curzon for the direction of his policy, or lack of it, during the years that Lloyd George held the Prime Ministry and, to a large extent, guided the foreign policy of Great Britain as well.

Austen Chamberlain was the third in the trio of British statesmen who captured Polish attention in these years. That he belonged to the Conservative Party, which Poland looked upon as friendly to her interests because the Baldwin government had in 1923 recognized her eastern frontiers, was to his advantage. But he and his government fell victim to sporadic outbursts of Anglophobia in the Polish press when he looked with favor upon the negotiations which culminated in the signature of the Locarno pacts. Poland, like the other non-revisionist states of East Central Europe, opposed the pacts at first. The Polish press, with few exceptions, attacked them as plans to divide Europe and compromise Poland's frontier with Germany. Divided on other issues, the Polish political parties were united in their fear of and opposition to the German arbitration treaty. Skrzynski's skill in winning ratification by the Diet cannot be overestimated. Chamberlain, however, never came in for the personal abuse and resentment that Poland had shown toward Lloyd George.

But there is some degree of truth to those arguments which claim that the reasons for failure of Britain's post-war diplomacy lay in a collapse of the national will which occurred simultaneously with the assertion of will-power by others. It was not so much a collapse of the national will, actually, as an atrophying of it with respect to the areas studied here. When Britain, on a few occasions, did choose to assert herself over the offensive policies of France, the degree of her success in both the Danzig and Upper Silesian questions was erratic and unpredictable.

To some, who had served in the Foreign Office and worked intimately with these Polish questions, the anti-Polish label that Britain had acquired was unearned. In theory, Britain had been as sympathetic to the Poles as France had, but France had not allowed her irritation with the Poles to get the better of her political sense. Britain "drifted" into the role of critic and found herself directly opposing Polish aspirations or asserting herself against her ally, France, and carrying on what Chesterton had once called a "tug of peace" with friends.

One assessment of the British policy of the first post-war decade as an "exploitation of victory," the first half of which was concerned with "plans for consolidating her gains,"[3] does not appear to be accurate when applied to the areas investigated here. It is correct only in the sense of exploitation as a self-serving use of circumstances without detriment to others. Britain used her dominant role in Danzig, for example, to expand her trade and involve herself in the financial reform of the Free City, but by so extending her interests, she made the Free City a beneficiary not a victim. Britain's post-war policy, in these areas generally, was one in which she expended too little effort and interest to ever be termed exploitative.

The early post-war British governments had been criticized by contemporaries for their failure to rely upon moral forces. "Never yet have we said in plain English that France's policy to Germany was morally indefensible and that we would do our utmost to thwart it."[4] One statesman of that era, Woodrow Wilson, had ostensibly acted under that motivation and had captured the imagination of men and women everywhere. But he also won the ire of many of his own compatriots who rejected the very Covenant he had fashioned, and he was mourned as a "singularly tragic embodiment of the New Diplomacy." Nations have seldom, if ever, acted in the first instance for what was good, but rather for what was worthwhile. Asking Britain to do so, then, would be to ask for a revolutionary change in her character--to muzzle France for the reestablishment of Germany, who had been wronged. She could do the same thing for more understandable reasons--to preserve German economic integrity as a basis for European stability and the expansion of British trade.

---

[3] W. N. Medlicott, British Foreign Policy since Versailles, 1919-1963 (London: Methuen & Co., 1968), p. 1.

[4] Manchester Guardian Weekly, October 26, 1923.

It was E. H. Carr who most correctly viewed British policy in East Central Europe in the years following the signature of the Treaty of Versailles by recognizing that as long as no single power emerged to dominate the continent, Britain was content to pursue no active European policy.

> Throughout the period in question, she was full of good intentions which she lacked the will (though not at first the power) to translate into deeds. She approved of self-determination, but was not prepared to quarrel with her former Allies in order to apply it for the benefit of former enemies. She wanted fair treatment of minorities, but was not prepared to embroil herself seriously with the minority states in order to secure it. She favoured a policy of reconciliation with Germany, but was not prepared to put pressure on France in order to bring it about. In all these issues, she was content with high-sounding words, mild gestures and occasional minor concessions.[5]

Britain thought with her heart and the new diplomacy; but she acted with her reason and the old diplomacy. She thought about protecting minorities and preserving the independence of Danzig. But she actively pursued a policy that favored the disposition of the Upper Silesian triangle more on the basis of economics than self-determination, made the pound sterling the basis for the new currency in a troubled financial community, and employed her armed forces to finish a job badly carried out by others. The Poles were wrong when they thought Britain was the inscrutable sphinx. She was, in fact, the Janus of international affairs--one face gazing steadfastly at the Treaty of Versailles and the other looking to the future and the evolution of events into a condition which might no longer correspond to that Treaty. Both of these faces converged at Locarno. Here Britain participated to varying degrees in negotiations that led to arrangements guaranteeing those German western frontiers which had been laid down by the Treaty of Versailles and envisioning a peaceful change of the eastern ones which had been laid down by the same Treaty but which, in the evolution of European affairs, were found to be alterable. Her participation had contributed to the "spirit of Locarno" that brought hope to Europe, but it had not been prompted purely by altruism. Chamberlain himself admitted that the peace and security of Great Britain were bound up with the independence and security of the nations whose frontiers she guaranteed and that, by guaranteeing those frontiers, she had insured her own.

---

[5] Edward Hallett Carr, Britain: A Study of Foreign Policy from the Versailles Treaty to Outbreak of War (London: Longmans, Green & Co., 1939), pp. 173-74.

In the end, Britain had not much changed. She had cast off splendid isolation, but her devotion to her security and self-interest remained intact. As Harold Nicolson said in his memorandum which assessed British foreign policy in 1925:

> In a situation of such incertitude the only sound line of British policy is the path of British interests. The road is too dark for any altruism or digression, it is our own security which must remain the sole consideration. Splendid isolationism is not today practicable policy.[6]

In the years 1919-1925 it was not in Britain's interest to condemn her French ally, to allow the economic disintegration of Europe, or to be the champion of the newly-independent, ostensibly democratic states. Their friendship would inevitably entail heavy commitments in a part of the world which, until recently, had not even existed for Britain. It is unfair, therefore, to label her shortcomings in these channels as failures. It was, however, in her interest to assist in the economic reconstruction of Germany, in which context her own trade would flourish. To this end she sponsored the transfer to Germany of an industrially rich Upper Silesia and the maintenance of Danzig as a literally Free City. If she is to be found wanting, it is in her failure to satisfy these objectives directly bound up with her own self-interest. As the Poles had put it earlier, in war Britain had learned that her defense began at the Rhine. She had yet to learn that it began at the Vistula as well.

---

[6] Nicolson memorandum (1925) in FO 371/10729, C 4049/459/18.

BIBLIOGRAPHY

Official Archival Records in the
Public Record Office, London

Great Britain. Cabinet Papers:

Cab 23/18 to 51 (The numbers immediately following the stroke in Cabinet and Foreign Office collections which are cited here indicate the volume number.)
Cabinet Minutes. A printed collection of Cabinet conclusions and Imperial War Cabinet minutes.

Cab 27/72 to 177
Cabinet Memoranda. A collection of reports and memoranda corresponding to the time span of this study.

Cab 29/42 to 80
International Conferences. Volumes 42 to 68 are part of the Conference of Ambassadors series and volumes 69 to 80 are part of the Heads of Delegations of the Five Powers series. This collection also contains papers on the meeting of Allied Prime Ministers in London, December 1922 and the British Empire Delegation at the League of Nations in 1920.

Great Britain. Foreign Office:

Foreign Office Confidential Print 11338. "Papers and Correspondence Dealing with the Establishment of Danzig as a Free City."

FO 371
The collection of general Foreign Office political correspondence. Hundreds of volumes relevant to this work have been consulted in both the files on Germany (Central Department) and Poland (Northern Department).

FO 373/3
A series of Peace Conference Handbooks which provides historical, geographical, and economic background on the three areas of Poland which were ultimately united in the new Republic of Poland.

FO 374
Acts of the Conference. This collection contains documents emanating from the Peace Conference in Paris, 1919. Most relevant of its volumes are the following: 1, the acts of the Supreme Council; 7, detailed and excellent maps; 10, documents of the Commission on Territorial Questions; and 20, a secret print containing miscellaneous papers prepared for the British Delegation to the Peace Conference.

FO 408/1 to 40
   Confidential print collection of correspondence dealing with Germany.

FO 411/1 and 2
   Prints of correspondence regarding the League of Nations in the years 1924 and 1925.

FO 417/9 to 19
   Poland: Confidential Prints. These volumes provide prints of the major documents dealing with the relations between Great Britain and Poland between the years 1919 and 1925 most of which can be found in the original in the FO 371 General Correspondence.

FO 566/1281 and 1282
   Two volumes which completely index the Foreign Office correspondence dealing with Poland in 1919-1920.

FO 608
   A large collection of 281 volumes containing papers of the Peace Conference of Paris.

FO 688/1 to 17
   The archives of the British Legation in Warsaw, 1919-1925. This contains the general correspondence with the Foreign Office and with the Polish Ministry of Foreign Affairs. Much of this material is recorded in FO 371 but has the additional value in this collection of containing the minuted observations of the British staff at the Warsaw Legation.

FO 840/1
   A small collection of papers of the British delegation to the Locarno Conference in 1925.

FO 890/Parts 1 to 16
   The archives of the Upper Silesia Plebiscite Commission, British Section. These papers are unbound and the parts appear as either boxes, packets, or folders. Especially valuable are Part 1 containing the Heneker-Stuart correspondence; 6-13 containing the diary accounts of British officers in the various towns of Upper Silesia where they were acting as administrators in the name of the Allied Powers; and 16 containing the diary of Colonel Percival who was the British Commissioner on the Plebiscite Commission until May 1921.

<u>Great Britain. Public Record Office:</u>

PRO 30/52
   League of Nations Assembly and Council Documents. A collection of over 300 volumes of papers of the London Office of the League of Nations. Contains <u>Official</u> <u>Journal</u>.

Great Britain. Treasury:

T 160/Box 132
   Finance files of the Treasury, 1920-1930. This box of files contains papers dealing with the financial questions involved in transferring Upper Silesia from German to Polish control.

T 163
   General Treasury Collection, 1920-1930.

Published Documents

Commission Interalliée de Gouvernement et de Plebiscite de Haute-Silésie. Journal officiel de Haute-Silésie. February 1920 to June 1922.

Danzig, Free City of. Abkommen vom 24. Oktober 1921 zwischen der Freien Stadt Danzig und Polen zur Ausführung und Ergänzung der Danzig-polnischen Konvention, 9.11.1920.

Danzig, Free City of. Zusammenstellung der zwischen du Freien Stadt Danzig unter der Republik Polen abgeschlossenen Verträge, Abkommen und Vereinbarungen. 4 volumes.

Great Britain. Department of Overseas Trade. Report on the Industrial, Commercial and Economic Situation in Poland by R. E. Kimens. London: His Majesty's Stationery Office, 1923.

Great Britain. Department of Overseas Trade. Report on the Industrial, Commercial and Economic Situation in Poland by R. E. Kimens. London: His Majesty's Stationery Office, 1925.

Great Britain. Department of Overseas Trade. Report on the Industrial, Commercial and Financial Situation in Poland in 1926 by R. E. Kimens. London: His Majesty's Stationery Office, 1927.

Great Britain. Foreign Office. British and Foreign State Papers, 1919-1925, Volumes CXII-CXXII.

Great Britain. Foreign Office. Documents on British Foreign Policy, 1919-1939, 1st series, 18 volumes. London: Her Majesty's Stationery Office, 1947-70.

Great Britain. Foreign Office. Documents on British Foreign Policy, 1919-1939. 1A series, 3 volumes. London: Her Majesty's Stationery Office, 1966-70.

Great Britain. Foreign Office. The Foreign Office List and Diplomatic and Consular Year Book. London: Harison, 1919-25.

Great Britain. Parliament. Parliamentary Debates (House of Commons), 5th ser., Volumes CXII to CXC (1919-1925).

Great Britain. Parliament. Parliamentary Debates (House of Lords), 5th ser., Volumes XXXIII to LXI (1919-1925).

Great Britain. Parliamentary Papers. (1925), Locarno Conference: Final Protocol of the Locarno Conference, 1925, and Annex of Treaties between France and Poland and France and Czechoslovakia. Cmd. 2525. London: His Majesty's Stationery Office, 1925.

Great Britain. Parliamentary Papers. Misc. No. 7 (1925), Papers Respecting the Proposals for a Pact of Security Made by the German Government on February 9, 1925, Cmd. 2435. London: His Majesty's Stationery Office, 1925.

Great Britain. Parliamentary Papers. Misc. No. 4 (1923), Report on the Twenty-fifth Session by Lord Robert Cecil, Cmd. 1921. London: His Majesty's Stationery Office, 1923.

Great Britain. Parliamentary Papers, (1919), Treaty of Peace between the United States, British Empire, France, Italy and Japan and Poland, Cmd. 223. London: His Majesty's Stationery Office, 1919.

League of Nations. High Commissioner. Decisions of the High Commissioner, League of Nations, Free City of Danzig, 1922-33.

League of Nations. High Commissioner. Summary of Subsequent Legal Effects of the Decisions by the High Commissioner. Danzig, 1928.

League of Nations. Convention germano-polonaise rélative à la Haute-Silésie faite à Geneve le 15 mai 1922. Geneva: Impr. A. Kundig, 1922.

League of Nations. Memorandum on Currency and Central Banks, 1913-1924. 2 volumes.

League of Nations. Official Journal: Minutes of the Council and Assembly. 63 reels.

Mantoux, Paul. Les Deliberations du conseil des quatre (24 mars-28 juin, 1919): Notes de l'officier interprete. 2 vols. Paris: Editions du Centre National de la Rechereche Scientifique, 1955.

Miller, David Hunter. My Diary at the Conference of Paris. 22 vols. New York: Printed Privately for the Author, 1924.

Poland. Monitor Polski: Dziennik Urzędowy Republiki Polskiej.
    [Polish Monitor: Official Daily of the Republic of Poland]
    February to May 1919.

Poland. Polish Bureau of Information. Poland after Five Years:
    Quinquennial Review of the Republic of Poland. New York:
    Polish Bureau of Information [n.d. 1923?].

Poland. Polish Commission of Work Preparatory to the Conference
    of Peace. Dantzig. Paris: Imprimerie E. Courmont, 1919.

Poland. Polish Commission of Work Preparatory to the Conference
    of Peace. Gdańsk and East Prussia. Paris: Imprimerie Levé,
    1919.

Poland. Polish Commission of Work Preparatory to the Conference
    of Peace. Union economique entre la Haute-Silésie et les
    autres territoires de la Pologne, 1919.

Poland. Polish Delegation at the Peace Conference. Economic
    Delegation. Memorandum. The Economic Situation of United
    Poland and the Necessity of Meeting Her Most Urgent Needs.
    Paris, 1919.

Poland. Ministry of Finance. Annual of Statistics. Warsaw, 1931.

Poland. Ministry of Finance. Report Submitted by Commission of
    American Financial Experts Headed by Professor E. W. Kemmerer,
    Warsaw: Ministry of Finance, 1926.

United States. Department of Commerce. Supplement to Commerce
    Reports. Bureau of Foreign and Domestic Commerce. Trade
    Information Bulletin. no. 32: "Public Finance of Poland" pre-
    pared by E. Dana Durand. Washington: Government Printing
    Office, 1922.

United States. Department of State. Papers Relating to the For-
    eign Relations of the United States. Volumes for 1919-1925.
    Washington, D. C.: Government Printing Office, 1935-1947.

Wambaugh, Sarah. Plebiscites since the World War: With a Collec-
    tion of Official Documents. Washington, D. C.: Carnegie
    Endowment for International Peace, 1933.

Private Papers: Archival Collections

Balfour Papers. British Museum. Correspondence of Lord Balfour and Peace Conference files. Add. Mss. 49683-49962.

Balfour Papers. Correspondence 1916-1922 arranged by country and other correspondence as Foreign Secretary and Lord President of the Council. London. Public Record Office. FO 800/201 to 217.

Cecil Papers. British Museum. Correspondence and Papers of Cecil of Chelwood. Add. Mss. 51071 to 51204.

Cecil Papers. Wartime and post-war correspondence of Cecil as Parliamentary Undersecretary of State and later as Undersecretary of State ranking directly below the Secretary of State. London. Public Record Office. FO 800/195 to 198.

Chamberlain Papers. (A. Chamberlain). Miscellanesous correspondence as Secretary of State for Foreign Affairs. London: Public Record Office. FO 800/256 to 258.

Crowe Papers. Papers of Sir Eyre Crowe as Senior Clerk in Western Department, Assistant Undersecretary of State, and Permanent Undersecretary of State. London: Public Record Office. FO 800/243.

Curzon Papers. Papers of Lord Curzon as Secretary of State for Foreign Affairs, 1919-1924. London. Public Record Office, FO 800/147 to 158.

D'Abernon Papers. Papers of Sir Edgar Vincent, Viscount D'Abernon as British Ambassador to Berlin and on special mission to Poland. British Museum. Add. Mss. 48922-48962.

Drummond Papers. Papers of Sir Eric Drummond as Senior Clerk and British Delegate to the Peace Conference, 1918-1919 and Secretary General of the League of Nations, 1919-1923. London. Public Record Office. FO 800/329 and 383-385.

Henderson Papers. Miscellaneous correspondence of Sir Nevile Henderson, 1924-25. London. Public Record Office. FO 800/264.

Lloyd George Papers. The Private Papers of David Lloyd George. London. Beaverbrook Library. 1,041 boxes.

MacDonald Papers. Papers of J. Ramsay MacDonald as Prime Minister and Secretary of State for Foreign Affairs. London. Public Record Office. FO 800/218 and 219.

Niemeyer Papers. Papers of Sir Otto Niemeyer collected between 1916-1930 during his career with the Treasury. London. Public Record Office. T 176.

Oliphant Papers. Papers of Sir Lancelot Oliphant as Undersecretary of State for Foreign Affairs. London. Public Record Office. FO 800/252.

Wigram Papers. One set of papers of R. F. Wigram on British foreign policy lectures. London. Public Record Office. FO 800/292.

Other Selected Primary Materials

Callwell, Major General Sir Charles E. *Field-Marshal Sir Henry Wilson, His Life and Diaries.* 2 vols. London: Cassell, 1927.

Chamberlain, Sir Austen. *Down the Years.* London: Cassell, 1935.

D'Abernon, Viscount. *The Diary of an Ambassador: Versailles to Rapallo, 1920-1922.* With historical notes by Maurice Alfred Gerothwohl. Garden City: Doubleday, Doran & Co., Inc., 1929.

D'Abernon, Edgar Vincent, Viscount. *The Eighteenth Decisive Battle of the World.* London: Hodder, 1931.

Gregory, John D. *On the Edge of Diplomacy: Rambles and Reflections, 1902-1928.* London: Hutchinson & Co., Ltd., 1929.

Hankey, Lord Maurice. *Diplomacy by Conference: Studies in Public Affairs, 1920-1946.* London: Ernest Benn Ltd., 1946.

Hankey, Lord Maurice. *The Supreme Control of the Paris Peace Conference, 1919: A Commentary.* London: George Allen & Unwin, 1963.

Hardinge, Charles Hardinge, Lord. *Old Diplomacy: The Reminiscences of Lord Hardinge of Penshurst.* London: Murray, 1947.

Haskins, Charles Homer and Lord, Robert Howard. *Some Problems of the Peace Conference.* Cambridge: Harvard University Press, 1920.

Headlam-Morley, Sir James W. *A Memoir of the Paris Peace Conference, 1919.* New York: Barnes and Noble, 1972.

Howard, Esme, Lord Howard of Penrith. *Life Seen from the Stalls,* Vol. II to *Theatre of Life.* London: Hodder & Stoughton, 1935.

Hutchinson, Lt. Col. Graham Seton. *Silesia Revisited*. London: Simpkin Marshall, Ltd., 1929.

Kaeckenbeeck, Georges. *The International Experiment of Upper Silesia*. London: Oxford University Press, 1942.

Lloyd George, David. *Memoirs of the Peace Conference*. 2 vols. New Haven: Yale University Press, 1939.

Lloyd George, David. *The Truth about the Peace Treaties*. 2 vols. London: Victor Gollancz Ltd., 1938.

Nicolson, Harold. *Curzon: The Last Phase, 1919-1925. A Study in Post-War Diplomacy*. New York: Houghton Mifflin Co., 1934.

Nicolson, Harold. *Peacemaking, 1919*. New York: Grosset and Dunlop, 1965.

Petrie, Sir Charles. *The Life and Letters of the Right Honourable Sir Austen Chamberlain*. 2 vols. London: Cassell, 1939.

Riddell, George Allardice, Lord. *Lord Riddell's Intimate Diary of the Peace Conference and After, 1918-1923*. London: Victor Gollancz, Ltd., 1933.

Skrzynski, Alexander. *Poland's Problems and Progress*. Washington, 1925.

Skrzynski, Alexander. *Poland and Peace*. London: George Allen & Unwin, Ltd., 1923.

Wilson, Trevor. (ed.). *The Political Diaries of C. P. Scott: 1911-1928*. London: Collins, 1970.

Selected Secondary Materials

Aubert, Louis. *The Reconstruction of Europe: Its Economic and Political Conditions. Their Relative Importance*. New Haven: Yale University Press, 1925.

Buell, R. L. *Poland: Key to Europe*. 2nd ed. revised. New York: Alfred A. Knopf, 1939.

Campbell, F. Gregory. "The Struggle for Upper Silesia, 1919-1922," *Journal of Modern History*, XLII (September 1970), 361-85.

Carr, Edward Hallett. *Britain: A Study of Foreign Policy from the Versailles Treaty to Outbreak of War*. London: Longmans, Green & Co., 1939.

Carr, Edward Hallett. *The Twenty Years' Crisis, 1919-1939*. London: Macmillan and Co., Ltd., 1939.

Clay, Sir Henry. *Lord Norman*. London: Macmillan, 1957.

Davies, Norman, "Lloyd George and Poland, 1919-1920," *Journal of Contemporary History*, VI (1971), 132-154.

Einzig, Paul. *Montagu Norman: A Study in Financial Statesmanship*. London: Kegan, Paul, Trench, Trubner & Co., Ltd., 1932.

Gatzke, Hans. *Stresemann and the Rearmament of Germany*. Baltimore: Johns Hopkins University Press, 1954.

Haus, A. and Bauer, A. *Gdynia: From Fishing Village to International Port*. London: n.d. [c. 1940].

Jones, Thomas. *Lloyd George*. London: Oxford University Press, 1951.

Kimmich, Christoph M. *The Free City: Danzig and German Foreign Policy, 1919-1934*. New Haven: Yale University Press, 1968.

Kudlicki, S. *Upper Silesia*. 2nd ed. revised. Perth, Scotland: Munro Press, Ltd., 1944.

Lévesque, Geneviève. *La Situation internationale de Dantzig*. Paris: J. Bière, 1924.

Lutz, Hermann. *Eyre Crowe der böse Geist des Foreign Office*. Berlin: Deutsche Verlags-Anstalt, 1931.

Macdonald, Gregory. "Polish Upper Silesia." Prepared for New Fabian Research Bureau, 1935. Unpublished manuscript deposited at Polish Institute and Sikorski Museum Library, London.

Mason, John Brown. *The Danzig Dilemma: A Study in Peacemaking and Compromise*. Stanford: Stanford University Press, 1946.

Medlicott, W. N. *British Foreign Policy since Versailles, 1919-1963*. London: Methuen & Co., Ltd., 1968.

Morrow, Ian F. D. *The Peace Settlement in the German-Polish Borderlands*. London: Royal Institute of International Affairs, 1936.

Nelson, Harold I. *Land and Power: British and Allied Policy on Germany's Frontiers, 1916-1919*. Toronto: University of Toronto Press, 1963.

Piernikarczyk, Josef. "England's Part in the Creation of Upper Silesian Industry," Baltic and Scandinavian Countries, III (May 1937) 270-73.

Pink, Gerhard P. The Conference of Ambassadors. Geneva: Geneva Research Center, 1942.

Reynolds, Warren H. "Britain's Relations with Poland, 1919-1939." Unpublished Ph.D. dissertation, Fordham University, 1959.

Rose, William John. The Drama of Upper Silesia: A Regional Study. London: Williams and Norgate Ltd., 1936.

Special Correspondent. "The Commercial War in Upper Silesia--I," The Economist, CI (October 10, 1925), 566-67.

Special Correspondent. "The Commercial War in Upper Silesia--II," The Economist, CI (October 17, 1925), 606-608.

Szyldrzynski, Jan. Anglia i Polska: w Polityce Europejskiej [England and Poland in European Politics]. Jerusalem: Orła Białego, 1945.

Thomson, Malcolm. David Lloyd George: The Official Biography. With the collaboration of Frances, Countess Lloyd-George of Dwyfor. London: Hutchinson, 1948.

Walters, F. P. A History of the League of Nations. 2 vols. London: Oxford University Press, 1952.

Newspapers and Periodicals

The Cologne Post [Upper Silesian Edition]. June 17, 1921 to August 6, 1921.

Czas. [Time]. Kraków. March 1 to July 24, 1919.

Danziger Neueste Nachrichten. March to August 1919.

The Financial Times, 1919-1925.

Głos Narodu [Voice of the Nation]. Kraków. January 1 to May 31, 1919.

Kattowitzer Zeitung. May to August 1919.

Kurjer Warszawski. January to July 1919.

The Manchester Guardian. 1919-1925.

The Manchester Guardian Weekly. 1919-1925.

Le Messager Polonais: Quotidien politique, economique et litteraire. Warsaw. 1925. [A semi-official organ of the Polish Foreign Ministry]

Polish Economic Bulletin. London. 1919-1923.

The Times. [London]. 1919-1925.

The Times Imperial and Foreign Trade Supplement. 1919-1922.

The Times Imperial and Foreign Trade and Engineering Supplement. 1922-1925.

INDEX

Access to sea, 7, 8, 10, 17
Admiralty Memorandum, 13-14
Administration, Allied, 53; cost of civil in Danzig, 147, 172, 174; moratorium on payment, 175, 177; payment, 190; provisional, 39, 40; cost of, 40
Alsace-Lorraine, 8
Amnesty, 48
Anglo-Polish Steamship Line, Ltd., 84
Appeals from High Commissioner decisions, 196
Arbitral Tribunal, 150, 152-53, 160
Attolico, Bernardo, 64
Autonomy movement in Upper Silesia, 46, 66-68, 152n, 181

Balfour, Lord, 138-39
Banca Commerciale Italiana, 145
Bank of Danzig, 179
Bank of England, 179, 180
Bank of Poland, 202
Benes, Edouard, 139
Bernezzo, Colonel de, 93
Bewick, Moreing and Co., 185
Bolshevik influences in Upper Silesian disorders, 42, 46
Bonin, Count, 103
Boundary Commission, 154-55; rectification in Upper Silesia, 185-86
Brockdorff-Rantzau, Count, 22

Calonder, Felix, 155, 159, 160
Carr, E. H., 79, 119, 215
Carr-Laroche Resolution, 82
Carton de Wiart, General A., 17, 32
Cecil, Lord, 7, 204
Cavallero, General Ugo, 40-41
Central Kassenactiengesellschaft, 179
Chamberlain, Austen, 206, 209, 213
Chantiers Naval Français, 142
Cheetham, Sir M., 131

Ciechanowski, Jan, 64, 87
Claims, to Danzig, 4, 5; to Upper Silesia, 4, 5, 6
Clemenceau, Georges, 35
Conference of Ambassadors, 54, 80, 108, 190
Corridor, 7, 8, 12, 205, 206, 210
Council of Four, 18
Council of Ten, 9, 17
Craig, J. I., 88
Cravens, Ltd., 121, 142, 143, 191
Crewe, Lord, 175
Crowe, Sir Eyre, 124, 131, 168
Currency, new in Danzig, 178-79
Curzon, Lord, 87, 131, 212-13
Curzon Line, 59
Customs union, 117, 119, 166, 169
Czechoslovakia, 203

D'Abernon, Lord, 61
Danziger Werft, 117, 143
Depression in Upper Silesia, 199-201
Diktat, 4, 207
Dmowski, Roman, 4
Draft Treaty at Versailles, clauses on Danzig, 21; German response, 23-24
Drummond, Sir Eric, 39, 153
Dubenskogrube massacre, 93

Eastern Frontiers of Germany, Commission on the, 25
Elections, municipal in Upper Silesia, 48
Ellis, Sir William, 191
Ethnic composition in Danzig and Upper Silesia, 13
Evacuation of Upper Silesia by Allies, 160
Execution of the Treaty, Commission for the, 39
Expropriation agreement, 159
Expulsion of Danzigers from Poland, 195

Federal Reserve Bank of New York, 180
Foch, Marshal Ferdinand, 103

Foreign policy of Danzig, 149, 194
Foreign representatives in Danzig, 148; of Danzig, 147-48, 194
Fourteen Points, 4
France, withdrawal from Danzig decision, 20
Franco-Polish Alliance, 52
Free City of Danzig, establishment of, 29, 63-64
Frontier closing, 170, delimitation 29, 33
Fry, B. H., 149, 166

Gdynia, 112-13, 114, 192-94
General strike in Danzig, 171
Geneva Protocol, 207
German-Polish Commission, 38
German-Polish Economic Convention, 154, 155, 159
Giolitti, Giovanni, 61
Goltz, General von der, 35
Goodyear, Col. Anson Conger, 45
Gosling, Cecil, 67
Gratier, General, 123, 131
Gregory, J. D., 3, 83, 167
Gregory-Massigli Resolution, 83
Grenzschutz, 43, 44
Gulden, 178-79

Haking, Sir Richard, assessment of Danzig situation, 55-56; evaluation of interim regime, 63; as High Commissioner, 65, 79-80, 114, 119-20
Haller, General Joseph, 53
Hankey, Sir Maurice, 153
Hanseatic League, 5, 10
Harbor, construction at Danzig, 35
Harbor and Communications Board, 58-59, 62-63, 171
Hardinge, Lord, 103, 133
Headlam-Morley, J. W., 6, 8, 170, 198, 205; on Danzig, 11, 14-15; on Upper Silesia, 43
Hemming, B. Villiers, 93
Henckel von Donnersmarck Beuthen Estates, Ltd., 185-86

Henderson, Nevile, 204
Heneker, General, 101, 110, 153
Höfer, Lt. Gen. Karl, 95, 122, 125, 127-28
Hope, Admiral Sir George, 33
Howard, Sir Esme, 7, 21
Howard-Lord Agreement, 10-11
Hurst, Sir Cecil, 148

Industrial triangle, 85, 88, 136, 139, 150, 162-63
Inflation in Upper Silesia, 173, 175, 178-79, 182
Insurrection of 1919, 44-46; of 1920, 68; of 1921, 92-97
International Engineering and Shipbuilding Co., 140-46, 190-92
Investment in Upper Silesia, 162-63
Ishii, Kikujiro, 80

Kaeckenbeeck, Georges, 159, 160
Kassubes, 31
Kimens, R. E., 159, 162, 199-201
Kisch, Col. Frederick M., 16
Korfanty, Wojciech, 65, 68, 70, 76, 92, 95, 97, 105, 108, 123
Korfanty Line, 95
Korfanty-Urbanek Agreement, 70
Krappitz Incident, 131

League of Nations, Council, 136-38, 148, 149, 150, 171
Lerond, General, 48, 72; report on plebiscite, 91
Lloyd George, David, 2, 9, 16, 105-106, 186, 212
Little Entente, 203
Loan to Danzig, 174-76
Locarno Agreements, 207, 208, 209-10

MacDonald, J. Ramsay, 203
MacDonnell, Mervyn, 170, 194, 195
Malcolm, General Neill, 31, 33
Mandate to defend Danzig, 80-84
Marinis, General de, 93
Martial law proclaimed in Upper Silesia, 93
Masaryk, Tomas, 3

Massigli, R., 83
Meissner, Dr., 179
Memel, 165, 205-206
Mezes, S. E., 20
Military Committee at Versailles, 103
Mission to Poland, British, 31, 51, 58
Mixed Commission, 150, 160
Müller, Max, 76, 205
Munitions in transport through port of Danzig, 59-61

Naval base at Danzig, Polish, 57-58, 84, 113-14
Naval Mission to Poland, British, 36
Naval presence, British, 31, 36, 63
Navy, Polish, 36
Neufahrwasser, 13
Neufahrwasser solution, 7, 12
Neutral zone plan, 93, 125-27
New Diplomacy, 2
Nicolson, Harold, 205, 212
Niemeyer, Sir Otto, 178, 180
Noë, Prof. Ludwik, 118, 143, 145, 191
Norman, Montagu, 180
Note of July 6, 131-33

Occupation of Danzig, 33-35, 40, 147, 172, 174; cost of 40-41; moratorium 175, 177
Occupation of Upper Silesia, arrival, 51; cost, 50-51, 184
Olszowski, Kasimir, 159
Oman, C. W. C., 7, 12-13
Ottley, Major L. E., 87, 99
Outvoters issue, 66, 74-77

Paderewski, Ignace J., 4
Parmoor, Lord, 204
Patek, Stanislaw, 52
Paton, H. J., 12, 31, 42-43
Percival, Col. Narold, 48, 69, 108-109
Percival-Marinis Report, 90, 91
Petersdorf Affair, 155-56
Pilsudski, Joseph, 4, 55, 161, 181

Plebiscite Commission, Inter-Allied, organization, 48-49; reorganization of 71-74; quells disorder 86; attempt to restore authority, 101-110, 123-29; after evacuation, 183
Plebiscite in Upper Silesia, proposed 24; Council of Four, 25; timing of 25-26, 66; preliminary arrangements, 66; conducted, 77-78; inconslusive, 85, 86-92
Plucinski, Leon, 169
Polish Affairs, Inter-Allied Commission on, 9, 11, 15, 17, 19
Polish National Committee, 4
Polish-Danzig Convention, 29, 37, 38, 56, 59, 116-17, 149, 176, 197
Polish-Danzig Economic Convention, 38, 46-47, 62, 200
Polski Bank Przemyslowy, 193
Porebski, A., 113
Port d'attache, 84, 113-14, 115-16
Posen, 8
Post Box Incident, 197-98
Postponement of Treaty of Versailles going into effect in Danzig, 54-55
Property, former German government, 29, 58, 62, 174
Prothero, G. W., 10

Quinones de Leon, J. M., 196

Railway in Danzig, administration of, 194-95; exploitation of workshops, 119-21, 142, 143
Rapporteur, 138, 196
Rawlings, Lt. Comm. H. B., 129
Reparation Commission, 47, 174
Repartition of Former German State Property, Commission for, 118-19
Revisionism, British, 167-68, 169, 189-90, 198-99, 203-10
Reynier, Col. James de, 167
Rhineland High Commission, 160
Rowe, Gilbert, 119, 143
Ruhr, occupation of, 165, 167
Rumania, 203
Rumbold, Sir Horace, 37

Russo-Polish War, 59, 68

Saar, 8
Sackville-West, Gen. C., 33
Sahm, Heinrich, 31, 191
Salvioni, Col., 94
Sapieha, Prince Eustace, 51, 62, 76
Schneider-Creusot and Hersant, 193
Seeckt, Gen. Hans von, 34
Selby, W. H. M., 167
Senate, Danzig, 171
Seyda, Maryan, 171, 178
Sforza, Count, 85, 107
Shortage of coal in Upper Silesia, 43-44
Sicherheitspolitzei, 65, 69
Siepmann, H. A., 180
Simpson, Capt., 93
Skirmunt, Konstantin, 120, 153
Skrzynski, Count Alexander, 166, 207-208, 209
Sobanski, Count, 36
Société de Construction des Batignolles, 142, 144, 193
Spencer, C. F., 143, 145, 191
Stadtnotgeld, 173
Stettin, 192
Sthamer, Friedrich, 87
Strasburger, Henryk, 177, 191
Stresemann, Gustav, 207
Strikes in Upper Silesia, 43, 45
Strong, Benjamin, 180
Stuart, Sir Harold, 110, 122-23, 156, 157-58
Supreme Council, delay of Upper Silesia decision, 90; on Upper Silesia boundary decision, 129, 133

Tariff revision, 201
Teschen, 139
Thelwald, F., 67
Thwaites, Sir W., 100
Tower, Sir Reginald, 40, 42, 53, 60
Treaty of Commerce and Navigation of 1923, 192

Troops, British in Upper Silesia, reinforcement of, 68, 99-101, 109-110, 130, 134; threat of withdrawal, 72-73
Tyrrell, Sir William, 16, 210

Ultimatum, London, 97, 98; to Höfer, 124-25
Urbanek, Dr., 70

Vickers, 112
Vilna, 55, 112, 171, 205
Volkmann, Dr. Ernst, 178, 179

Washington Naval Conference, 131
Wilson, Sir Henry, 40, 79, 99
Wilson, Woodrow, 204
Wirth, Joseph, 152
Wojciechowski, Stanislaw, 166, 193
Wyndham, Sir Percy, 31

Young, Hilton, 201

Zamoyski, Count Maurice, 193
Zloty, 202